FICTION WRITING
Master Class

*Emulating the Work of Great Novelists
to Master the Fundamentals of Craft*

WILLIAM CANE

**WRITER'S
DIGEST
BOOKS**

www.writersdigest.com
Cincinnati, Ohio

FICTION WRITING
Master Class

*Emulating the Work of Great Novelists
to Master the Fundamentals of Craft*

WILLIAM CANE

For more resources for writers, visit www.writersdigest.com.

22 21 20 19 18   9 8 7 6 5

Distributed in the U.K. and Europe by F+W Media International
Brunel House, Newton Abbot, Devon, TQ12 4PU, England
Tel: (+44) 1626-323200, Fax: (+44) 1626-323319
E-mail: postmaster@davidandcharles.co.uk

ISBN-13: 978-1-59963-916-1

Edited by Scott Francis
Designed by Claudean Wheeler and Bethany Rainbolt
Illustrations by Joshua Roflow
Production coordinated by Mark Griffin and Debbie Thomas

DEDICATION

For Marilyn, my wife,

Who ate up my words,

And Kate, my daughter,
Who often ate the manuscript.

TABLE OF *Contents*

INTRODUCTION

So many people today are banging their brains out against their keyboards and asking themselves, "Why can't *I* write like the greats?" when the simple answer is that you can. First, though, you need to come to grips with the fact that the greats were educated quite differently from you and me.

Unfortunately, during the past eighty or so years writers have not received instruction in a vital training method that their predecessors routinely employed to improve their skills. Indeed, this neglected technique is one of the most important training methods ever developed for writers, a technique which was used with spectacular results for two thousand years but which was suddenly dropped from the curriculum. Almost every great writer studied these methods, but you were probably denied access to them by a recent change in our educational system. Chances are that when you discover this lost technique, and practice this forgotten art, the experience will have an explosive impact upon your writing and will do for you what it did for Chaucer, Shakespeare, Milton, Pope, Swift, T.S. Eliot and countless others, infusing new life into your work and jump-starting your creative career.

Wouldn't you like to know the biggest difference between *your* education and that of these well-known writers? I'm going to tell you in a moment, but first let me ask one question. How often did you hear the word *originality* mentioned when you were in school? In other words, how frequently were you urged to do new work, break new ground, and write in your own voice? Like most students you were probably slapped silly by demands that you avoid plagiarism, be authentic, and above all do original work. "Let me hear your *voice!*" professors would say. Most of us can still hear the echoes of those demands ringing through the halls of academia.

And *that*, believe it or not, is the problem.

You cannot become a terrific writer just—*poof!*—out of thin air. It takes something preexisting, some structural savvy, some foundation in technique, some underlying sense of the *possibilities* of language before you can strip off your topcoat and tap dance across the pages like Fred Astaire.

Before I explain exactly *what* was left out of your education, let me tell you how I stumbled upon this deplorable state of affairs in the first place. It all started in those long years before I went to law school, years when I roamed the musty library stacks during my stint in college. Because I was president of the debating society, it was my job to dig up as much evidence as I could against the other teams. So I would stand for hours sifting through government documents on the sweltering third floor of the library at Boston College. Then, for fun, because I was also working at the college radio station, I would browse around looking for material that I could use in the radio plays I directed. And it was in this manner that one evening I stumbled upon a shelf—actually shelves upon shelves—of books about ancient rhetoric. It turns out that these dusty volumes contained a gold mine of ideas that we could employ in various soap operas which we broadcast to a small group of loyal listeners.

But the other thing I discovered was that this subject—the subject of ancient rhetoric—was *not* being taught in any college writing classes; not, at any rate, in any that I could find. Rhetoric had been relegated to the speech communications department, where we got some pretty tedious lectures on Aristotle, Cicero, and Quintilian. The upshot of my little digression is that rhetoric is the subject that has been neglected in writing education; indeed, according to Edward P.J.

Corbett, widely regarded as the most accomplished living scholar in this field, the key components of rhetoric were phased out of American education around 1930.[1]

Why should you care whether rhetoric was phased out? After all, isn't rhetoric simply sound and fury signifying nothing but persuasion? Sure, it may be that, but it's also much more than verbal volleyball and pontificating propagandism. Rhetoric also encompasses methods of being felicitous with words as well as techniques for mastering style. In its purest form rhetoric also deals with the arrangement of material and the selection of topics for clear, artful, entertaining presentation. Rhetoric, among other things, teaches how to contrive an introduction that will seduce a reader, take him by the nose, and never let him go until he reaches the last paragraph. You want to do that don't you? Of course you do!

Allow me, then, to introduce you to one *aspect* of rhetoric, one teensy-weensy aspect of it that can literally salvage your writing career, infuse your style with new vim and vigor, and give *you* a voice equal to the voices of the best and brightest who came before you. It's all in this book about the classical rhetorical technique of imitation. Yes, this is a book about imitation, a method of writing instruction that has dropped off the map, fallen through the floor, and disappeared from the face of the earth as far as modern education is concerned.[2] And yet imitation is arguably (according to Aristotle, Cicero, and numerous other authorities) the most *effective* rhetorical device for learning your licks as a writer.[3]

Too simple to be true? Well, consider for a moment that musicians, such as the Beatles or the Beach Boys, or whoever else you download onto your iPod, learned their craft by doing covers of other artist's songs. Put more simply, they began their own careers by *imitating* the

---

1. Corbett 1971:32-33, 627.

2. As one highly-respected contemporary novelist—who knows the secret—points out, "[I]n the eighteenth century imitation was the chief way of learning to write" (Gardner 1983:26).

3. Cicero, for example, called imitation his first principle of rhetoric (Murphy, Katula, Hill, and Ochs 2003:172).

work of other artists. Only after they had mastered these basics did they venture to write their own material. Why, then, aren't writers allowed to do the same? Why aren't they *instructed* and *encouraged*, for heaven's sake, to do the same? That's the lesson taught by the classical technique of imitation.

And that's the lesson of this book. You too can imitate the greats, and in the process absorb elements of their style that will make your writing sing. The point is that the rhetorical device of imitation will help you grow as a writer, just as it helped Milton, Melville, Flaubert, Faulkner, Dickens, and Shakespeare. More importantly, you cannot expect to reach your *full* potential as a writer unless you learn to absorb from other writers by using the technique of imitation.[4]

This book explains this time-tested method of improving your output that modern writers never learned in school, a method of helping you write better that can work wonders and transform producers of plodding prose into Salingers, Hemingways, and kindred butterflies, all of whom flutter through their stories as if doing so were the easiest thing in the world. To be sure, the techniques taught in this book will help you in your work like *nothing* you've ever learned before. As a professor of English, I've used these techniques to coach a generation of students. I *know* these methods work, and by the end of the book so will you.

The chapters that follow will make up for what you missed in school. I'm going to introduce you to the classical device of imitation by examining the work of twenty-one notable writers, pointing out exactly how you can adopt their techniques in your own writing. Like a painter absorbing the elements of style necessary for composition, tint, and tone, you'll learn the fundamentals of your craft—including how to master the essentials of prose rhythm, character portrayal, and story development, among many other topics—so that you can advance in skill and ability and learn from those who have gone before, just as they learned from the greats who preceded them.

---

4. Many great writers not only practiced imitation but sang its praises, freely admitting that it helped them in their work. Dante, for example, stated that "To attain perfection we must copy the great poets of the past" (Reynolds 2006:59).

The ultimate goal of this book is not to make you become a clone of these other writers but to help you learn their secrets so that you can express yourself with confidence, style, and your own unique voice. For once you use imitation to master the tools of the trade that are set out for you in the following pages, your inner voice will emerge in a way it could never have done without this crucial foundation.

No, I'm not going to hesitate to say it. I've been waiting to say it ever since I stumbled upon those dusty books in the library so many years ago. You have in this volume a work that has the potential to put you light-years ahead of your contemporaries. May the experience of reading and using this book be filled with the delight, enjoyment, and excitement of discovery.

CHAPTER 1

WRITE LIKE
Honoré de Balzac

Balzac was a klutzy writer. His sentences are awkward, his phrasing clumsy, his style unappealing—and yet he was very successful. How can we explain this?

The answer lies in the fact that Balzac had many other talents: his writing is filled with realistic people, intricate plots, and plenty of romance. As a result, readers forgave Balzac for his clumsy, ornate prose. They turned the pages to find out what was going to happen to Eugène de Rastignac, Père Goriot, Eugénie Grandet, and a circus of other characters, all of whom seemed to come alive in the pages of his fiction. The greatest French novelist in terms of sheer literary production; the most ambitious in scope; the most amorous in his personal life; the most bizarre in his peccadillos; the highest paid writer of his day and at the same time, through prodigal error, the most impecunious—the man who stands at the forefront of French literature was in many ways strangely and barbarously self-centered. This, as we shall see, is one of the keys to understanding his work and to discovering how to adapt *his* most successful devices to your *own* uses.

Born in 1799, a firstborn with two younger sisters whom he loved dearly, Balzac studied law but, like Kafka, found its practice unbearably dull. To the chagrin of his father he stopped practicing law and set out to become a writer. Ambitious and full of wild business schemes (all of which failed) he had no choice but to write because writing brought him money, vast sums of money; enough money, in fact, to make him a wealthy man many times over—except for the fact that he was a prodigal genius, as one biographer termed him, and could not resist throwing money away on gloves, expensive clothes and, like so many of his characters, the pursuit of aristocratic women. As a result he was in debt to the end of his days. An incurable romantic, perhaps *the* most romantic of all the writers in this book, a man for whom numerous love affairs were a way of life (including one with Olympe Pélissier, a high-priced courtesan whose stories and famous acquaintances provided him with plots for a good number of novels),[1] Balzac was in many ways a very modern writer, one whose sensibilities resonate with our own age.

HOW TO OVERCOME A KLUTZY STYLE

Nothing is so off-putting to a reader than a style that wheezes and moans its way from start to finish of a story. The ideas may be good but if the writing is dull, heavy-handed and stumbling, its chances of being well-received are considerably diminished. For this reason it is incumbent upon even good writers to strive always to make their work more felicitous; to learn tricks of composition; to edit and accept editing suggestions, and, in short, to do everything possible to make prose have a certain rhythmic flow. The result will be music to the ears of your readers, so much so that if the story occasionally happens to drag, they can listen to the poetry.

Balzac's clumsy style began almost as a joke at the start of his career. Looking for some means of earning a living he noticed a group of young men who had hit upon the scheme of writing books together as co-authors and sharing the proceeds. They were selling their work to local publishers, and seeing their success Balzac told his sister that he was going to join the fray; the only difference being that he would write entire books *himself* and keep *all* the money. He set to work like a madman, writing at a furious pace.

---

1. Gerson 1972:103-104.

What he discovered was something of great importance to his future as a writer: he could write as fast as he talked and this was very fast indeed. He wrote a novelette in two or three weeks, working in long timeless stretches; he boasted that he could wear out ten crow-feather pens in three days, in his rapid hand that dashed like black rain across the uncorrected pages. He could hardly keep up with his fantastic invention and he did not care much how it all read. It was all offal, he said, but it poured out. [His father] was amazed but his mother was horrified. She had been brought up with a regard for syntax and prose style and his careless clichés shocked her. They got worse as he succeeded.[2]

If you fear that you, too, may have some element of awkwardness in your writing, if your sentences don't sound musical, if your prose is sometimes stolid and leaden, take heart. While it is important to try to fix these faults, they should *not* stop you from writing. After all, they never stopped Balzac.

It is no use to try to give examples of this difficult prose style. For one thing all his work was written in French and most English-speaking writers are going to read him in translation anyway, where the *translators* are the ones who have to struggle through his garbled syntax and run-on sentences, often rendering them into much more palatable prose than the original. For another thing the enumeration of countless examples of stolid prose will not stimulate your imagination or fire your writing the way that it needs to be stimulated and fired so that you, too, can turn out a story in record time. The point to be made, however, is that a klutzy writing style was not a bar to Balzac's success; in fact, the time he saved by not worrying about style was time he devoted to churning out more text. For the beginning writer who is facing his first novel, the example of Balzac can prove heartening.

Let's say you happen to lack a certain ear for the music of words ... should you, on that account, give up trying to be a writer? Far from it! You can still motivate yourself to get that first draft done. Sit down, pick up the pen, and don't look back. One of the most difficult aspects

---

2. Pritchett 1973:51-52.

FICTION WRITING *Master Class*

of writing a novel is getting that first draft done, and on this score if Balzac can't inspire you no one can.

Sometimes a klutzy style will improve over time; in fact, it's almost inevitable that the more you write the better you'll write. There's no way that you can sit down at a desk four to six hours a day, writing your heart out, and *not* become a better writer. Get yourself a blog and post your ideas and thoughts, and even chapter drafts so that you can see your work professionally formatted. This by itself is bound to help your writing. A well-known writing coach once confided to me that his students were mostly deficient in the area of prose style. "They have no ear for the music of words, for the rhythm of prose, for the way words sound. The meter and repetition necessary for writing totally escapes them." This is something that, unfortunately, can't be taught too easily and is best learned by the student on his own through more writing. Which is why you may wish to take a lesson from Balzac and write as much as possible.

HOW TO USE EMOTIONAL TAGS

If, like Balzac, you have some problems with your prose style, you can compensate like he did by using other strengths which you may possess. For example, Balzac was a master of emotion; his writing is filled with emotional tags—little references to the feelings of his characters. In *Père Goriot* (1834) Balzac constantly delves into the hero's mind to reveal Eugène de Rastignac's feelings: "*His bitter thoughts* were dispersed by the *pleasure that he looked forward to* in dining at the viscountess's."[3] Balzac jam-packs sentences with emotional comments, two of which I've emphasized. To add power to your writing, include emotional tags like this and readers are likely to overlook small stylistic faults and other compositional errors.

Emotional tags were perfect for the novel Balzac was writing in 1834. The story centers on the status-seeking Eugène de Rastignac, a young man who climbs the social ladder in France mainly through

---

3. Balzac 1834:123 (emphasis supplied).

his association with aristocratic women. Modeled on Balzac, who was always on good terms with a number of aristocratic women, de Rastignac is sometimes shallow, sometimes uncertain, but always seeking a way up out of the muck. He has one redeeming quality: although he will sleep with any woman to advance his status, he ignores the advice of Vautrin, a criminal, and vows to make his mark on society without committing murder.

As de Rastignac prepares to go out for the evening, Balzac describes the young man's narcissistic pleasure in seeing his own charming features, and in doing so he uses emotional tags. "Eugène *enjoyed all the little pleasures* of which young men dare not speak for fear of being laughed at, but which flatter their vanity." Later, at a ball, he feels highly self-satisfied because he's conquered the Baroness de Nucingen, and Balzac tells us quite directly that "he for the first time enjoyed the *pleasures of smugness.*"[4] If you've noticed a pattern here, it's all for the better. Even with his emotional tags Balzac is rather clumsy; in fact, he uses *the same word* to describe half of the emotional reactions of his characters: Pleasure! pleasure! and pleasure! If you see a pattern you know Balzac has hit his stride. Like a soldier marching to the tempo of a drumbeat, Balzac issues the reports of his characters' emotions with a metronomic drone that can sometimes be humorous when its mechanical similarity is noted. And yet, when such drops in the bucket are separated by a few pages, as they are here, the reader doesn't notice; only the critic (and the budding novelist) sees through to the essential simplicity of the device. Simple, yes. But also effective? successful? and wonderful when used in context? *Absolument!* We can say that the technique comes off with resounding success, causing generations of critics to rave about the vitality of Balzac's writing (despite its klutzy prose!) and the lifelikeness of his characters—their essential *reality*, their truth, their naturalness! Can such a thing be wrought with such a simple clockwork of repetition, such an inconspicuous little device, such a small thing as the emotional tag? Not *everything* is achieved through the little emotional

---

4. Balzac 1834:154.

tag, but a considerable amount of the vitality and essential humanness of the characters is brought to the fore by this little trick of the trade—a trick which Balzac uses to his decided advantage.

The method of using emotional tags is so well entrenched in the literature of our day that there are even manuals of the tags you can use, which you can purchase and refer to (like a dictionary or thesaurus) to inspire your writing when you're too tired to do the thinking needed to hit upon an elegant or inventive tag.[5] Perhaps Balzac could have benefited from such a dictionary, had they been available in his day. But you can easily make up emotional tags with the advice you'll learn from him. The first thing to realize is that the tags should be used to describe emotions. The more violent the emotion, the stronger the tag can be and the more effective. After the criminal is revealed to have murdered someone who was standing in de Rastignac's way, the young hero feels guilty and Balzac paints his emotion in the strongest terms with a brilliant emotional tag. "Eugène had gone out to walk, to breathe fresh air; he felt he was suffocating." And as he continues to walk by the Luxembourg Gardens we learn that "he thought himself tracked by a pack of dogs."[6] This is the depths, the bottommost emotion, the core of negativity, and Balzac uses emotional tags at just this moment to fix, as it were, the beating pulse of this emotion upon the map of the human heart he is drawing. We can learn from him, and notice that the next time the character feels an upward swing, the elevation of spirits, a rise to the treetops of delight, an emotional tag is again employed. "Eugène took Delphine in his arms, and, folding her in a close embrace, *he wept with happiness.* This final contrast between what he had seen and what he saw now, in a day which had brought so many *irritations both to his head and his heart, made him break down completely.*"[7] The technique, as used by this early master of the form, is to emphasize both your highs and your lows with emotional tags.

---

5. One of the best of these manuals is *The Romance Writer's Phrase Book* by Jean Kent and Candace Shelton.

6. Balzac 1834:198.

7. Balzac 1834:213 (emphasis supplied).

When a *powerful* emotion affects a character, a tag is brought out to vivify the emotion and make it stand in stark relief from the surrounding placid narration. Balzac's practice of dredging the depths and seeking the heights should suggest something of maximal effectiveness and value to you; namely, that you can resort to the emotional tag whenever you hit any peak of emotion. At the point where your story is rolling along at a normal pace and everyday things are happening, no emotional tags are needed; but when the pace accelerates, when characters react with anger, pride, hubris, longing, love, envy, hatred, or any number of other pivotal and strong emotions, *that's* when you want to blow air into your sails and give readers the emotional tag. If you have a few stock tags they're going to be better than none at all. If you can be creative, all the better; but if you can't think of anything splendiferous or unique enough to please your inner ear, don't despair. Balzac was in your shoes, and look what he did! With his stormy heart and flair for the bon mot, he often simply resorted to the quickest emotional tag that came to him, and left it at that—not going back to revise for felicity, for variation, for variety. So should *you*, when the moment is right, strike while the iron is hot and don't let the opportunity slip by; instead, drive home one or two nice turns of phrase, letting readers see into the hearts of your characters by virtue of the fact that you add an emotional tag or two to light the way.

BALZAC'S SECRET METHOD FOR WRITING

A man of immense creativity and endless ideas, Balzac was yet a creature of habit; indeed, a fixed routine was a large part of his success. He isolated himself from the world so that he could concentrate on his writing. He did this in two ways: first, by staying in his home with the blinds drawn,[8] and second, by working at night while the world slept. Unless

---

8. The first floor of his home at 13 Rue des Batailles was empty and in order to gain admission his guests needed a secret password. This was to avoid creditors as well as to ensure privacy. Balzac lived and worked upstairs on the second floor (Maurois 1965:273).

you distance yourself from the ceaseless distractions of the everyday world, like most successful writers (Conrad locked himself into a room, Salinger wrote in a concrete bunker, Fleming completed all the Bond novels in a Jamaican hideaway), unless you take steps to isolate yourself from the madding crowd, distractions are liable to make sustained work impossible. But perhaps even more than isolation, Balzac's secret was coffee.[9] His procedure was to keep himself alert during the wee hours of the night with murderously black and concentrated and above all thick-brewed coffee, which he made in a big coffeepot and sipped while he worked. He was so fond of coffee that he devoted a chapter to it in a scientific treatise on modern stimulants, singing its praises in glowing terms.[10] "[C]offee is a great power in my life," he confessed. "I have observed its effects on an epic scale."[11] It kept him awake at night and enabled him to write. It stimulated his creative powers. It allowed him to marshal his thoughts. It gave him so many ideas he could barely keep up with them and his fingers flew across the pages, writing novel after novel at breakneck speed.[12]

It is hardly my purpose here to advocate the kind of coffee consumption that Balzac indulged in—drinking cup after cup of sludge—for just as surely as the caffeine inspired him it also, as he admitted, "roasts your insides"; indeed, it was the cause of numerous stomach maladies in his later years and he was specifically advised by his physician to cease his abuse of the stimulant.[13] The point to be made, however, is that isolation and concentration are probably two prerequisites to success as a writer, and obtaining them—whether by force of will, meditation, or through the occasional use of nootropics—is a necessity for many writers.[14]

---

9. Gerson 1972:162. *See also* Boon 2002:174.

10. Balzac 1838a.

11. Balzac 1838b:273.

12. Ayn Rand reportedly used amphetamines for a similar effect (Branden 1989:348).

13. Balzac's early death was attributed, in part, to his abuse of coffee (Boon 2002:175).

14. Nootropics, also known as smart drugs, are a class of supplements that boost cognition and brain functioning. Described by Ray Kurzweil in *Fantastic Voyage: Live Long Enough to Live Forever*, they include coffee, tea, vinpocetine, huperzine, pregnenolone, and numerous others, many of which are more effective than coffee and have fewer side effects.

WHERE BALZAC GOT IDEAS

Balzac's ideas were fantasies drawn from his own life and transmogrified in the pages of his fiction into the amorous escapades of his heroes: young men on the cusp of maturity, young men who associate themselves with aristocratic women in an effort to pull themselves up by their own bootstraps into a position of respectability and power, young men who yearn for the spotlight and who will do anything (or *almost* anything) to attain the kind of prominence they so ardently desire. That de Rastignac stops short of murder is not to say he is totally guileless; on the contrary, even today in France to call someone a Rastignac is to impute vanity, aggressiveness, and the avariciousness of a social climber to the individual, a clear tribute to the lasting nature of Balzac's portrayal, and tribute to Balzac's own ego.

As Christopher Booker observes in *The Seven Basic Plots* (2004), the story of de Rastignac is a departure from the morality tales of the seventeenth century; indeed it's a departure from the long line of literary creations stretching through Shakespeare and Dante and reaching back to the ancient Greeks and Homer—literature that rang out with a moral and a meaning, stories that traced the development of a hero through various stages and saw him mature and grow as a person, eventually (with the exception of tragic heroes) becoming an individual who had vanquished his adversary and learned something of value about what it means to be a human being. Balzac, on the other hand, was part of the great change that came over modern fiction generally, part of a movement toward egocentric stories and sentimentality that defines Hollywood even today. The prolific French novelist traces not *maturing* characters (despite what we shall say about character change later), but rather characters who act in accord with the author's own peculiar fantasy life. These characters don't learn anything of significance about themselves nor do they come into their own as good men; instead, they are an egocentric projection of the author's own fantasy life and, as such, they can do no more than represent what the author wished to achieve. Young de Rastignac, like the young Balzac, wishes to conquer women; like Balzac he yearns for wealth;,and like his creator he wants to rise into the stratosphere of high society—and he pursues all these goals with an obvious self-centered interest.[15] Eugène de Rastignac's interpersonal relations were marred by egocentricity and they lack any real connection, except for fleeting romantic interludes during which he fancies himself in love, and a sentimental affection for Père Goriot. But even de Rastignac's love is used as a tool for social climbing, and the hero never relates completely with any woman, never makes a happy marriage and, on the whole, strikes thoughtful readers as rather infantile and puerile.

So the secret for getting ideas and for developing a varied plot—a moving, dynamic plot like Balzac employs—is letting your own fantasy life wander where it will. Is it likely that through the employment of this technique you will write Homeric works, Shakespearean morality tales, or Ovidian stories that show deep metamorphosis in your characters? No, you will instead write the modern tale, the tale of a soul plunged into a society and running for his life, scrambling after something he considers the ultimate desideratum, his own self-advancement. In the composition of tales like this, the example of Balzac will guide you like no other.

But Balzac can help you even if you wish to write another *Pilgrim's Progress* with a moral and a developing character who grows and changes. The idea is to let your fancy roam across the landscape of your own interior life; let imagination carry you where your ego wishes to go, and utilizing remembrances from your own life—situations where you failed, moments where you triumphed—you will craft a series of scenes that relate to the acquisition of some goal peculiar to the protagonist's ego. Then it is up to you—the logical, editing, thinking writer—to craft from that amalgam of ego-driven scenes a plot and a message and a moral. But for that we will have to look at the work of other writers. Balzac teaches the zest, the driving force of novel writing,

---

15. It is noteworthy that Balzac imitated Stendhal, whose writing was part of the new vanguard that dropped moral development and focused on the egocentric plots that characterize so much of modern storytelling (Booker 2004:352).

but he has little to say about how to infuse a moral into a work or how to make a character grow into a human being. Ego is the name of the day but also the quickly changing plot necessary to engage a modern reader. From Balzac these essential skills can be learned as they can be learned from few other writers.

MODERN CHARACTER CHANGE

There is nothing writing teachers like to dwell upon more than the necessity of illustrating character change and development. It is, to listen to them, the writer's holy grail, the be-all and end-all of fiction, the mark of accomplishment without which all else is meaningless. "If you don't create the potential for change, the character will feel predictable and the reader will quickly lose interest" they warn.[16] And yet anyone who surveys the field of modern fiction will tell you that character change and development has been curiously lackluster during the past hundred or so years. The kind of changes that David Copperfield goes through don't occur in Holden Caulfield.[17] The kind of maturation that Jane Eyre experiences is absent from most modern fiction. Character development has become a relatively small "turn" or epiphany, something characters experience fleetingly, and critics make mountains out of molehills when they see any kind of change take place in a character. Sure, de Rastignac learns a few things about how to run after women of rank, but this can hardly be called fundamental character change or maturation.

Eugène de Rastignac starts out as a young man who wishes to advance himself in society and he ends the same way. All throughout the book he is ready to *use* people, including his relatives, as stepping stones to his own personal advancement. He never has a long-lasting relationship with anyone and he winds up no better than he begins: he is still avaricious, grasping, mean and hungry. He is neither married nor

---

16. Reissenweber 2003:34.

17. Which may be one reason why J.D. Salinger ironically has Holden disparage David Copperfield in the first sentence of *The Catcher in the Rye*.

in love, he is neither morally nor ethically wiser than when he began, and he has not learned any character-enhancing lessons. Balzac pays mere lip service to character change throughout the book, especially near the end. Indeed critics have made much of the last paragraph of the novel, which describes how de Rastignac climbs a hill and looks down at Paris.

> His eyes were fixed almost avidly on the area between the columns in the Place Vendôme and the dome of the Invalides, the region of that high society in which he had sought to make his way. Upon this humming hive he cast a look which seemed already to suck the honey from it, and he gave utterance to these portentous words: 'Between us the battle is joined henceforward.'

In other words the young man still has within his heart a desire to claw his way up, ever up. He is not satisfied, he has not reached any position of balance, he has not changed in any significant way. To claim that this is character change is to misunderstand the nature of change. Balzac's hero is still the same callow youth he was in the first chapter, where we are told that de Rastignac came "to understand the stratification of society. He begins by admiring the carriages which pass along the Champs-Elysées, and before long he craves a part in the procession." Eugène de Rastignac has craved and wished and scraped his way up into the higher reaches of society *all throughout the book*, and he epitomizes the kind of shallow young man who *always* wants more. But he has not changed. He ends the way be began: a clawing, striving ego-driven ambitious young rake.[18] The only scrap of sentimentality he evidenced through the book was his attempt to help Père Goriot, but

---

18. It's no surprise that de Rastignac is often compared with Stendhal's Julien Sorel from *The Red and the Black*, another ambitious young man *who remains virtually unchanged emotionally and psychologically throughout the novel*. See, e.g., Higonnet 2002:82. See also Christopher Booker's penetrating analysis in *The Seven Basic Plots: Why We Tell Stories*, which finds much similarity between de Rastignac and Sorel. "As de Rastignac climbs his way ruthlessly up the social ladder, there are no signs of any inner transformation, any development towards wholeness and maturity: merely the acquisition of new and sharper weapons in the war of self-aggrandisement" (Booker 2004:353).

even that led to nothing and was mixed up with his longing to use one of the old man's daughters to foster his own egocentric goals.

Our discussion of the almost total absence of change in Balzac's hero is not meant to be totally negative; on the contrary, there are many fine flourishes that a modern writer can learn from his novels, most notably how even a modest suggestion of change will do the trick. And here is precisely where modern writers can learn the most from Balzac. Despite Christopher Booker's criticism (brilliant as it is) this slight shading of personality is often how contemporary writers present character change. It's advisable to learn the technique directly from Balzac and the modern writer would be wise to study his work on just this point. The reason is that contemporary writers have been absolved, because of the direction of modern fiction, from showing the kind of exaggerated fairy-tale like character development that occurs in a story such as Cinderella or Snow White ... or David Copperfield, and most writers can get by with the kind of subtle flourishes that Balzac gives us. A flash here, a sentence or two there, a little phrase now and then, especially at the end—and that should suffice; indeed, most modern editors will consider you perceptive and insightful. They will in all likelihood find this minimalist technique tasteful and sufficient, so that there is really no need to give them mountains of character development. As Balzac teaches us, today a subtle little suggestion of change goes a long way toward making modern characters come alive.

CHAPTER 2

WRITE LIKE
Charles Dickens

When he worked as a professor at Wellesley College and Cornell University, Nabokov lectured on Dickens, urging his students to read him as one reads a revered saint and "to bask in Dickens."[1] Why did Nabokov, one of the masters of contemporary prose style, admire Dickens?[2] What is it about Dickens that inspired readers to line the street waiting for the ship to bring installments of his books to America? And most importantly, for our purposes, what can we learn from Dickens about how to write?

No author since Shakespeare has created a cast of characters so vast, so startling in their variety, and so engaging in their many permutations of human behavior. More than this, Dickens regales us, like Shakespeare, not only with engaging stories but also with the music of his language so that even when the story flags the sound of the words carries us along. Born in 1812 to middle-class parents, his circumstances took a turn for the worse financially when his father was sent to debtor's prison. The family joined the breadwinner in jail and the young Dickens had his first taste of the low life that would haunt his fiction ever after. Sent to work in a factory after his father's release, he experienced even more of the harrowing life of an indentured servant. Later he studied law, was admitted to the bar, yet worked as a journalist. Most of his major novels appeared in serial form.

---

1. Nabokov 1980:63.

2. Kuzmanovich 2005:13.

Today it's a clear mark of success for a novelist to be compared to Dickens and almost every major novelist (except for those coming out of writing programs who prefer to be called minimalists) vies for that comparison. Tom Wolfe recently said that he thought John Irving wanted to be compared with Dickens and was jealous when *he* was.[3] Writers in the know recognize that Dickens has a few tricks up his sleeve. And these tricks of the trade are yours for the asking. We'll discuss four of the most useful aspects of Dickens's style that you can immediately adopt in your own writing. And you won't have to write a jot about poor boys forced to work in miserable surroundings because the beauty of Dickens's method is that it can be applied to almost any type of story you care to create. The techniques we'll consider include the construction of character in a state of conflict, the use of humor, mastery of pathos, and the conscious integration of suspense into mainstream stories.

CHARACTERS IN CONFLICT

When characters are the soul of your story, people look forward to reading your work. Every Dickens novel is character-driven, and it's primarily his characters (like Scrooge, Pip, and Uriah Heep, for example) that people remember. Call someone a "Scrooge" today and everyone knows what you're talking about. Dickens may have used outlines to plot months in advance for serial publication, but he was first and foremost a caricaturist (with a strong sense of plot, to be sure), always on the lookout for ways to embellish a portrait.[4] And his character portraits, while certainly dependent on a fanciful and fruitful imagination, were grounded in reality and the grit and grime of his day.

How can you use the same technique to depict character as realistically as Dickens, especially in light of the fact that modern readers won't sit still for paragraphs or even extended passages of description?

---

3. The comment appears in Wolfe's funny and incisive essay "My Three Stooges" (Wolfe 2000:153).
4. An interesting discussion of how Dickens planned chapters in advance, with samples of his short outlines, can be found in Ford and Monod's "A Note on the Text" in Dickens 1853b:777-799.

To paraphrase Emanuel Lasker, one of the world's best chess players, "When you think of a good description, look for a better one."[5] Instead of settling for something routine, stretch your imagination, and above all, have a sense of humor, a sense of the absurd, and a sense of satire. Poke fun at your own creations, give them humorous and ironical names, describe them in whimsical ways. Your readers will enjoy being in on the joke *with* you.

"He is of what is called the old school—a phrase generally meaning any school that seems never to have been young—and wears knee breeches tied with ribbons, and gaiters or stockings," says Dickens in describing Mr. Tulkinghorn, Sir Leicester's lawyer. "One peculiarity of his black clothes and of his black stockings, be they silk or worsted, is that they never shine. Mute, close, irresponsive to any glancing light, his dress is like himself. He never converses, when not professionally consulted."[6] Dickens begins by painting this dreary portrait of Mr. Tulkinghorn, but he hardly stops there. His next strategy is to get his elaborately carved chess pieces into some tight corners and big conflicts. That is the key to all his scenes, and that is the problem you must solve if you are to make *your* story work. Before long Mr. Tulkinghorn is in conflict with Lady Dedlock, threatening to reveal her secret to her husband—and we're off and running.[7]

Another perfect example of conflict is the argument between Dombey and his wife, Edith, in chapter forty of *Dombey and Son* (1848). Their conflict is described in excruciating detail, with many a revelation of their thoughts to show that Dombey totally misunderstands his wife and thinks she is in *awe* of him. In actuality she is holding her tongue to protect her daughter, Florence: "She bent her eyes upon him steadily, and set her trembling lips. He saw her bosom throb, and saw her face flush and turn white. All this he could know, and did: but he could not know that one word was whispering in the deep recesses of her heart, to keep

5. Lasker, of course, said, "When you see a good move look for a better one."

6. Dickens 1853a:10.

7. Chapter 41.

her quiet, and that the word was Florence."[8] Telling us an inside secret makes the conflict all the more interesting.

Dickens's technique is not that difficult to master. It has two components: The first involves character portrayal through satire, physical description, or other observations. You can paint your characters hot or cold, black or white, young or old, as long as you trim the length of your descriptions and keep such descriptions relatively brief. Study Dickens, yes; but then abbreviate the length of your descriptions for your modern audience. The second step for creating conflict is to follow Dickens in pitting major characters against each other in both physical, verbal, and mental antagonism. Remember how Dickens keeps some conflict *hidden* and *below the surface*, as in the contest between Edith and Dombey, or as in the lurking Tulkinghorn, who hovers around Lady Dedlock trying to discover her secrets. These muted conflicts can then be allowed to erupt into verbal fireworks, the kind of open conflict that readers enjoy.

MAKE THEM LAUGH

"Make them laugh, make them cry, make them wait," was Dickens's motto and his method. The techniques used in the execution of this method bear careful scrutiny for they were integral to the work of the master storyteller. Unfortunately, the use of humor escapes many writers today, especially those who seek to write serious fiction. Eschewing low humor, they mistakenly neglect the high. Dickens was a master of high humor—satire, puns, wordplay, and a curious method of characterizing that poked fun at his own creations even as he fleshed them out with life and a persona all their own.

The humor in Dickens begins with the little touches in character portraits, such as in *Dombey and Son* where Mr. Perch is described "shutting the door, as precisely and carefully as if he were not coming back for a week."[9] The portrait of Uriah Heep in *David Copperfield* (1850) is a classic of humorous description: "I observed that he had not such a thing

---

8. Dickens 1848:651.

9. Dickens 1848:377.

as a smile about him, and that he could only widen his mouth and make two hard creases down his cheeks, one on each side, to stand for one."[10]

The satire Dickens lavishes on the upper class in *Bleak House* is often laugh-out-loud funny. For example, his description in chapter 12 of Sir Leicester: "Sir Leicester is generally in a complacent state, and rarely bored. When he has nothing else to do, he can always contemplate his own greatness. It is a considerable advantage to a man, to have so inexhaustible a subject. After reading his letters, he leans back in his corner of the carriage, and generally reviews his importance to society."

You can use the same techniques employed to such good effect by Dickens to add outright humor to your work. The way to take advantage of this device—introducing humor into your story—is to develop your sense of the incongruous. Try to exaggerate your characters a bit and use a satirical tone. If all else fails, read Dickens and underline passages that strike you as particularly funny. Then use a similar *tone* or *approach* when describing one of your own characters, especially people you wish to poke fun at. This type of humor will not, it is important to underscore, detract from the high tone or seriousness of your subject. Instead, it will add a much appreciated human element to otherwise serious writing.

MAKE THEM CRY

The second element of Dickens' famous dictum revolves around his use of pathos, or strong emotion. As Aristotle pointed out in his *Poetics*, emotional appeals are one of the chief devices of the orator and, by extension, of the novelist. Novels weren't invented back in Aristotle's time, but drama was, and he pointed to examples from the ancient Greek dramatists where the evocation of pity and fear in the audience was planned in advance by the dramatist. In a similar way a novelist can learn from Dickens how to make readers feel strong emotions.

When Esther learns that her mother is Lady Dedlock, she is surprised. But Dickens knows that surprise is not enough, and he milks

---

10. Dickens 1850:190.

the scene for all it's worth. He knows that a mother and child relationship will be moving, especially one in which a child discovers its mother after a long absence during which the girl was in ignorance. But he has the skill to ratchet up the emotion by having Lady Dedlock tell Esther that they must never speak again and that she (Lady Dedlock) cannot give any help to Esther. Here is a scene calculated to wrench the tears from even a hardened heart.

Our jaded age may find it harder to cry, but Dickens was a master of situations that bring on the sympathy needed to cause reader emotion. The very memorable death of Nell had Americans lining the docks to get their hands on the installment of the magazine with the resolution of that part of *The Old Curiosity Shop* (1841). But Dickens worked himself into a state of near despair to write the scene, turning away offers from friends to visit. In composing that scene he probably went back in his mind to a trauma he had suffered when he watched helplessly as seventeen-year-old Mary Hogarth, his sister-in-law, died in his arms some years earlier.[11] The message is clear: to create emotion you must feel emotion. Do not hesitate to use memories from your own life; indeed, you must do so to produce real emotion on the page. Transmuting your own experiences, you will create art and affect your readers as deeply as you yourself have been affected.

MAKE THEM WAIT

I have to admit that mystery novels were never my cup of tea. My mother and sister dote on them, but I usually find them rather formulaic; I honestly couldn't care less who killed who, and the characters don't interest me since they're simply vehicles for the story to reach a conclusion. I say this not to try to convince anyone *not* to read mysteries but rather to illustrate that even writers who couldn't care less about mysteries *should* pay attention when Dickens tells them that an element of mystery—an *element*, mind you; merely an

---

11. Preston, quoted in Dickens 1841:xv.

element—is *essential* to a well-told story. Who am I, after all, to argue with Dickens!

In a wonderful little book, *Charles Dickens as Serial Novelist* (1967), Archibald C. Coolidge Jr. advances the very convincing proposition that the serial form of publication put certain pressures on Dickens that forced him to solve a typical novelist's problems (such as how to maintain reader interest) in strikingly bold ways. What this means is *very* good for you. It means that Dickens was forced to use his talent to discover and use techniques integral to the novel in a way that are so bold, so striking, and so exaggerated that other writers should find studying his work almost a textbook example of what to do, how to craft stories, and how to create characters people will remember—and care about.[12] One of his most important techniques and one which is often overlooked by writers who prefer *literary* fiction is the use of an element of mystery and suspense. If, like me, you don't respond well to mystery, you may discount its effectiveness in a mainstream story. But this would be a mistake! It behooves us to learn from the master. Dickens called it his mystery story technique. "He solved the problem of the constant need for advance in plot by creating a mystery … which had alternating sublines."[13] An example of the mystery that runs through *Bleak House* (1853) is the identity of Esther's mother. The story also unfolds with many mysterious doings by Lady Dedlock and her husband's attorney, Tulkinghorn. By the time the truth is revealed, the reader is worked up to a fever pitch of interest. The resolution of the mystery is revealed when Lady Dedlock tells Esther that *she* is her mother. The scene is given added poignancy when Lady Dedlock warns Esther that they must never speak again! Not only does Esther find her mother in a dramatic way, at the end of a big mystery plot, but she *loses* her in the same scene. Leave it to Dickens to twist the loose ends of his stories together, interweaving the resolution of the mystery with the fate of Esther.

---

12. Coolidge 1967:4.

13. Coolidge 1967:10.

To provide a mystery in your mainstream novel, you might choose some aspect of the story that can be concealed from the reader. Then play the part of the omniscient writer, who knows all, and do *not* reveal too much … only tell as much as is needed.

In *Great Expectations* (1861), the mystery of the identity of the person giving Pip the money is woven into the story. Pip assumes it is Miss Havisham, the woman who is the guardian of Estella, whom he adores. The mysterious money allows Pip to travel from his humble home to London, where he begins to make a man of himself. The mystery is kept alive by continuing references to the money and to what it does to lift Pip out of poverty. Dickens even uses the word "mystery" occasionally to talk about the mystery! In chapter 40 we are told, from Pip's viewpoint, "Words cannot tell what a sense I had, at the same time, of the dreadful mystery that he [Magwitch, the convict] was to me. When he fell asleep of an evening, with his knotted hands clenching the sides of the easy-chair, and his bald head tattooed with deep wrinkles falling forward on his breast, I would sit and look at him, wondering what he had done." When the mystery is finally resolved and we learn that Magwitch is Pip's secret benefactor, the story gets a jolt of energy because Pip is thrust back into the Miss Havisham plot, and the fact that he had worried about *her* being benefactor requires him to visit her again to find out what she really means to him.

You can use the same Dickensian mystery story technique in your own work by purposefully withholding crucial information, such as who a friend (or enemy) of your hero really is. You can even lead readers in the wrong direction, provided one of the characters legitimately believes the wrong thing, as Pip does when he suspects that his benefactor is Miss Havisham.

Sometimes, the less you tell the more readers love it. So, by all means, make them wait.

CHAPTER 3

WRITE LIKE

Herman Melville

If poetry is what you're after, go to school in the pages of Melville. Along the way you'll learn how to use symbols and create memorable characters. It is no accident that he has been called one of the greatest American novelists.

Born to patrician parents in 1819, Melville grew up surrounded by brothers and sisters in a loving family that was more aristocratic than well-off.[1] During high school he excelled at composition and enjoyed writing essays.[2] His father died when he was twelve, after which his older brother took over much of the responsibility for the family. At nineteen Herman could often be found writing at his desk in the attic.[3] Shortly before his twentieth birthday he went to sea as a cabin boy and enjoyed the experience so much it became a way of life for him during the next few years. On numerous sea voyages he visited the Polynesian Islands, deserted ship to live among cannibals, and worked on a whaler—all of which would become part of his novels and stories. In 1847 he married and shortly thereafter moved to Pittsfield, Massachusetts, where he eventually raised four children and focused much of his time on writing. In Massachusetts he also

---

1. Melville had a brother three and a half years older, a sister two years older, a sister two years younger and, after that another brother and then two more younger sisters, the last of whom was eight years distant.

2. Robertson-Lorant 1996:60.

3. Robertson-Lorant 1996:67. *See also* Milton Meltzer's wonderful biography for a riveting account of Melville's life and work.

befriended Nathaniel Hawthorne, who was to have a profound influence on his prose style.

MELVILLE'S FIRST DRAFT SECRETS

One of his secrets was to put aside all worries about what others might think or criticize in his work.[4] Isolation helped and so did regular working hours. His wife noticed that he couldn't concentrate if he stayed up past midnight and she began encouraging him to adopt a regular schedule.[5] While working on *Moby-Dick* (1851) he sequestered himself away from family and friends to concentrate on the first draft.

> In a week or so, I go to New York, to bury myself in a third-story room, and work and slave on my 'Whale'… *That* is the only way I can finish it now, – I am so pulled hither and thither by circumstances. The calm, the coolness, the silent grass-growing mood in which a man ought always to compose, – that, I fear, can seldom be mine.[6]

Another secret was his method of *resuming* work with gusto after an extended interruption. The first draft of *Moby-Dick* had been interrupted for weeks, but he was determined to jump right back into it. "I'm going to take him by the jaw, however, before long, and finish him up in some fashion or other."[7]

Melville was not above learning from good writers who preceded him; in fact he admitted that he discovered how to write narration from Nathaniel Hawthorne:[8] "I feel that this Hawthorne has dropped germinous seeds into my soul."[9] As one critic observed, "cultivated by a quick intimacy, the seeds developed into the narrative technique of

---

4."Once Herman made up his mind to be a professional writer, he would make a conscious decision not to let the concern for how things might look to other people spoil his 'mood for composition.' Becoming a writer was Melville's way of telling his own truth" (Robertson-Lorant 1996:132).

5. Robertson-Lorant 1996:176.

6. Parker 1996:841. This technique of isolating oneself is used by many writers, most notably J.D. Salinger. Many rent rooms in hotels or lodging houses to work in quiet.

7. Parker 1996:841.

8. Howard 1994:71-72.

9. Melville, quoted in Howard 1994:72.

Moby-Dick."[10] Part of what Melville absorbed from Hawthorne was how to put his convictions and feelings into a work, ensuring that more than a surface tale is told; as a result, *Moby-Dick* is replete with meaning, symbolism, and emotion.

HOW TO BE POETIC

Melville's style crashed onto the scene like a tsunami, smirking at tradition and ultimately bolstering the reputation of the American novel. *Typee* (1846) uses "a limpid, poetic prose style" that sets it apart from other more "prosaic factual travelogues so popular at the time."[11] *Mardi*'s (1849) breathless opening leads into some of the innovator's most lyrical passages:

> We are off! The courses and topsails are set: the coral-hung anchor swings from the bow; and together, the three royals are given to the breeze, that follows us out to sea like the baying of a hound. Out spreads the canvas—alow, aloft—boom-stretched, on both sides, with many a stun' sail; till like a hawk, with pinions poised, we shadow the sea with our sails, and reelingly cleave the brine.

Writing like this brought out the worst in Melville's critics. In fact he was so often the target of literary brickbats that he became defensive. When *Typee* was lambasted as improbable and fabricated, he begged an acquaintance to submit a rebuttal ghostwritten by himself.[12] About the novel one critic opined, "These discursions, these graces, this flowery style, festooned, twisted into quaint shapes, call to mind the arabesques of certain writing masters, which render the text unintelligible."[13] On the whole, however, there were more positive than negative reviews.[14] If nothing else the laudatory comments on his poetic style should encourage you to take risks with your own prose.

---

10. Howard 1994:72.

11. Robertson-Lorant 1996:141.

12. Robertson-Lorant 1996:144.

13. Chasles 1849:171.

14. According to a modern critic, "the style was universally praised by the reviewers" (Branch 1997:4).

One of the techniques Melville used, which can be adapted by modern writers, was to infuse his books with the rollicking rhythms and lilting notes of poetry, employing both meter and alliteration in countless passages.[15] In a letter to a friend, he stated:

> It will be a strange sort of book, tho', I fear; blubber is blubber you know; tho' you may get oil out of it, the poetry runs as hard as sap from a frozen maple tree; – & to cook the thing up, one must needs throw in a little fancy, which from the nature of the thing, must be ungainly as the gambols of the whales themselves. Yet I mean to give the truth of the thing, spite of this.[16]

What Melville is admitting here is that he used poetic techniques consciously: The rolling meter and alliteration didn't just pop into his head unbidden; he worked as hard for these effects as a poet. But do *you* have to be a *published* poet to do the same? Certainly not; all it takes is some sensitivity to sound and sense.

Here's an example of what we're talking about. Before the main action of *Moby-Dick* gets underway, the narrator arrives, in chapter thirteen, at the whaling town of New Bedford. The fifth paragraph contains a profusion of alliteration.[17]

> New Bedford rose in terraces of streets, their ice-covered trees all glittering in the clear, cold air. Huge hills and mountains of casks on casks were piled upon her wharves, and side by side the world-wandering whale ships lay silent and safely moored at last; while from others came a sound of carpenters and coopers, with blended noises of fires and forges to melt the pitch, all betokening that new cruises were on the start; that one most perilous and long voyage ended, only begins a second; and a second ended, only begins a third and so on, for ever and for aye. Such is the endlessness, yea, the intolerableness of all earthly effort.

---

15. We will see Nabokov using somewhat similar techniques a hundred years later. It is also highly relevant to note that much of Melville's stylistic bravura is a result of his creative imitation of other writers, including Hawthorne, Virgil, Shakespeare, and Mary Shelley's *Frankenstein* (Delbanco 2005:126-131, 138).

16. Quoted in Branch 1997:24.

17. I'm indebted to Andrew Delbanco for pointing this out in his excellent biography (Delbanco 2005:128-129).

Looking at this passage, one biographer compared Melville's work to the best of poetry. "In the long second sentence, the range of alliterated initial consonant sounds mimics the 'blended noises' of men laboring on the docks. ... seven pairs and one triplet of alliterated words that perfectly convey the ceaseless repetition of the dockside work. ... He achieves here a mastery of verbal effects that one expects from only the most accomplished poetry."[18] A modern writer may wonder whether he has the nerve to dare anything quite so bold. Melville has thrown down the gauntlet though few have been the brave souls who have picked it up. Yet the careful use of alliteration appears in some of the most powerful prose works of the twentieth century, including novels by Nabokov, Bradbury and Roth.[19] Often the best use of alliteration, however, is that which readers do not consciously notice.

HOW TO USE SYMBOLS

Some modern novelists fail to make effective use of symbolism, as if they were afraid that using a symbol might label them as striving after literary significance. But the fact is that symbolism, if used judiciously, can infuse added meaning into a work and lead to greater reader satisfaction.

Melville is a good writer to study to learn how to use symbolism, not only because he used many symbols but also because he wove them into his work to support a central vision. The whale is clearly a symbol of the Self, a Jungian archetype of the integrated personality.[20]

---

18. Delbanco 2005:128-129. Delbanco's book presents an excellent analysis of the poetry in Melville's prose and is well worth reading for its analysis.

19. Alliteration and other poetic devices in Nabokov's *Lolita* are analyzed in Proffer 1968. Bradbury's *Something Wicked This Way Comes* is probably his most poetic work. Roth begins *The Great American Novel* with a first sentence clearly a homage to Melville and a first paragraph that uses alliteration more than forty times. The character's psychiatrist warns him to *reduce* his use of the poetic device. *See also* Baker 2004.

20. Booker 2004: 358-364. Booker's reading puts to shame a generation of critics who have flailed about trying to decipher the great mystery of what the whale means. For example, the whale has been interpreted as symbolizing "another world" (Sherrill: 1986:89). Naturally it *could* potentially mean anything to anybody, but when you have a good fit and a meaning that explains the entire work it's probably best to stick with it.

Ahab lacks this integrated personality and is driven by a lopsided madness, often referred to as monomania because he is focused so intently on destruction. Revenge has blinded him to any acceptance of his fate as a cripple. One critic suggests that "Captain Ahab is an embodiment of that fallen angel or demigod who in Christendom was variously named Lucifer, Devil, Adversary, Satan."[21] That might be close to the mark, but perhaps closer still is to suggest that Ahab symbolizes the failed attempt at self-integration, the neurotic over-emphasis on hatred that ruins everyone else's life. Because of Ahab all the sailors, except the narrator, perish.

Once the central symbol of your work is discovered, peripheral symbols can be manipulated to provide a constellation of heightened meaning and significance. If the whale symbolizes the Self, an integrated personality that men long for,[22] we can see why Ahab does *not* reach the goal: He has not allowed forgiveness into his heart; he has never gotten over his mad lust for revenge. No man can live a good life like that. Queequeg then become clear as a symbol of the man who comes *closer* to the ideal, a "noble savage," as Melville terms him in chapter thirty-four. As one critic observes, Queequeg symbolizes Melville's mature appreciation of "brotherhood, religious tolerance, the beauty of the instinctive."[23] Ishmael is then "the symbol of Everyman."[24] He too seeks the integrated personality, the white whale. But why does he alone survive? The answer lies in his *difference* from Ahab: Ishmael does not let himself become swept up in the unreasonable, tyrannical savagery of the mad captain. He maintains a sense of moderation and knows his

---

21. Murray 1956:10.

22. The most moving and persuasive interpretation of this book that I have read, and I've read them all, is that proposed by Christopher Booker. "Moby Dick is god-like: the image of a mighty creature at one with life and with nature; in perfect harmony with the great spirit that moves the universe; a complete symbol of the transcendent Self. And the total opposite to this is that dark, murderous embodiment of the human ego personified in the demonic madman now bent on his destruction" (Booker 2004:363).

23. Vincent 1949:78. Vincent's analysis of symbols in Melville is excellent. *See also* Booker 2004:359.

24. Vincent 1949:339.

FICTION WRITING *Master Class*

limits, something Ahab does not. Ishmael also knows right from wrong, while Ahab is blind to any morality but his own. Ismael controls his impulses, but Ahab *cannot* control his.

Modern writers should be emboldened by Melville's work and inspired to use symbolism. There is no use feeling inferior simply because *he* did such superb work; although that's often a response writers slip into upon seeing brilliant craftsmanship.[25] You can use Melville's technique in your own work, especially if you have a central character who embodies dark elements—lack of insight, vengefulness, monomania, and other egotistical qualities. By creating counterbalancing light characters[26] you can set them up as foils to the heavy.[27] In this way you can move back and forth from work on the particulars of characterization to the abstract concept (the symbol) in a process which Ayn Rand referred to as the quick dance a writer does "between abstractions and concretes."[28] Abstractions are the symbolic meanings of a character or thing; concretes are the descriptions of the characters and things and their actions in the narrative. By working on both processes simultaneously you can free your creativity and avoid being smothered by just one or the other. The creation of symbols works best when it goes hand in hand with the detailed creation of character and plot. As you do this work you will discover deeper meanings in your own story, which is part of the joy of writing.

---

25. For example, J.D. Salinger felt inferior to Kafka. Keats was worried about his inferiority to Shakespeare, but he developed a ten-year plan to read and outshine Shakespeare. Brian Wilson of the Beach Boys fell into a deep depression upon hearing the Beatles' *Rubber Soul*, worrying that he would never be able to surpass such a perfect album.

26. The concept of light and dark characters is taken from Christopher Booker. Like Northrop Frye, Booker excels at explicating how literature embodies archetypes. His *Seven Basic Plots* provides one of the most helpful approaches to interpretation for the working writer. *See* Booker 2004, especially chapters thirteen and eighteen for a discussion of dark and light characters.

27. Melville used symbols for a wide range of other effects, including to attack Transcendentalism (Vincent 1949:151, 155), to present a Freudian death wish in the person of Ahab (Shneidman 1986:553), and to personify reason as a guiding light for mankind in the character of Bulkington, who is otherwise not integral to the plot (Gleim 1938:64-65). All these symbols are peripheral to the central symbol of the whale as the integrated Self.

28. Rand 2000:52-55.

SECRETS OF CHARACTERIZATION

Melville was sometimes accused of using hyperbole and exaggeration in drawing his main characters. "The characterizations in *Moby-Dick* also suffered the charge of extravagance. Ahab, especially, was labeled exaggerated, though many reviewers accepted his monomania as reason enough for his wild actions, and they admitted the need for an extraordinary human being to do battle with the white whale."[29] For the student of characterization, however, no better model exists than Melville, in large part because the brushstrokes are so bold that they can be seen and studied much more easily than the work of more subtle masters of character.

The portrait of Ahab is one of the most famous in all literature. It is also one of the most technically accomplished. Melville uses four literary devices to characterize, the first of which is *complexity*, meaning that Ahab is described with conflicting characteristics. For example, he is said to be both good and bad, sane and insane, knowable and unknowable. The second device is that of *unreliability* since we're hearing about him from other characters (including Captain Peleg and Captain Bildad, both of whom have a biased view of Ahab). As a result the characterization has a nebulous uncertain quality. Put more simply, readers need to sift fact from fiction if they are to know Ahab. Using the device of unreliability draws readers into the tale and usually creates heightened reader interest. The third device Melville employs is *selection*, meaning focusing on only a few main traits, such as zeroing in on madness and monomania to limn Ahab. And finally, Melville uses the device of *mystery*, by stating that there are things that are unknown or unknowable about Ahab, leading readers to wonder what more there is to learn about this man.

The description of Ahab begins with macabre echoes and intimations of madness. A conversation with another captain furnishes Ishmael with some facts about the mysterious Ahab. Note how heavily Melville relies on the device of complexity in this initial description

---

29. Branch 1997:27-28.

(as I have indicated in the passage below), although he also uses mystery, unreliability, and selection.

> I don't know exactly what's the matter with him [*mystery*]; …a sort of sick. … In fact, he ain't sick; but no, he isn't well either [*complexity*]. … He's a queer man, Captain Ahab–so some think–but a good one [*complexity*] … He's a grand, ungodly, god-like man [*complexity*], Captain Ahab. … Ahab's been in colleges, as well as 'mong the cannibals [*complexity*]. …his crazy, widowed mother … died when he was only a twelvemonth old. … I know Captain Ahab well … I know what he is [*unreliability*]–a good man–not a pious, good man [*complexity*] … but a swearing good man [*complexity*] … on the passage home, he was a little out of his mind for a spell [*selection*]; but it was the sharp shooting pains in his bleeding stump that brought that about, as any one might see. I know, too, that ever since he lost his leg last voyage by that accursed whale, he's been a kind of moody–desperate moody, and savage sometimes [*selection*]. …it's better to sail with a moody good [*complexity*] captain than a laughing bad one.

After studying Melville you would be perfectly within your rights to experiment with the same literary devices. Remember, you never hear boxers say, "Oh, I'm not going to use a jab. That was Muhammad Ali's technique." That would be the height of folly. The same argument holds true in writing. Sure, you want to strive for originality, but you can't ignore the foundation. It would be just as fatal for a writer to ignore successful literary devices as it would be for a boxer to get in the ring and fail to use jabs. The bottom line is that these literary devices are not beyond the ken of anyone reading this book, and they are also not copyrighted. True, Ahab is one of the most successfully developed characters of all time, but that doesn't mean you can't use the same devices in characterizing.

Be fearless about employing similar techniques in layering various aspects of characterization. Don't forget to include complexity and contrary impulses in the same character. An all-bad or all-good character is far less compelling than one (like Ahab or, for that matter, Holden Caulfield) who is composed of both good and bad. Don't make your hero too perfect; allow him his imperfections and foibles and readers will welcome him into their hearts, seeing in him a reflection of themselves.

At the same time include mystery in your characterization, leaving some things undefined and unexplained. Have characters wonder about other characters, about their motives, their actions, their goals. This suspense and mystery adds another layer to the character and builds a more realistic portrayal of a person.

If possible add some element of unreliability, either with an unreliable narrator or through the reflections and ruminations of other characters. Using this literary device will involve your readers in creating the character since they have to figure him out for themselves. Readers find this enjoyable, and they'll thank you for letting them have fun when reading your work.

And last but not least use selection, focusing on just a few main traits. Don't try to create three-dimensional characters by throwing in the kitchen sink like the naturalists. Doing so, as Ayn Rand observes, you'll wind up, ironically, with characters who "are overdetailed and never fully real."[30] The two or three traits you select will suffice to create your own Ahab.

---

30. Rand admires the naturalists as good writers but observes that their overdetailed character portraits fail to provide anything more than a kitchen-sink approach and leave us with too much detail. Better to select a few traits that define your characters, and your readers will come away with a stronger and more vivid portrait (Rand 2000:81).

CHAPTER 4

WRITE LIKE

Fyodor Dostoevsky

There's one thing Dostoevsky does better than any other writer. He immerses readers in a vividly imagined world in which humiliation and shame figure as the overarching emotions, a world in which characters become disorganized and disoriented because of their feelings. "[H]e develops a narrative strategy that involves his readers' immersing themselves in the experience of shame."[1] As we will see, the technical accomplishments that allow him to do this can enable you to write powerful scenes focusing on *any* emotion, not only shame and humiliation.

Fyodor Dostoevsky was born in 1821 in Russia, the second of seven children. His father was a physician prone to alcoholism and bursts of violent temper. Dostoevsky excelled at languages in school and by the time he was twenty-two had translated Balzac's *Eugénie Grandet* into Russian. Arrested for participation in a liberal political group, he was scheduled to be executed by firing squad, but at the last minute a pardon was granted. For the rest of his life he suffered epileptic fits, a characteristic he imparted to Prince Myshkin in *The Idiot*. When he was forty-six Dostoevsky married his twenty-year-old stenographer, and their marriage brought much needed stability to his life.[2]

---

1. Martinsen 2003:12.

2. Simmons 1940:180–181.

DOSTOEVSKY'S SUPERB
VIEWPOINT CONTROL

To tell stories with nerve-racking intensity Dostoevsky shifts from mind to mind in a carefully calculated manner. This allows him to tap into whatever emotion is most relevant for any given scene. He employs a specific method that involves scene setting, penetration into one mind, and then shifting to the next mind. Once you master the technique you'll find that you can write your own intense scenes, filled not only with shame and humiliation, like Dostoevsky, but with any emotions you find appropriate to *your* story.

Dostoevsky begins setting the scene in part five, chapter four of *Crime and Punishment* (1866). This is one of the most wonderful sections of the novel, narrating how Raskolnikov reveals to his girlfriend Sonia that he is a killer. He fully expects her to reject him forever. Instead, he's surprised when she tells him that she loves him and that she feels sorrow and pity because he has harmed *himself* so dearly by doing this stupid thing! The scene is set swiftly in a friend's apartment. "[H]e quickly opened the door, and looked at Sonia from the threshold. She was sitting with her elbows on the table, hiding her face in her hands; but when she saw Raskolnikov she got up quickly, and went toward him as though she had been expecting him." Even the setting of the scene has a sense of urgency. It is written with an eye toward letting the reader clearly know *who* is present and where they are in relation to each other so that we can then visit the minds of each individual in turn while still remaining oriented to the scene.

The next step is to penetrate into the mind of one of the characters. It helps if the person is in the midst of turmoil and strong feelings, and certainly that is the case here. Raskolnikov has just confessed that he is the one who killed Lizaveta, and Dostoevsky jumps into his mind: "As soon as he said it ... he ... remembered clearly Lizaveta's expression as he approached her with the ax and she backed away from him toward the wall with her arm raised in front of her and a completely childlike fear in her face."[3] This description is the height of craft: It is a brilliantly

---

3. Dostoevsky 1866:391.

timed penetration into the mind of Raskolnikov and it reveals deep emotion. Typical of Dostoevsky, it expands upon the theme of shame because Raskolnikov is rightly ashamed of what he did; he is embarrassed about having to reveal to his girlfriend that he is a killer, and he begins to feel ashamed of the fact that he is a murderer. The boldness of the inner turmoil reveals Dostoevsky at his best.

The final step is to switch to the next character. Dostoevsky waltzes through the process as if it were the easiest thing in the world. Once we have heard the inner workings of Raskolnikov's mind, we are told: "Sonia looked at him quickly. After the first passionate and agonized feeling of sympathy for the unfortunate man, the terrifying idea of the murder once again stunned her. In the altered tone of his words she suddenly heard the murderer. She looked at him with astonishment. She still did not know why or how or for what it had been done."[4] Notice the artful way Dostoevsky makes this shift. He doesn't do it when Sonia is thinking any *ordinary placid thoughts;* on the contrary, he makes the shift *when she is at the height of her passion,* when she is *beside herself with emotion,* when she is *stunned* with the news of the murder and her mind is in *a whirlwind of conflicting and confusing thoughts and feelings.* Notice also, which is significant and useful for a writer, that he does not simply pile up thoughts and overburden us with them. Instead he alternates Sonia's thoughts with her *actions,* so that we are told, *in the midst* of her thoughts, exactly what she does: "She looked at him with astonishment." Then back to her thoughts: "She still did not know why or how or for what it [the murder] had been done." This alternation between thought and action keeps the reader alert to *who* is thinking and to what she is *doing* while thinking, which greatly enhances *the illusion of reality.* We *see* her, and we are *in her mind* … the process is complete! With this one device—seamlessly moving from mind to mind *within a scene*—you can move mountains; but even more importantly *you can move readers.* This is what novels are best at—rendering the inner workings of the character's soul, of their mind, of their "central nervous system"![5]

---

4. Dostoevsky 1866:393.

5. "But the real point of view, in which the audience feels that it is inside the mind, or the central nervous system, of a character—movies have *never* been able to do this." Novels and nonfiction do this better than any other medium (Wolfe, quoted in Scura 1990:51).

DOSTOEVSKY'S TRANSITION SECRET

Transitions are another device Dostoevsky uses with consummate skill. Admittedly this is a device that all story writers must master, but in the intervening century since he wrote, writers have made no advances in writing transitions; in fact, most contemporary writers do a more *awkward* job at it than the Russian master! Dostoevsky is fast, efficient, and almost cinematic in cutting from scene to scene. But he also has an added secret that you're going to love—for it ensures that your transitions work smoothly.

Let's consider an example of this transition secret from one of Dostoevsky's early works. The fact that he was using it so early, and that he continued to use it throughout his career, suggests that he found it vitally important and useful. In *Notes From Underground* (1864) one chapter closes with the antihero taking a coach to a hotel party. The transition at the top of the next chapter is sketched swiftly for us.

> "I knew in advance that I would be the first. But now it was no longer a question of who was first.
>
> "Not only were none of them there, but I had difficulty in finding our room."[6]

The cut is made efficiently because there is no excess verbiage. We are simply at the new location. But more importantly Dostoevsky brings us there through the *consciousness* of his narrator, and as a result we are ushered into the new location by both a physical description, which is actually minimal, and by the emotional *significance* of his being there, which is much more significant. In fact Dostoevsky's use of *emotion* in transitions is a sophistical technique that most modern writers never use because they simply don't know about it.

Let's look at another example. The same sophisticated transition is used in *The Brothers Karamazov* (1880). In book two, chapter one, we learn of the arrival of Pyotr Miusov and Pyotr Kalganov at a new location. Dostoevsky has one of the men arrive in an undecided state,

---

6. Dostoevsky 1864:83.

reflecting about whether he should enter a university. The other man arrives late. In two swift moves the transition has been accomplished in a way that propels us forward into the new location with the *emotional baggage* that the men bring with them: undecidedness and lateness. We're not simply told that we are someplace new; instead, we are injected into this new location *through the emotional feelings* of the two characters.

An even more brilliant example of Dostoevsky's transition prowess occurs at the close of *The Idiot* (1868) when Prince Myshkin arrives at the house where he will find the woman he loves murdered. Dostoevsky begins with his usual efficient technique:

> About fifty paces from the hotel, at the first crossing, someone in the crowd suddenly touched his elbow and said in a low voice directly into his ear:
>
> "Lev Nikolayevitch, follow me, brother. I want you."
>
> It was Rogozhin.

Then Dostoevsky sets his transition trap: The prince is in a *jovial* mood, so that when he sees the murdered woman the *change* in his emotions are sharp and jarring. "Curiously enough, the prince began joyfully telling him—babbling away and barely getting the words out—how he had expected to see him just now in the corridor at the hotel."[7] In two blinks of an eye the scene is switched and the prince is no longer alone; snatched out of the crowd, so to speak, by the murderer, the prince is in a good mood. This quick transition, with the *emotion* of the prince highlighted, draws us into the new scene with the force of an explosion; a perfect segue into a set piece where the prince will lose his mind.

To use Dostoevsky's transition method, ignore the work of most modern writers who simply change localities. Yes, they do this *efficiently* enough, but Dostoevsky adds a twist that will take your readers' breath away. Remember, first of all, to make your transition quick. Then add to that change in location some *emotional element,* preferably in the heart of the protagonist or focus character. This two-pronged approach

---

7. Dostoevsky 1868:630.

is sure to make your transitions effective. Using Dostoevsky's method you'll achieve more than admirable cinematic *quickness* as you cut from one locale to the next. You'll also keep readers *engaged* and *involved* as you make the transition because everyone responds to emotion—much more so than to mere description. As a result your two-step transitions will bridge the gap between scenes with a force rarely encountered in modern fiction. And if you can add the master touch of *reversal* of emotion as you transition from one scene to the next ... well, then in the next edition of this book we'll be writing about *you*.

MAKING READERS LIKE YOUR VOICE

Voice is a term of art used for a writer's unique tone, feeling, and individuality that is expressed through word choice, style, and other linguistic devices. Dostoevsky uses two secrets to make readers *like* his voice. First, when employing a first-person narrator, he often has them admit their sicknesses, frailties, and weaknesses. This same device is used to good effect by J.D. Salinger in *The Catcher in the Rye* (1951), by Hermann Hesse in *Steppenwolf* (1972), by Mark Twain in *Adventures of Huckleberry Finn* (1884), and by Hunter S. Thompson in *Fear and Loathing in Las Vegas* (1971). The second technique is to get cozy with readers—the Uncle Albert-style of storytelling. Clearly both techniques are as valid today as they were when Dostoevsky used them. In other words, relying on these devices won't make your work sound old-fashioned; it will instead electrify readers and make them lean forward to hear every word.

Remember that J.D. Salinger used one of these techniques: Holden tells us all his own weaknesses and foibles. Well, guess who Salinger learned that from? Good old Dostoevsky. The fact is that Dostoevsky is a past master of making readers like his voice. In *Notes From Underground* the main character begins with the famous opening:

> I am a sick man. ... I am a spiteful man. An unattractive° man. I think my liver hurts. But actually, I don't know a damn thing about my illness. I am not even sure what it is that hurts. I am not in treatment and never have been, although I respect both medicine and doctors. Besides, I am

superstitious in the extreme; well, at least to the extent of respecting medicine. … No, sir, I refuse to see a doctor simply out of spite.

The narrator is highly unlikable, has numerous faults, and is in many ways difficult to comprehend. Yet the very fact that he *has* problems and that he *admits* this frankly is what overcomes our resistance and makes us curious. *Such an oddity!* we think. *Surely this is going to be one hell of a story.* By obtaining this kind of a response from readers Dostoevsky gets us to turn pages. We're hoping to put all the pieces together and find a method in the character's madness. That's how he works his magic with a first-person narrator.

Dostoevsky's second method is to cozy up to the reader in a roundabout way with a voice that's more like *speech* than edited prose. As one critic points out:

> The polyphony of *The Brothers Karamazov* extends to the narrative voice. Dostoevsky chose a personalized narrative voice. The narrator's manner is that of a "conversation with the reader," and his vocabulary and syntax tend to be those of an improvised oral narrative: sentences and paragraphs are not well-constructed and well-balanced, but appear as " 'chains of sentences' in which thoughts are grasped, as it were, step-by-step … as though the author were gradually … groping his way toward a definitive formulation of his ideas."[8]

This folksy verbal style may make it more difficult for readers to *follow* what is happening, but it certainly compensates for this by increasing reader *interest* and *enhancing reader participation* in what is happening. The bottom line is that readers respond to the warmth and personality of the voice.

WHY DOSTOEVSKY'S CHARACTERS ARE SO MEMORABLE

Dostoevsky's characters are memorable for many reasons, not the least of which is that they are described in a way that reveals their personality.

8. Terras 1981:87, quoting Braun 1976:271, 272-273

"Dmitry Fyodorovich, a young man of twenty-eight, of medium height and pleasing aspect, looked, however, much older than his years."[9] With this first sentence Dostoevsky piques our interest. Why does Dmitry look older than his years? What does this mean? What *can* it signify, since everything *should* have meaning in a well-constructed novel? "He was muscular, and by all appearances, physically very strong; nevertheless, there was something sickly about his face. For all the resolute intensity of his protruding, rather large dark eyes, there was a certain indecision in them." Things get curiouser and curiouser the more we *see* of Dmitry. For Dostoevsky knows that in a novel what is on the outside is what is on the inside. Put more simply, a character's physical description reveals his or her inner personality. Writers who realize this can tailor their descriptions to unmask subtle personality traits.

Dostoevsky's characters are also remarkable because of their violent and hectic thoughts. In *Notes From Underground* the narrator meets a prostitute, Liza, and is acutely embarrassed when she comes to visit him. He is ashamed because he is impoverished and living in a hovel. "I stood before her, crushed, humiliated, sickeningly ashamed, and, I think, smiling as I struggled desperately to wrap myself in my tattered quilted robe."[10] Passion and confusion mark the character as a man apart. The same hectic quality and whirlwind thoughts define Raskolnikov, Dmitry, and Prince Myshkin; indeed, all Dostoevsky's major characters experience similar disoriented mental processes, drawing readers into the whirlpool of their disjointed lives.

No discussion of Dostoevsky would be complete without touching upon the *actions* of his characters—the outlandish things they do and the stunningly bold paths they follow. Raskolnikov murders for the sake of murder simply to prove he is a superman who *could* commit such a crime. What could be more bold, more stunning, more dramatic! The Underground Man decides to sleep with a prostitute and then tries to *humiliate* her by giving her money, only to find that in

---

9. Dostoevsky 1880a:85.
10. Dostoevsky 1864:138.

the end *he* is the one who is ashamed and humiliated—by her and by her love for him! Prince Myshkin offers to marry Nastasya Filippovna, then finds her murdered by his rival ... and as a result he loses his mind! Dmitry nearly murders his own father as they become rivals for the love and affection of Grushenka! The outrageous actions of the characters, the boldness of the plot twists, the violent passion his protagonists feel—all this marks Dostoevsky's characters as exceptional.

To access the same devices in your own work, set your sights beyond the norm. Once you have thought of an action, stop and ponder whether you can up the ante by making it bolder, more striking, even more outrageous. Add telltale descriptions and whirlwind thoughts into the mix. Then and only then will you have achieved the Dostoevsky touch so that your characters *will* be memorable.

SPEED UP YOUR READER'S PULSE WITH DOSTOEVSKY'S METHOD OF WRITING DESCRIPTIONS

The nineteenth century was the crucible of realism in fiction, and writers like Balzac, Dickens, Zola and Tolstoy piled on details and created worlds familiar to readers of their day. As Tom Wolfe argues, realism was the single most important discovery that set the novel on the right course and it is the *only* course which will assure its continuing success.[11] Dostoevsky is part of this grand tradition, but like all nineteenth-century novelists he wrote much wordier descriptions than typical modern writers. In the middle of chapter three in part six of *Crime and Punishment*, for example, Raskolnikov leans his "chin on the fingers of his right hand" and stares "intently at Svidrigailov." Then the reader is regaled with a 116-word paragraph describing the landowner, Svidrigailov, before having the scene resume with the rest of their conversation.[12] Today, such wordiness would probably be out of place, but

---

11. Wolfe complains that "there are talented people [today] writing stories where the hero has no social background or social context. He's just a hero and people don't speak in any language that would betray a social background." In no uncertain terms, says Wolfe, "It's ruining certain careers" (Wolfe, quoted in Scura 1990:34).

12. Dostoevsky 1866:445.

the description itself could be shortened to fit a modern audience. For example, these touches could easily be employed to intrigue readers: "It was a strange face, rather like a mask." And later in the paragraph, "There was something terribly unpleasant about this handsome and unusually well-preserved face." Notice that these descriptive passages are loaded with emotional overtones and connotations: The face was *strange* and like a *mask*; there was something *unpleasant* about it.

Introducing emotion into description is one way Dostoevsky makes his portraits effective and moving. But he also links physical description to the *meaning* of a character, as we have already mentioned. "Rarely is a detail of physical character deployed merely to establish the character's corporeal credentials. ... Instead, external details serve a symbolic function by betraying the inner, spiritual world."[13] Alyosha in *The Brothers Karamazov* is described in a way that illuminates his inner goodness and nobility. "Alyosha was at that time a personable, red-cheeked youth of nineteen with a bright gaze and bursting with health. He was in those days even very handsome—well-proportioned, of average height, with dark-brown hair and a straight, though somewhat elongated oval of a face, brilliant wide-spaced dark-grey eyes, most reflective and to all appearance most calm."[14] Dostoevsky goes on for quite a while, continuing this physical description and commenting upon it in a perambulating manner that might be out of place in a modern novel, but the salient points could easily be incorporated into a modern writer's work by highlighting the positives when describing a character for whom you wish your readers to have a positive reaction, and vice versa.

But perhaps Dostoevsky's most stunning technical accomplishments in the realm of description include those aspects of the horrible and pulse-pounding that pertain to the violent acts of his characters. The murders in *Crime and Punishment* are described numerous times: first when they are anticipated, second when they actually happen, and

---

13. Leatherbarrow 1992:85.
14. Dostoevsky 1880b:38-39.

FICTION WRITING *Master Class*

then repeatedly from different psychological angles as Raskolnikov thinks about them and worries about what he has done and begins to feel guilty about the brutal slaying of two elderly women. The death of Nastasya in *The Idiot* is another triumph of florid yet realistic description, which begins with the ominous words: "The prince took another step forward, then another, and stopped dead." Dostoevsky does a brilliant thing with his descriptions, he extends them when they are emotional, to milk the scenes and the descriptions for all they're worth. As with the repetition and recurring nature of the murders in *Crime and Punishment,* the murder of Nastasya in *The Idiot* is dwelt on for the space of many pages as the prince and the murderer, Rogozhin, sit in the apartment with the corpse, talking earnestly while the prince begins to lose his mind.

The numerous devices Dostoevsky uses to wring meaning from simple description can be incorporated into modern writing by imitating his method of introducing emotion and symbolic meaning into physical description. When you have a memorable or violent scene, repeat it in the mind of your characters for added effect. Do not hesitate to milk the description for all it's worth, having characters remain at the location of the horror or the violent incident. In this way, you will gain the kind of mileage from a description that will make readers remember it.

Dostoevsky is a writer's writer. His work, while somewhat wordy for modern tastes, nevertheless has timeless value for storytellers. No fiction is complete without penetration to the heart and soul of characters, and Dostoevsky shows us how to accomplish this, how to transition effectively, how to use a voice readers will embrace, and how to describe physical and mental states of characters affected by powerful emotion. This is Dostoevsky's legacy and his gift to contemporary writers.

CHAPTER 5

WRITE LIKE

Knut Hamsun

If you yearn for something new in literature, for a writer who is a bold and fearless innovator, you'll likely embrace the work of Knut Hamsun. In addition to developing an ingenious way of portraying multidimensional and lifelike characters, he also broke new ground in presenting the passage of time in stories. But he wasn't simply seeking change for the sake of change. He also developed a theory of literature upon which his work was based.[1]

Born in 1859 in Norway, Hamsun was a middle child. He traveled to the United States a number of times, finding employment as a streetcar conductor and in various menial jobs. His most ambitious project in America, however, was offering a series of lectures on the novel. He believed that the conventional novel, with its focus on a static character who has a dominant trait, was seriously flawed and not true to life. Like Tom Wolfe, he had a clear *theory* of the novel (although, unlike Wolfe, he did not prioritize realism), and he hoped to put his theory to practical use in novels of his own. Eventually he returned to Norway and continued to speak on the topic of the contemporary novel. Hamsun was excited about his controversial new ideas (some would say disconcerting new ideas), and he would use this new approach to write a new kind of fiction. His books would break from the traditional linear

---

1. See the "Introduction" to Sverre Lyngstad's 2001 translation of *Mysteries*, which discusses Hamsun's lectures and his article "From the Unconscious Life of the Mind" (Hamsun 1892:xv-xvi).

progression of a story and include Dostoevskian emotional content, internal monologue that shifts quickly between two or more time periods, and dream sequences that let him portray the inner state of his characters with a dazzling faithfulness to the flickering and unpredictable light of consciousness.

CONQUERING WRITER'S BLOCK

In stark contrast with his innovative view of the novel, Hamsun had a very traditional view of the role of women—in life and in literature. "In his novels, women are happiest as mothers, while education, civilization, and travel destroy and spoil them."[2] His first marriage ended in failure, in part because of his insistence that his wife give up her independence. His second marriage "was much more successful. However, the cost to [her] of holding the marriage together was enormous. She gave up her career as an actress and agreed to move with Hamsun to a remote location in order to experience Hamsun's dream of unspoiled wondrous nature."[3] Like Herman Melville, J.D. Salinger, and numerous other writers, Hamsun left his wife "for months at a time" so that he could work on his books "in hotels or boarding houses instead of at home."[4] Indeed, he believed that he could get over his frequent bouts of writer's block by impulsively leaving home for a new location from which to set up shop and write. The technique usually worked, too, and he wrote some of his best material after leaving familiar surroundings.[5]

THE MAN WHO TAUGHT HEMINGWAY AND KAFKA

Despite early success as a writer Hamsun ran into significant political difficulty during World War II. He was so adamantly anti-British

---

2. Zagar 1998.

3. Ibid.

4. Ibid.

5. Unfortunately the technique did not *always* work for him, although it usually did and he found a new location a stimulus to creativity (Ferguson 1987:282).

that he went so far as to support Hitler, even when the Germans rolled their tanks into Norway and occupied the country. After the war he was fined for supporting the Germans and he lost a considerable amount of money. His work was also slighted and ignored, especially in England and America. This neglect was an unfortunate result of his strong political views. It was not so much that Hamsun was pro-Germany—in fact, when Norwegians were being executed, he met with the Germans to try to have the killings stopped—instead, it was his anti-British feelings that caused him to lose perspective and rather uncritically and unconditionally support the Nazi invasion. Because of this controversial position, his work fell into disfavor after the war, and he is relatively unknown today in America.

Hamsun won the Nobel Prize in 1920 for *Growth of the Soil* (1917); ironically, one of his most uninspired books.[6] Much more technically interesting for our purposes were his novels *Mysteries* (1892) and *Victoria* (1898), both of which took significant risks with character portrayal and the innovative use of language. Hamsun has been called "a veritable prose poet, as well as a pioneer of the psychological novel."[7] Often he presents two characters who represent two sides of a single personality, a literary device known as a doppelgänger, and one which was used to good effect by Hermann Hesse (an admirer of Hamsun) in much of his work.[8]

Although he had political problems at home, Hamsun's writing was read closely by British and American novelists, including D.H. Lawrence, Hemingway and Kafka.[9] They sought to learn the

---

6. In a thoughtful essay Edmund White observes that Hamsun's best work was done early in his career with books like *Mysteries, Pan*, and *Victoria*. Later in life Hamsun only hit the high notes of his youth with two inspired books: *Under the Autumn Star* and *On Overgrown Paths*. Indeed, White characterizes *Growth of the Soil* as "tedious" (White 1996:25).

7. Buttry 1982:1.

8. For example, in Hamsun's novel *Mysteries* Nagel and the dwarf are two facets of the same man. In his short story "Hemmelig Ve" [English title "Secret Suffering"] "both men are two facets of a single personality" (Buttry 1982:3). Hesse employs the doppelgänger prominently in *Narcissus and Goldmund* (1930), *Steppenwolf* (1927), and *Demian* (1919).

secrets of his style and to apply his technical mastery of emotional content to their own work. From Hamsun they discovered that the emotional life of a character can be conveyed by dream sequences, by poetic writing, and by abandoning a linear plot to adhere more closely to the vagaries of the human heart. From Hamsun modern writers can learn some of the most sophisticated methods of getting to the heart of the changeable nature of human consciousness. If you seek to write about people in a way that respects their multifaceted complexity, Hamsun can show you how to break free from the common and ordinary method of portraying a character with one or two dominant traits in favor of a technique that more closely mirrors the quick and frequent changes that characterize all human minds and hearts.

Hamsun surely was right when he criticized modern fiction. Most novels do tell a story in a linear fashion, beginning at one point in time and moving forward through a series of linked episodes or scenes which are causally connected and which affect one another like a string of dominos falling one after the other once the inciting incident sets the whole shebang in motion. True, modern writers often employ the device of flashbacks, but this can be seen as a background device, little more. How close does this get to the psychic experience of a real person, who often views the world in terms of his own memories and who experiences events in an emotional web which may very well distort linear time into an unrecognizable format? Knut Hamsun favored a dreamlike and introspective approach over the linear and rational. No wonder writers like Hemingway and Kafka admired and studied his

---

9. Despite his relative obscurity in our time, the range of writers influenced by Hamsun is impressive. D.H. Lawrence's *Lady Chatterly's Lover* was heavily influenced by Hamsun's *Pan* (1894) (Fjågesund 1991:421). Charles Bukowski admitted that he imitated Hamsun to such a large degree that he could call Hamsun a "crutch" (Harrison 1994:217). Hamsun's biographer points out that the young Ernest Hemingway "apprenticed himself to" Hamsun, learning to write in crisp, clear sentences from the early works of Hamsun (Ferguson 1987:24). Other admirers of Hamsun include Sherwood Anderson, John Galsworthy, H.G. Wells, Thomas Mann, Bertolt Brecht, Hermann Hesse, Henry Miller, and Maxim Gorky. Hemingway even went so far as to recommended that F. Scott Fitzgerald read Hamsun to pick up a few pointers (Ferguson 1987:228, 301).

work, hoping to learn a few new tricks of the trade that could make their own writing more powerful.

BEYOND THE "DOMINANT TRAIT" APPROACH

Norwegians "stubbornly continue to read and love even the most flawed Hamsun novels."[10] There is no doubt that his work is becoming more accepted now that we have some distance from the Second World War. The critic Edmund White, for example, has strong praise for Hamsun's work: "Knut Hamsun is one of my favorite writers. ... he remains for me a touchstone of lyric beauty and of fidelity to the irrational patterns the spirit can describe. And I know of no one who writes better than he about passion—the sting of physical desire, the fear of rejection, the tragicomedy of courtship."[11] One of the things White admired most in Hamsun's work was the way the Norwegian Nobel Prize winner broke the mold and struck out in a new direction when attempting to portray the human soul. Hamsun's method can be called expressionist; that is, a style that seeks first and foremost to give voice to the complexities of the multidimensional and multifarious human personality. Another way of saying this is that the expressionist distorts reality to give voice to the emotional content of his subjects.[12]

One of Hamsun's major contributions to literature was a rejection of Zola's approach to character; in fact, Hamsun openly derided the naturalist's method of delineating characters with a dominant trait. Hamsun felt that saddling a character with a dominant trait was an artificial and inauthentic device. Strongly influenced by Dostoevsky, whose characters were quite flexible and unpredictable, Hamsun claimed that none of his characters could be pinned down to a "dominant trait"; instead, they are changeable, like quicksilver, and reflect flashes of one trait and

10. Rees 2008:110.

11. White 1996:21.

12. It is not surprising that the paintings of Edvard Munch, an expressionist artist, have been used to illustrate the covers of Hamsun's novels *Victoria* and *Mysteries* (Penguin editions).

then another in rapid, often bewildering, succession.[13] In many ways a strikingly unique and modern writer, Hamsun presents a Zen-like portrait of human consciousness.

In *Mysteries*, for example, the main character, Nagel, is an enigma. He appears in town in a yellow suit and does not tell anyone much about his background. He lives in a dive, yet he is wealthy; he claims he's not talented, yet he plays the violin with virtuoso skill, and although he tries to keep to himself, he falls madly in love with the village beauty (who happens to be engaged to another man) and pursues her like a demon. His protean nature is contrasted and compared with a village dwarf, Miniman, who possesses dark characteristics and who Nagel befriends. Near the end of the novel, Nagel tries to kill himself by taking poison but fails. The reader thinks he has died, but an extended hallucinatory passage delves into his mind. At the end of the story, Nagel, disappointed in love, manages to commit suicide by jumping into a lake.

Hamsun's technique throughout the novel is a departure from the usual linear plot development. He also departs from the prevailing literary approach of making a character represent only one psychological type. Nagel is a boaster and a braggart, a shy man and an impetuous lover, a fool and a genius. He is a bully to a judge, a friend to a downtrodden midget, and a mystery to his neighbors. He is a man with a secret, alternately depressed and manic ... and finally a suicide. Hamsun's modern translator highlights some of the charm of the book: "As a whole, *Mysteries* succeeds in creating an intensely immediate sense of the day-by-day, hour-by-hour, stream of thought of the central character, who is poised on the brink of annihilation. ... In *Mysteries* Hamsun shows little concern with some of the most essential elements of the traditional novel: a coherent plot, causality, fullness and consistency of characterization, plausibility, and point of view."[14] For those writers seeking a more immediate way to portray their central character, *Mysteries* is a book worth studying.

---

13. White 1996:22.
14. Lyngstad 2005:34–35.

THE MULTI-"TIME ZONE" TECHNIQUE

Hamsun's novels often follow a pattern. As Edmund White observed: "the hero is a loner who arrives at a village, where he falls in love with a local young woman … She is frequently frightened by his eccentricities but never indifferent to his appeal (Hamsun was a handsome giant of a man and his protagonists are always physically magnetic)."[15] But following this plot pattern is neither necessary nor particularly helpful when using Hamsun's techniques. His modern stylistic brilliance can be employed in any type of story that attempts to present the fickle play of the human mind, and modern writers can have a field day adapting his most innovative techniques in their own work.

Hamsun's books are "stunning improvisations, pages torn out of a romantic egotist's heart."[16] This is, in part, due to the fact that he mixes past and present in his characters' minds more easily than most novelists, even those who, like Joyce and Woolf, are known for the stream-of-consciousness technique. In fact, in the mind of Hamsun's characters the past and present don't simply swirl around one another, they merge and meld with bewildering psychological power. When characters become confused, so do readers. In fact, this mental confusion is all part of Hamsun's technique. For example, in *Victoria* the romantic male hero, Johannes, overhears an insult uttered by his rival, the Lieutenant, who is engaged to Victoria, the woman Johannes loves. Earlier still, years ago, Victoria had kissed Johannes. Now, thinking over the insult he has overheard, Johannes's thoughts meld together three distinct time periods: Victoria's kiss in the distant past, the Lieutenant's insult in the recent past, and the fact that the Lieutenant and Victoria are currently walking together in the park without him:

> *One day she had kissed him, once upon a time, one summer. It was so long ago, God knows if it was even true. How was it, weren't they sitting on a bench?*

15. White 1996:23.
16. White 1996:25.

They talked together for a long time, and when they left he came so close to her
that he touched her arm. Then, in front of an entrance, she kissed him. I love
you! she said. ... <u>By now they had walked past, perhaps they were sit-</u>
<u>ting in the pavilion.</u> **The Lieutenant would give him a smack on**
the ear, he said. He heard it quite clearly, he wasn't asleep; but
he didn't get up and step forward either. An officer's hand, he
said. <u>Oh, well, it didn't matter....</u>[17]

In the original, this passage is all in roman type, but in order to show
how the passage melds three time "zones," I have italicized the time
period from the distant past (when Victoria kisses Johannes), I have
set in bold type the time period from the recent past (when Johannes
overhears the Lieutenant insult him), and I have underlined the present time period (when the Lieutenant and Victoria are walking in the
park). In this way you can see graphically how Hamsun jumps from
time zone to time zone within the passage. This kind of blending of
distant past, recent past, and present time produces a very intimate look
at the actual processes of the human mind under duress and under the
power of deep emotion, humiliation, and memory.

Hamsun's novel was made into a film by director Bo Widerberg, famous
for his masterpiece *Elvira Madigan*, another lushly romantic movie. There
are many similarities in the two stories; both are about lovers who cannot fulfill their love. In Hamsun's novel the major obstacle is the fact that
Victoria is not true to her deepest feelings; she represses her powerful love
for Johannes so that she can marry a wealthy lieutenant and save her father's
castle. Sartre would have accused her of acting in bad faith. As a result of
her lack of conviction, both she and Johannes are doomed to a life without true love. A deep emotional gulf widens between them, and yet they
are inextricably entangled and involved on an emotional level. This emotional conflict allows Hamsun to move in with a literary microscope and
moil over the thoughts of Johannes, his protagonist. The fact that Hamsun
employs this literary device when his protagonist is under enormous emotional stress suggests that in order to use Hamsun's most successful stylistic

---

17. Hamsun 1898:54-55.

tools it helps to have characters in conflict who are experiencing emotional turmoil. One naturally thinks of Dostoevsky in this context, another writer who often focuses on emotional humiliation, fear, and shame.

To emulate Hamsun's style is, admittedly, to run the risk of momentarily confusing your readers. But when such confusion mimics the confusion felt by a central character, the risk is perhaps worth taking. You can achieve the same powerful effect that Hamsun achieved by carefully deciding *when* to use the device of dipping into the mind of a character. If you employ the device of peering into the mind like Hamsun does, when your characters are in the midst of emotional upset, you will be much more likely to succeed. At such moments of heightened tension and conflict, you can present the interior thoughts of a character, roaming freely between one or more past time periods and the present. If those past interludes are themselves filled with emotion (such as the time when Johannes was kissed by Victoria, or the time when he was insulted by the Lieutenant) so much the better. Your reveries will have the double effect of presenting a character's thoughts and also of thrusting a reader into the mind of a character in mental chaos.

The device of presenting multiple time periods is sophisticated and depends on creating a complex character with a history of emotional upheavals. But it cannot be stressed strongly enough that Hamsun's technique, masterful though it is, can be copied freely and adapted by any modern writer at will. The method of portraying vivid characters who will strike readers as lifelike and surprising is a three-step procedure. First, the writer needs to imagine a series of incidents in the character's life, incidents which carry emotional weight. Second, the writer will want to ensure that the emotions are not trivial but, instead, powerful and deeply moving. Emotions like humiliation, shame, fear, and longing were pressed into service repeatedly by Hamsun (and by Dostoevsky before him, with equal success). Finally, the writer will want to choose the times when he will dip into the character's psyche carefully, making sure that the moment is ripe for the explosion of inner angst and feeling that will be portrayed.

Writers wishing to employ this multiple time zone approach might wish to browse through *Mysteries* and *Victoria*, seeking those passages where Hamsun uses the technique. Notice how he switches seamlessly from present to past to distant past and back to present time again. Examine how he exaggerates reality, departs from it in dreams, and returns to normal time. Look at his punctuation, his paragraph length, his use or avoidance of quotation marks and other surface devices—all of which can show you the way to achieve similar effects with your own material. While Hamsun's complex rendering of inner life is not for everyone, those on the cutting edge of fiction, and writers who wish to achieve powerful expressionist effects, will find studying Hamsun a lesson like no other. You will not learn how to do these things in a fiction class. No books will teach you the technique.[18] The lesson must be learned by studying the master himself. But by learning it from *him* you will emulate the best.

DREAMS

To peer even deeper into the minds of characters in turmoil, Hamsun borrowed a device from Dostoevsky, the integration of dream sequences into a story. In *Mysteries* he employs the technique on the last pages of the book in such a way that the reader does not realize it is a dream sequence until it is over. Earlier in the novel Hamsun uses a similar technique when he leads the reader to believe that Nagel, the hero, is committing suicide by drinking poison from a vial he carries about his neck. Unknown to the hero (and also unknown to the reader) the poison has been removed from the vial by Miniman, his friend and nemesis. Hamsun gives us a thrilling emotional ride, however, as we are led to believe that the protagonist is becoming sick and approaching death. The reader believes that Nagel is dying, and so does Nagel. "How his eyes were growing dim already!" Hamsun tells us.[19] Hamsun also includes a multitude of other exciting details in the scene so that the reader is absolutely convinced that the hero is about to

---

18. One book, however, that deserves mention because it does a wonderful job of critically analyzing how authors portray the mental lives of fictional characters is Dorrit Cohn's *Transparent Minds: Narrative Modes for Presenting Consciousness in Fiction* (1978).

19. Hamsun 1892:245-248.

perish. A few pages later the truth is revealed, and the hero wakes up, as if from a dream. At this point, so does the reader.

This expressionist technique of departing from reality with dreams or hallucinatory sequences allows Hamsun to penetrate to the central nervous system of his protagonist and render frantic and despairing thoughts in a Dostoevskian manner. What is important is not reality, Hamsun suggests, but the feelings of a character under stress. The device also allows him to move the story along at an exciting pace. For example, when Nagel awakens from his attempted suicide, readers are immediately curious about what he will do next: Will he be disappointed? Will he learn a lesson and wish to live? Will he try again? Few writers use thoughts and dreams with such narrative power. Even Joyce's extended stream of consciousness and Woolf's complex interior monologues don't have such profluence, the power to move a story forward.

HAMSUN'S LEGACY

Near the end of his life Hamsun was tried in a court of law and found to be a traitor. He was also sent to a mental institution where doctors attempted to catalog the psychological problems they imagined he had. In fact he was sane all along and "considerably more intelligent and subtle of mind than his observers."[20] He wrote a final book about his experiences, *On Overgrown Paths* (1949), a work of sensitivity which exposes the errors that lawyers and doctors can make when attempting to analyze an artist. Robert Coles, author and psychiatrist, observes that "once again he is pointing out how insulting and humiliating people can be to other people. No one has done a better job of documenting the simple-minded, abusive and condescending questions a breed of psychiatrists can ask and inflict on their patients."[21] It is precisely this sensitivity that informs all of Hamsun's best work, and it is his gift to modern writers. In his novels this sen-

---

20. Coles 1967:23.
21. Coles 1967:23-24.

sitivity bursts forth like the light of consciousness itself. Descriptions can only hint at the power of his writing.

By studying Hamsun's work a modern writer can learn the value of developing the same kind of sensitivity and subtlety, and should you choose to do so you might find a way to break the mold and penetrate to the inner core of the human heart and mind. At the same time, Hamsun's legacy is certainly a challenging one for he teaches how to write without tying yourself to the commonplace "dominant trait" school of literature. "He doesn't show individuals as always acting in character."[22] It may be risky to break the mold, but all great writers take risks and set goals that are beyond the norm. By daring to follow some of Hamsun's pathways—as Hemingway, Kafka, and Hesse did—you put yourself on the cutting edge of modern fiction. This doesn't mean that you have to totally reject realism or scene structure or even major characters who have dominant traits; but it does mean that you will start to look beneath the surface and seek to portray characters in a way that is more faithful to the human condition.

22. White 1996:23.

CHAPTER 6

WRITE LIKE
Edith Wharton

Few novelists craft sentences with such care and unobtrusive poetry as Wharton. Unfairly criticized for a lack of complexity vis-à-vis her friend and "mentor" Henry James, and for failing to render New England with sufficient veracity, she actually achieved more lifelikeness in her characterization than James, wrote with more spontaneity, and outshone her critics with the expressionism of her stories.

Born in 1862, Wharton grew up in Manhattan with brothers eleven and sixteen years older.[1] By the time she was six she was living in Paris where she discovered the joys of writing and was already displaying such a prolific imagination that her parents were surprised and alarmed.[2] Married unhappily for many years to Edward Wharton, she eventually had an affair with Morton Fullerton, a bisexual journalist,[3] and then, after divorcing her husband, formed deep bonds of friendship with a number of prominent male artists, including Walter Berry ("the love of my life") and Henry James.

Even this brief biographical sketch suggests that Wharton poured her soul into creating fictional replicas of the real-life relationships she experienced. All the romantic angst her characters felt was in actuality

---

1. Benstock 1994:3.
2. Benstock 1994:21. It has been convincingly argued that Wharton, reared by nannies and governesses, experienced a deprivation of a normal mother-child bond that led to her artistic endeavors and multiple affairs (Erlich 1992:6).
3. Erlich 1992:xii and chapter three.

part of her own psyche. This then is the first lesson a writer can take away from Wharton: Even before we look at her technical accomplishments, it is useful to remember that a writer needs a life outside the written page for the raw material that is to be transmuted into art.[4]

CONCISION

In being concise Wharton was using a trick of the trade that all professional comedians hone to a fine art. The same technique will serve the writer well. True enough, not all writers strive for concision. One need only think of Faulkner or Joyce to see evidence of a contrary trend; however, Edith Wharton clearly had a *literary reason* for concision. Powerful examples of this stylistic device can be found in *Ethan Frome* (1911).

What one critic refers to as "Wharton's exemplary thrift and concision"[5] was no accident of style; instead, it was a carefully contrived effect. "Wharton writes in her autobiography of going through her early prose on an 'adjective hunt,' to achieve 'concision and austerity,' and she noted how George Eliot's *Romola,* for example, was rendered lifeless by its weight of description: 'for all its carefully studied detail,' she wrote, '[it] remains a pasteboard performance.'"[6] Wharton's first major novel, *The House of Mirth* (1905), was initially serialized and then published in book form, and Wharton revised to achieve greater concision for the book version. "Changes in the book version are often toward greater economy of expression or more precise description."[7]

Ethan Frome is the story of a tragic affair between the relatively inarticulate Ethan (a man of "clumsy words") and his wife's cousin Mattie. The girl comes to work in Ethan's house to care for his sickly wife, Zeena. Ethan promptly falls in love with Mattie and they wander through the snowy New England woods wondering how they can

---

4. This is the process of emotion recalled in tranquility, as Wordsworth described it. "Poetry is the spontaneous overflow of powerful feelings: it takes its origin from emotion recollected in tranquillity" (Wordsworth 1802:l).

5. Wegener 1995.

6. Hughes 2005:387 (references omitted).

7. Lewis 1986:1322.

deal with the complexity of their hopeless infatuation. Finally they decide that the only solution is to kill themselves. They take a sleigh ride down a steep hill and purposefully crash into a tree that ironically fails to kill them but leaves them both mangled and disfigured for life. The bleakness of the conclusion is characteristic of Wharton.

Let's examine some examples of the kind of concision we're talking about. After Mattie comes to stay in his house, Ethan falls in love quite quickly. "All his life was lived in the sight and sound of Mattie Silver." Not only is the sentence short and sweet, it's also poetic with its use of alliteration—the repetition of the L and S sounds. When Ethan and Mattie are heading for their fateful crash with the tree Wharton doesn't slow down with an extended description, she comes right to the point: "There was a last instant when the air shot past him like millions of fiery wires; and then the elm …" The sentence is direct, free of convoluted additions, and powerful. Perhaps Robert Southey, one of the British Romantic poets, said it best: "It is with words as with sunbeams—the more they are condensed, the deeper they burn."

LOVE AT FIRST SIGHT—AND BEYOND

Wharton's influence can be felt to this day, especially in stories of romance and love.[8] One traditional technique she relied upon is the device of love at first sight. As soon as Ethan meets his wife's cousin he is smitten with her. "He had taken to the girl from the first day, when he had driven her over to the Flats to meet her, and she had smiled and waved to him from the train, crying out, 'You must be Ethan!' as she jumped down with her bundles."[9] The device also appears in *The Children* (1928), a Lolita-like story—absent Nabokov's explicitness—in which a middle-aged engineer falls in love with a fifteen-year-old. He first sees the girl as she's carrying one of her siblings up a series of steps on a cruise ship:

---

8. According to Esther Lombardi, Wharton influenced many novelists of her day as well as many contemporary writers. *See also* Coard 1985.

9. Wharton 1911:23.

Men of forty-six do not gasp as frequently at the sight of a charming face as they did at twenty; but when the sight strikes them it hits harder. Boyne had not been looking for pretty faces but for interesting ones, and it rather disturbed him to be put off his quest by anything so out of his present way as excessive youth and a rather pathetic grace.[10]

Another device for investigating romantic themes is delving into the mind of a character to reveal longings and desires which are hidden from other characters. In *The Age of Innocence* (1920) both Newland Archer and Countess Olenska are married to other people. The countess is the cousin of Archer's wife, and at one point Archer goes to meet her at a train station. Wharton delves into Archer's mind to set up the romantic prelude to the scene:

In his senseless school-boy happiness he pictured Madame Olenska's descent from the train, his discovery of her a long way off, among the throngs of meaningless faces, her clinging to his arm as he guided her to the carriage, their slow approach to the wharf among slipping horses, laden carts, vociferating teamsters, and then the startling quiet of the ferry-boat, where they would sit side by side under the snow, in the motionless carriage, while the earth seemed to glide away under them, rolling to the other side of the sun. It was incredible, the number of things he had to say to her, and in what eloquent order they were forming themselves on his lips...[11]

As Dorrit Cohn points out, one of the most convenient methods of rendering thoughts is to mark the "psycho-narration" passage (that is, the passage telling the character's thoughts) with a phrase such as "he thought" or "it occurred to him that ... he asked himself whether ..."[12] This is an easy way for a writer to slip into the mind of a character. Wharton does it effortlessly here in the first sentence of the above quotation with the

---

10. Wharton 1928:11.

11. Wharton 1920:242.

12. Cohn, in a fascinating study, observes that these overt markers of thought can become monotonous. For this reason, and to delve further into the character's psyche, writers typically move from psycho-narration (which is an author's *report* of a character's thought) to quoted monologue (a character's direct mental discourse) (Cohn 1978:38).

words "he pictured," and once those introductory words are uttered, she has free reign to wander into his mind and describe what he thinks, all of it supremely romantic.[13]

Romance can also be embodied in dialog, such as when Archer tells the countess, "I want–I want somehow to get away with you into a world where words like that–categories like that–won't exist. Where we shall be simply two human beings who love each other, who are the whole of life to each other, and nothing else on earth will matter."[14] Dialog such as this will never go out of style. Neither will the device of love at first sight. Together with presenting a character's thoughts, these techniques can be studied in Wharton and used in the most contemporary stories to portray love and romance.

HOW TO REPEAT CRUCIAL INFORMATION

There's a fine line between telling too much and telling too little. Sometimes it helps to watch a successful novelist to see how to repeat crucial information.

In *Ethan Frome,* for instance, Wharton initially mentions a few details about the hero's abbreviated education: "He had taken a year's course at a technological college at Worcester." When Ethan is described a few pages later as falling in love with Mattie, Wharton reiterates the point about the unfinished education: "His unfinished studies had given form to this sensibility and even in his unhappiest moments field and sky spoke to him with a deep and powerful persuasion."[15] The technique is to repeat using different words and to embed the repetition in a meaningful context. The point about his education drives home his sensitive side, which is highly relevant to his affair with Mattie. One of the things Mattie likes about him is this sensitivity.

13. We could easily compare Wharton's passage to many similar ones in *Madame Bovary* in which Emma thinks of the romantic life she could enjoy with her various lovers.
14. Wharton 1920:247.
15. Wharton 1911:19, 23.

Another crucial bit of information is the sickliness of Ethan's wife. The reader must be aware that Zeena is somewhat of an invalid. We are told in chapter one that "Zeena had always been what Starkfield called 'sickly.'" And then in chapter eight, when Ethan has second thoughts about deserting Zeena, it is because she is sickly. "He was a poor man, the husband of a sickly woman, whom his desertion would leave alone and destitute."[16] In this case the repetition uses the same key word and this poses no problem since the instances are separated by many pages and chapters.

Other things that are repeated in the book, which are key points, include Mattie Silver's fine appearance and her kindness, as well as the barren and snowy landscape, which will play a crucial part in the climax of the story. In novels it is essential that crucial information be repeated. By varying the phrasing, by embedding the information in a meaningful context, and by separating repetitions with intervening material, a writer can achieve the kind of thematic significance that makes repeated material meaningful and supportive of a novel-length story.

WHEN TO DESCRIBE SETTING

In addition to being a novelist, Edith Wharton was also a gardener and interior decorator; in fact, her first book was a work of nonfiction, *The Decoration of Houses* (1897). You don't have to be an interior designer in order to write about beautiful clothes, large mansions and romantic settings. All you need is the ability to translate physical sensations into a story using three tools: selection, condensation, and integration.

Selection refers to the process of choosing what to report. The eye sees millions of things, the ear hears a multitude of sounds, and the other senses are similarly bombarded with input. From this cacophony a writer selects what is important. When *Ethan Frome* opens, we find Ethan walking through the snow to meet Mattie. "The village lay under two feet of snow, with drifts at the windy corners. In a sky of iron the points of the Dipper hung like icicles and Orion flashed his cold fires." There are trees but Wharton does not describe them. There

---

16. Wharton 1911:23, 103.

is a horizon but she does not need to say a word about it. There are other details, but Wharton, like a painter, has selected the details that matter. She uses light to good effect, describing how the illumination from the church windows threw beams along the snow banks: "and the basement windows of the church sent shafts of yellow light far across the endless undulations." Once these carefully chosen details have been introduced, the world will come alive for readers and the characters can be envisioned within it.

Condensation refers to the technique of making words tell. You needn't go on at length in describing something if a few words will encapsulate the idea. In chapter thirty-three of *The Age of Innocence* when the countess is leaving for Europe and the final separation between her and Archer is taking place, Wharton condenses the description to just enough details to leave a vivid impression. The countess is in a carriage, the interior of which is dark, and Archer has not had a chance to talk with her before she is to leave his life forever. In one swift sentence Wharton severs the connection between the two lovers (lovers in the emotional not physical sense). "For a moment, in the billowy darkness inside the big landau, he caught the dim oval of a face, eyes shining steadily—and she was gone." Condensed and distilled to the essence! You can obtain similar condensation by omitting words, paring down descriptions, and sharpening focus. If everything is leading up to something (a departure or an arrival, for instance), when you get to that big moment condense instead of expand and you may achieve similar effects.

Integration is perhaps the most sophisticated technical device Wharton employs in setting a scene. It is a method of describing the background location here and there during the course of the action. The most poetic examples probably occur in *Ethan Frome* when the barren snowy environment is woven into the mix of the narrative, yielding an eerie otherworldly effect. In chapter two Ethan has gone to pick up Mattie at the dance and bring her home. When she comes outside he slips his arm through hers. "It was so dark under the spruces that he could barely see the shape of her head beside his shoulder." The background trees are brought in to give a feel for the darkness and to suggest romantic isolation. Later we are told, "They walked on in silence through the blackness of the hemlock-shaded lane, where Ethan's saw mill gloomed through the night." Again setting is seamlessly integrated into the action for a feeling of isolation which makes their relationship all the more meaningful. In chapter nine just before their fateful sled ride they hear the ringing of a church bell, a detail that adds a sense of finality to the scene: "Through the stillness they heard the church clock striking five." By working details like this into the story, dropping them in where needed to keep the setting alive and also to heighten meaning, a writer can achieve effects that go well beyond mere description.

FORESHADOWING

Ethan Frome is a bleak story of tragic love. To prepare us for the conclusion Wharton drops hints that foretell what is to come. In the middle of the story Ethan chances upon the gravestones of his parents. Wharton says, "he wondered if, when their turn came, the same epitaph would be written over him and Zeena." This prevision of his death actually goes beyond the novel's time frame, although his fate in hitting the tree and disfiguring himself and Mattie is also a kind of death.

In *The Age of Innocence,* immediately after his marriage to May, "Archer suddenly felt himself looking at her with the startled gaze of a stranger." In the same paragraph shocking imagery describes May: "The blood that ran so close to her fair skin might have been a preserving fluid." No casual detail. Both are examples of foreshadowing. May will turn out to be a stranger to her husband, a cold and calculating destroyer who manipulates people to prevent Archer from leaving her.

Ironic foreshadowing is Wharton's forte, and the marriage chapter closes with May remarking, "Ah, it's just our luck beginning – the wonderful luck we're always going to have together!" Actually just the opposite will be their fate and Archer will come to see that he is married to a woman he has little in common with except social class and that his true love, the countess, is finally beyond his reach.

The trick of using foreshadowing is to not overdo it. But here and there, perhaps as many as a dozen times in a novel, let drop a hint of what is to come. The hint need not register consciously with readers. But nevertheless its tone and tenor will communicate a sense of what is ahead, whether good or bad, and readers will savor the pleasure of being in a structured universe.

EPIPHANIES

As Christopher Ricks points out, the only one who can't go to a Bob Dylan concert is Bob Dylan. If he were in the audience there would be no show! Somewhat similarly (and somewhat sadly) the only one who may not be able to enjoy reading for the sake of reading is a writer. To paraphrase critic Harold Bloom, all strong writers can only read themselves.[17] This means that anytime you read something you are reading like a writer—analyzing, tearing apart, scrutinizing, finding out the secrets of those who have written works you admire. Maybe that's one reason why Samuel Beckett, the consummate stylist, was addicted to mystery novels. He had to escape into something different from his own work. But this curse of the writer is also his greatest strength. Other people will simply read *The House of Mirth*. You will read it to analyze the character arc of Lawrence Selden. Others will simply enjoy its story. You will pick apart the brains of the novel and see how Wharton achieves character development through a series of epiphanies. You will then start to use epiphanies in your own work. Suddenly you've aligned yourself with a long literary tradition that can help your own work achieve the kind of backbone that fascinates readers.

Most people associate the literary device of epiphanies with James Joyce. An epiphany is a moment when a character has an insight into his world. It's an enlightenment or an awakening, an ah-ha moment. Joyce used epiphanies in many of the stories from *Dubliners* (1914), such as when Eveline has that horrifying moment of realization that she cannot follow her boyfriend onto the boat and venture into a new

17. Bloom 1997:19.

world and a new life with him. That crushing realization is an epiphany, a moment when she sees things clearly. Wharton learned about epiphanies from Joyce but there was much in his work she did not like. She considered it self-centered, narcissistic, and sensationalist. But she was savvy enough to know that there was something of value even in the material she didn't like and she seized that device out of the books of Joyce the way a fisherman cuts a pearl out of an oyster. Moreover she used ephipanies in her work in a more traditional way, to advance plot and illuminate character development. Whereas Joyce's epiphanies—especially in later works like *Ulysses* (1922) and *Finnegans Wake* (1939)—are moments of light that simply flash without illuminating any moral development, Wharton always used her character illumination moments to advance plot and develop character.[18]

In the same way Stanley Kubrick planned movies by saying, "We need to have six or seven big moments," Wharton planned six or seven points of illumination and then structured a novel around an awakening mind. This is known as a character arc. But whereas character arc is a more comprehensive term, encompassing the beginning, the middle, and the end of the arc—as well as all the little steps along the way—the concept of an epiphany is easier to grasp and easier to employ in your work because an epiphany is the smallest unit of a character arc. It is the moment when the straight line of a character's development bends. Instead of thinking of character arcs, it might be more helpful to think of a series of straight lines that curve into a fractured arc (see the illustration on page 70). At the node of each curve is an epiphany or "lightnings of intuition," to use Joyce's term.[19]

The Age of Innocence tells the story of Newland Archer's betrayal by his aristocratic wife. Archer is a patrician New York lawyer who is terribly constrained by the rules and beliefs of his class. When Countess Olenska drifts into his orbit he is so distracted and has so many epiphanies that it's as if she were the spark igniting a series of firework

18. *See* Kim 2006.
19. Joyce 1916:205.

CHARACTER ARC

This chart illustrates changes in a character throughout a story.

EPIPHANY

A flash of intuition and an instance of character change

CHARACTER ARC

A series of six epiphanies are graphically represented along one character arc. The arc segments are of unequal length because epiphanies are not evenly spaced out in a narrative but may occur whenever needed by the demands of the story or the progression of character development. After each epiphany the direction in which the character moves is altered because character change has occurred as a result of the insight or realization that happened during the epiphany.

BEGINNING OF STORY

displays in his mind. There are many moments where Wharton shows Archer having a flash of intuition. One of the earliest and most significant is when he defends the countess against someone who criticizes her for living with another man after she separated from her husband. "He stopped and turned away angrily to light his cigar. 'Women ought to be free–as free as we are,' he declared, making a discovery of which he was too irritated to measure the terrific consequences."[20] Wharton closes chapter five with this epiphany and opens chapter six with a further investigation of the meaning of Archer's insight: "With a shiver of foreboding he saw his marriage becoming what most of the other marriages about him were: a dull association of material and social interests held together by ignorance on the one side and hypocrisy on the other."[21] It is clear that this moment of insight is central to the story for it begins the character arc and is the first major turn in that arc.

In order to incorporate epiphanies into your own stories you can slow down and polish those moments when a character is having an insight. The device of using epiphanies can be consciously developed. Just as an athlete can work on a particular aspect of a sport, such as lifting weights to strengthen the biceps for javelin throwing, so too can a writer flex the ability to write epiphanies by practicing the process of writing these sections. Because Wharton "made epiphany central to her theory of fiction," studying her use of the device may be one of the most efficient ways to learn the technique.[22]

---

20. Wharton 1920:38.
21. Wharton 1920:40.
22. Kim 2006:150.

CHAPTER 7

WRITE LIKE

W. Somerset Maugham

Whenever you find your writing becoming flamboyant and ornate, you might try reading Maugham. "I believe the modern writer who has influenced me most is Somerset Maugham, whom I admire immensely for his power of telling a story straightforwardly and without frills," said George Orwell. Because Maugham's work is never complex stylistically, he has been called "one of the first masters of the plain style."[1]

Born in 1874 to a mother and father who would die before he was eleven, Maugham was thereafter sent to live with a rather cold and demanding uncle.[2] Although he went to medical school in order to satisfy his uncle's wishes, he was always more interested in writing. By the time he was twenty-three he had published his first novel, *Liza of Lambeth* (1897).[3]

Maugham had an early sexual experience with a young man in Germany while studying in Heidelberg and he later acquired another male lover, Frederick Haxton, with whom he remained until Haxton's death, when Maugham was seventy. Maugham also fathered a daughter with Syrie Wellcome, who was married at the time. The scandal caused her husband to divorce her in 1917, after which Maugham married her. They divorced in 1927.

---

1. Curtis 1974:245.

2. Morgan 1980:8-11.

3. He was also accused of plagiarism for the work (Morgan 1980:57).

During World War I he was employed as a spy for Great Britain. He then moved to the United States, where he worked in Hollywood. His literary output was enormous and includes plays, short stories, essays, and twenty novels.

CHOOSING CHARACTERS LIKE MAUGHAM

The characters a writer chooses should not be picked at random. The key goal when choosing characters is balancing character *types* so that there are contrasting personalities. Woody Allen's favorite book on plotting, Laios Egri's *The Art of Dramatic Writing* (1960), suggests that characters must be *orchestrated*. "If all the characters are the same type—for instance, if all of them are bullies—it will be like an orchestra of nothing but drums."[4] Variety for the sake of variety is not the goal, instead you are aiming to achieve the kinds of differences that will lead to interpersonal conflict. Maugham is a master of orchestration.

In *Of Human Bondage* (1915), the hero, Philip Carey, is a doctor and a sensitive young man. Maugham based the character on himself. The other major character, Mildred Rogers, is the opposite of Philip. Brash, wanton, and cruel, she is in constant conflict with him. In fact as their relationship blossoms she becomes sadistic and Philip responds with almost masochistic pleasure. "They seemed to be always on the verge of a quarrel. The fact was that he hated himself for loving her. She seemed to be constantly humiliating him."[5] Two characters have never been so perfectly orchestrated because they are always annoying each other.

The same technique is employed in *The Moon and Sixpence* (1919), Maugham's roman à clef about Paul Gauguin. In the novel the painter is named Charles Strickland and is portrayed as brutal and unfeeling, a man who cares only for art and to whom human beings are nothing. He has no respect for his wife and leaves her to travel to Paris in

---

4. Egri 1960:114.

5. Maugham 1915:309.

order to further his artistic career. The other major character in this section of the novel is Dirk Stroeve, a second-rate artist who befriends Strickland. The two men are orchestrated beautifully and are opposites, despite the fact that they're both painters. Strickland is unfeeling and uncaring, Stroeve kind and compassionate. Strickland pays Stroeve back for his kindness by stealing his wife. When he gets tired of her he drops her, and in desperation—though Stroeve is waiting for her to return to him—she kills herself. Could two men be more at odds? Keep in mind how Maugham orchestrates the contrast between these two painters and compare that to two of your main characters. Can you honestly say that you've achieved similar contrasts and opposites? Only when the answer to that question is "yes" should you feel satisfied enough to stop tinkering with your characterization.

ORGANIZING CHAPTERS

One of the most overlooked technical devices is the alternation of fast and slow chapters. It stands to reason that putting all the action chapters first followed by all the analytical chapters can lead to an unbalanced effect.[6] By alternating dramatic material with thoughtful sections you'll produce a more pleasing reader experience.

Maugham alternated fast and slow material in all his work. *The Razor's Edge* (1944) is about Larry Darrell, a young man who seeks spiritual enlightenment. Early in the novel there is a dramatic scene in which Larry shocks his fiancée by telling her that he wants to study instead of go into business. The dramatic content of the chapter is intensified because his fiancée doesn't wish to reveal her disappointment. "Her heart was beating madly and she was sick with apprehension."[7] She

---

6. A famous example of the failure to alternate chapters is Norman Mailer's *The Armies of the Night* (1968). The first half of the book is exciting and dramatic, culminating in Mailer's arrest at the Pentagon. The second half is a slow-paced analysis of the methods of organizing a march. Despite the fact that the book ultimately won a Pulitzer Prize and the National Book Award, the second half was so different from the first and so "dry" that *Harper's*, which had published the first half as "The Steps of the Pentagon," rejected it (Dearborn 1999:235).

7. Maugham 1944:76-77.

pretends to take the news calmly, but she decides not to marry him and offers to return his engagement ring. This dramatic chapter is followed by a slow chapter in which the girl talks calmly with family and friends about her broken engagement. The same type of alternation occurs near the end of the novel. An extended slow chapter is devoted to the narrator's listening to Larry tell about his spiritual quest. This relaxing almost serene chapter is immediately followed by two short chapters describing the violent death of one of Larry's girlfriends, Sophie MacDonald. The juxtaposition of serenity with violence is certainly the result of careful planning.

The same alternating technique can be found in *Of Human Bondage*. Philip takes Mildred to the theater and then walks her home. He pines for her. "He did not know how he was to get through the hours that must pass before his eyes rested on her again."[8] Then she snubs him and they part with Philip in despair. These dramatic scenes are followed immediately by an extended section in which Philip mulls over the whole affair and feels lonely. Then, like the beat of a heart, the end of chapter fifty-nine plunges us once again into a dramatic scene in which Mildred humiliates Philip. Clearly the alternation between fast and slow pace can occur within, as well as between, chapters.

This alternating effect can also be accomplished by varying paragraph length between chapters.[9] Increased paragraph length often signals a slower pace. Indeed, an entire chapter can be written with short paragraphs followed by an entire chapter with long paragraphs. Maugham used the latter technique in chapters fifty-one and fifty-two of *The Moon and Sixpence*. Chapter fifty-one is dramatic and written in short paragraphs and dialogue. It tells how Strickland is in Tahiti and is introduced to a seventeen-year-old, whom he begins a relationship with by threatening to beat her. This fast-moving chapter is followed by a slower-moving chapter filled with fat paragraphs. The slow chapter summarizes the next three years of Strickland's life, a time of

---

8. Maugham 1915:297.

9. Browne and King 2004:164-165.

harmony with the girl. This is followed by a quick-moving chapter in which Strickland is seen living amongst the natives, working on his art surrounded by young girls and boys who are his models.

MAKING NARRATIVE FLOW

One way to make narrative flow is to put characters into situations where they must make difficult decisions. Readers will naturally want to know what happens next.

Maugham uses this technique in the middle of *The Razor's Edge*. Larry is on a farm and he has met two women, Ellie and Frau Becker. Frau Becker obviously likes him. One night a woman climbs into his bed ... and Larry makes love to her, thinking it must be Frau Becker. But he discovers to his chagrin that it's actually Ellie. This turn of events forces Larry to make a decision. The reader naturally wonders how he will handle the situation.

In chapter thirty of *Of Human Bondage* Maugham puts another character into a difficult situation, forcing her to make a decision. Cacilie, a sixteen-year-old, is having an affair with an Asian. The proprietor of the boarding house objects and threatens to have the girl removed. Cacilie must decide what to do. After much conflict she and her lover elope. The conflict moves the story along and makes readers turn pages in a desire to find out what the girl will do in response to the pressure put upon her to stop seeing her lover.

An even more powerful example occurs in the middle of the same novel. Philip has decided that he has had enough of the humiliation and shame that Mildred constantly showers upon him, and he leaves her for the caring and maternal Norah. He fancies he loves Norah because their relationship is friendly and comforting. Then suddenly, just when the reader thinks that Philip has forgotten Mildred, she reappears. She confesses that she's miserable because her new lover left her. Suddenly all Philip's desire for her is reawakened.

What should he do? Who will he choose? The reader turns the pages to see how he will resolve the conflict.[10]

In addition to putting characters in a position where they must decide what to do, narrative can be made to flow more quickly by piquing curiosity about future events and setting up expectations by "advertising" what is going to happen.[11] At the start of *The Moon and Sixpence* the narrator tell us that he knew Charles Strickland intimately and that he discovered secrets about him when he happened to visit Tahiti during the war. "I find myself in a position to throw light on just that part of his tragic career which has remained most obscure." Anyone with even a passing interest in human nature, and everyone with an interest in the artist, can now be expected to have their appetite whetted and be eager to know more. What *are* the obscure details that the narrator knows? What revelations lie ahead? When will these gossipy tidbits be thrown our way? Can a reader ever hope for more from a novelist? This *promise* of gossipy revelations is one of the things that keeps us turning pages.

Maugham resorts to the technique again, in chapter eight, when he tells us that Strickland deserted his wife and left her to run off to Paris with another woman. This puts the reader in a state of anticipation. What will his wife do? Will she divorce him? And what is Strickland's life like now that he lives in Paris? We turn the pages because Maugham has promised that there is more to come in the sordid life of Charles Strickland.

Nine years after the death of Strickland, the narrator, in chapter forty-five, tells us that the exigencies of war took him to Tahiti. Could there be a more clear advertisement to the reader that something of moment is going to be disclosed? Naturally the narrator makes inquiries in Tahiti and soon he discovers those who knew Strickland well, including a doctor who diagnosed Strickland with leprosy. The doctor

---

10. *Of Human Bondage*, chapters 66-69.

11. The concept of "advertising" future events is derived from the field of screenwriting (Howard and Mabley 1993:74-76). Advertising is similar to foreshadowing in that they both relate to future events; but foreshadowing is only a hint, advertising is a promise.

gives an account of Strickland's death and the "beautiful and obscene" paintings of his last days—completed when he was blind!

You can employ both Maugham's techniques for ensuring reader interest and making your narrative flow in your own writing. The first device can be set into motion when you have a character choose between two alternatives. The key to keep in mind is that the character who has to make this choice must be faced with a life-defining decision of some sort, a choice that is in some way difficult and challenging. When Larry discovers he has made love to a woman he does *not* love, he must choose what to do, and his choice defines him as a man. When Cacilie is discovered having an affair, she must choose what to do because the world turns against her. Her decision to elope is life-defining. When Mildred comes back to Philip he has to choose between her and Norah, and his decision changes the course of his life. Don't make things easy for your characters; saddle them with difficult choices that will steer them in life-defining directions. Following your characters down the new paths they decide to take will be exciting for readers and will keep them turning pages.

When you employ the second technique, promising something that will happen in the future, remember that Maugham always makes sure it is something of pivotal interest, something integral to the plot, and something that will impact characters in a major way. When the narrator reveals that he knew Strickland personally and that he visited Tahiti to find out about the man, the reader is in effect being given a promise. "Upcoming in the story," Maugham is telling us, "will be exciting details about the hero, and revelations that will be central to understanding him." If you tell readers what to expect, and if what you promise is intriguing and exciting, they will read with eager interest.

CREATING SURPRISE

Surprise is a key ingredient of storytelling. Writing is a game of revealing only so much of the story as is necessary and holding back other events that will ultimately surprise the reader.

Just when we think that Larry and Isabel are going to be happy, Maugham reveals that Larry is more interested in finding truth, enlightenment, and wisdom. Just when we think Philip Carey is going to be content with Norah, Mildred reappears. Just when Strickland seems to have found a woman he loves by stealing Stroeve's wife, he casts her aside and causes her to kill herself.

Each of these surprises shocks the reader and produces heightened interest. In each case the surprise leads to a major turning point and major character revelations. When Larry tells Isabel he wishes to study with the wise men of the world, she breaks their engagement and sets him free. What will he do now, readers wonder. His character becomes clearer to us—here is an unusual man, indeed! He has rejected a beautiful young woman who loves him...for what? for a chance to read the classics? for an opportunity to study ancient wisdom? What *kind* of man is this?

When Mildred reappears we are as shocked as Philip. We then see more clearly into *his* character. He is a man who relishes the woman who was strictest with him. Perhaps he is also somewhat of a masochist. This revelation tells us worlds about the hero and enhances our interest.

When Strickland causes the death of Stroeve's wife, the reader is not only surprised but desperate to know what he will do now that he has hurt Stroeve. And what will Stroeve do? Will he retaliate? What kind of monster *is* Strickland? How can he have become such a magnificent painter when he is such a brutal human being?

Using surprise can work to your advantage as long as your surprise is related to the story. Notice that Maugham doesn't simply have a ton of bricks fall on anyone to effect his surprises, he always makes sure that something plausible occurs. You can achieve the same effect by making sure the surprising plot twist is fully motivated and integral to your story. It is plausible that Mildred would return, for instance, even though surprising. That dovetails into the plot. We know that Mildred is a needy person and that she liked Philip, so while it is surprising that she shows up at this point, it is also plausible. We know that Strickland is a brute—he demonstrated it by deserting his wife—so while it is surprising that he should leave Stroeve's wife, we have been prepared for it. And while it is surprising that Larry prefers studying to marriage, we have been prepared for it by being told he is an intelligent, thoughtful young man. In each case, make sure your surprise is prepared in advance.

In addition to plausibility, make sure that the surprise throws light on character. Larry's announcement certainly fleshes out his enlightenment-seeking character. Mildred's return and Philip's embracing her over Norah tells us worlds about him. And Strickland's abandonment of Stroeve's wife portrays him as even more of a brute, making us see him more clearly, even if we (like the narrator) do not fully understand his complex motivation. If you keep these considerations in mind, your surprises will shock and fascinate readers and, at the same time, add greater resonance to your plot and characters.

PUTTING YOURSELF INTO YOUR WORK

Maugham was fond of putting himself into his work. "I have put the whole of my life into my books," he admitted. In some ways he was one of the most autobiographical of writers. He is the narrator of *The Razor's Edge*. In that novel he even pokes fun at himself, having Sophie call him "a stuffed shirt."[12] It is widely known that *Of Human Bondage* is a closely autobiographical novel, following the life of a medical student whose personality and escapades are patterned closely on Maugham's own life. The stutter that Maugham suffered as a child was transformed into Philip's club foot. One of the pleasures of this novel is that it offers such intimate insights into the sensitive mind of Maugham. In addition the narrators of *The Moon and Sixpence* and *Cakes and Ale* (1930) are based on Maugham's life.[13]

In *The Summing Up* (1938) Maugham admits that fact and fiction are so commingled in his work that there is no way to tell them apart.

---

12. Maugham 1944:192

13. Meyers 2004:9. *See also*, Cordell 1961:37.

"In one way and another I have used in my writings whatever has happened to me in the course of my life. ... Fact and fiction are so intermingled in my work that now, looking back on it, I can hardly distinguish one from the other. It would not interest me to record the facts, even if I could remember them, of which I have already made a better use."[14] In effect he is admitting that his works are a psychological portrait of himself.

All writers base various aspects of their stories on their own lives, but some writers rely more heavily on their own experiences than others. What lessons can be learned from Maugham's practice of putting himself into his work? One thing to note is that Maugham did not, like the Gonzo Journalists, radically distort his experiences or exaggerate them; instead, he rather faithfully transformed his life into fiction.[15] The trick when doing this with your own work is, of course, to avoid libel suits from others who might recognize themselves in your pages. It can help to disguise people by combining two characters into one or by putting them into different occupations or locations.

KEEPING TO A SCHEDULE LIKE MAUGHAM

It should come as no surprise that Maugham, a medical doctor, took good care of himself physically. As a result of keeping to a schedule (including waking early and caring for his health with regular visits to spas) he lived to the age of ninety-one.[16] But perhaps the most telling fact of Maugham's professional life is Garson Kanin's observation that "Maugham carefully explained that he rises at eight o'clock every morning—no matter where he is—has his breakfast and so on, and at nine o'clock sits down and writes for four

---

14. Maugham 1938:1.

15. To see the difference one need only compare *Of Human Bondage*, which parallels Maugham's life, with Hunter S. Thompson's *Fear and Loathing in Las Vegas* (1971), which is based on Thompson's real-life adventures but which clearly exaggerates and distorts reality for comic effect.

16. Morgan 1980:287-288.

hours."[17] During this time he exploited his own vast storehouse of personal experience. The regularity of his writing routine never detracted from his pushing himself to have a full personal life. In this he was like Balzac, who lived a full life and had intense relationships, but who also kept regular hours for writing. Indeed when advising a young writer, Maugham said, "If you want to become a writer it is very necessary to expose yourself to all the vicissitudes of life, and it isn't enough to wait for experience to come to you, you must go out after it. Even if you bark your shins now and then, that again will be grist for the mill."[18] This combination of plenty of personal experiences together with a regular writing routine helped Maugham produce a prodigious amount of material, including more than thirty plays.

Maugham was also interested in meditation. One of the techniques of meditation is to meditate while doing daily activity. Maugham may have transferred this meditation technique to his writing practice, for he said that, "The author does not only write while he's at his desk, he writes all day long, when he is thinking, when he is reading, when he is experiencing, everything he sees and feels is significant to his purpose and, consciously or unconsciously, he is forever storing and making over his impressions."[19] This constant preoccupation with writing is a habit that can be cultivated and developed.

There is a twofold lesson to be learned from studying Maugham's professional life. If you can write regularly, you are more likely to be productive and successful. Secondly, you need to incorporate personal experiences into your work, which means you will need to live deeply and embrace human relationships. Even while having such experiences, you can, like Maugham, reflect upon them and place them into your own work in some fashion. This constant attention to the process of writing is certain to be rewarding for it is the work of the true artist.

---

17. Kanin 1966:33.

18. Maugham, quoted in Morgan 1980:509.

19. Maugham, quoted in Silverman 1999:65.

CHAPTER 8

WRITE LIKE

Edgar Rice Burroughs

The man who created Tarzan thought of himself primarily as an entertainer, but Edgar Rice Burroughs was much more than that. He was a craftsman whose storytelling skills enthralled the world. His mastery of pace, conflict, and romance still offer important lessons for contemporary writers seeking to inject life and excitement into their literary creations.

Born in 1875 in Chicago, Edgar Rice Burroughs was the last of four brothers. He certainly fits the mold of lastborn creativity, inventing some of the most memorable characters in speculative fiction. Creator of numerous science-fiction series, his work continues to influence some of the top writers working today. At the outset, though, Burroughs could not find a career and he tried his hand at various jobs, including ranching and working for his brothers. One day he read a story in a pulp magazine and told a friend, "Even I could do better than that." His friend challenged him to try and the result is history. His first novel, *A Princess of Mars* (1912), launched one of the most successful science-fiction series of all time. It is centered around the fictional world of Barsoom (which is what Mars is called by its many inhabitants). Burroughs wrote fast-moving stories, many set in faraway locations such as Mars and Venus, where elaborate civilizations flourished and different races vied for power. Into these worlds Burroughs introduces a heroic Earthman who must learn about the alien civilization and its customs, fight for his freedom, and establish his right to live.

There is inevitably a beautiful princess, usually dressed in the merest scrap of wardrobe, who becomes his bride. This formula worked time and again for Burroughs and it was one which allowed him to exercise his imagination in creating peoples, beasts, and settings that continue to amaze readers. The same kind of fantasy went into the Tarzan novels, which also became successful films.

Although Burroughs is primarily a SF writer, his craftsmanship can teach writers in any genre. We'll examine how he started stories, named characters, paced narratives, employed conflict, and used romance to engage reader interest.

WHAT YOU CAN LEARN FROM TARZAN

One thing Edgar Rice Burroughs does better than most writers today is start a story right. He doesn't open a narrative with repellent or disagreeable character names or exotic and confusing locations. Even mainstream and literary novelists fall into this trap all the time. It's as if they want to wow you right off the bat with a dazzlingly different fantasy world or with their creativity in thinking up bizarre names. The fact is they're alienating readers and making it difficult to get into the story. Burroughs never does that. Instead he usually begins in familiar territory, like a friend putting an arm around your shoulder and talking to you from the heart. He begins in *this* world before he talks about another world. He begins with the familiar before he introduces the unfamiliar. In this way he treats you to a rare joy, namely, the pleasure of starting in the world we know and then gradually transitioning into another world. This is how he prepares you for the unexpected and makes his new settings believable.

Tarzan of the Apes (1912), the first in the Tarzan series, for example, doesn't begin with an ape man who can speak to animals. That would be too abrupt a beginning. Instead the story opens describing how an Englishman, John Clayton, Lord Greystoke, travels to Africa and is stranded in the jungle with his wife. They eventually have a baby, which is stolen and raised by a female ape. That baby becomes Tarzan.

The novel illustrates the classic theme of the noble savage, suggesting that the trappings of society debase man from his true goodness. Tarzan, who has not been exposed to Western or European society, is strong and good and essentially a model of what a human *could* be and *should* be. The fact that Burroughs begins the novel with an extended narration of the adventures of Tarzan's biological father and mother, who are human, eases us into this fantastic tale. By the time we see the young infant snatched up by a female ape, we have suspended our disbelief and the rest of the story flows rather naturally from that point.

There are countless other examples of this important technique in Burroughs's oeuvre. In the first John Carter novel, *A Princess of Mars*, we begin on Earth. The foreword is written and signed by Edgar Rice Burroughs himself; it tells about his Uncle Jack, a very convivial man. This is certainly easy enough to digest! But then the story interjects a hint of what is to come: When Uncle Jack dies he instructs his nephew, Burroughs, to put him in a coffin with a hinge that "can be opened *only from the inside.*" We then begin with the manuscript of John Carter (Uncle Jack), who prospects for gold in Arizona and is eventually chased by Indians. Escaping into a cave he passes out. All this is rather easy to follow too. We understand John Carter and his world because it's the world we all know. Then when the transition comes and we find ourselves on Mars, we're not disoriented because we're still with John Carter, a character we have come to know rather well in the beginning section of the book.

My favorite example of this technique is the opening of *Pirates of Venus* (1934). "If a female figure in a white shroud enters your bedchamber at midnight on the thirteenth day of this month, answer this letter; otherwise do not." The incredulous recipient of that comment in a letter puts it aside and forgets about it. But on the appointed day the woman arrives! So begins the story, taking us from a common earthly situation (a man receiving a letter) to an unearthly planet and strange customs, warring Venusian armies, and alluring alien women. In this way Burroughs handles introductions like a pro. What a shame that his books, in those wonderful Ace editions, are not readily available today. If modern writers had access to them our current crop of novels might begin in a more reader-friendly manner.

WHY NAMES ARE CRITICAL

One of the chief pleasures of reading a book by Edgar Rice Burroughs is the names. The women sound euphonious, the heroes strong, the villains dastardly. The hero always has a solid sounding masculine name: John Carter (the Mars series novels), Tarzan (the Tarzan books), Carson Napier (the Venus books), Gordon King (*The Land of Hidden Men*), Bowen Tyler (the Caspak series), David Innes, Abner Perry and Jason Gridley (the Pellucidar series). The names of the women are as alluring as their descriptions and beauty: Princess Dejah Thoris of Barsoom (*A Princess of Mars*), Nah-ee-lah (*The Moon Maid*), Valla Dia (*The Master Mind of Mars*), Duare (*Pirates of Venus*), and many others equally exotic. Remember that your characters' names will be seen throughout the book, and if you select something unappealing it may even hurt sales since many people flip through the pages before making a purchase. Luckily, an ear for names can be acquired. Highly recommended is *The Name Game* (1977) by Christopher P. Andersen, which reveals the subliminal and unconscious psychological associations of names. Written to help people name their babies, its insights are actually of unique value for creative writers.

HOW TO PACE NARRATIVES LIKE BURROUGHS

Edgar Rice Burroughs was a master of pace, but he didn't know all the tricks right off the bat. In fact he had to write a few books before he acquired the knack of making readers turn pages. True, his plots were always exciting, but the key pacing tools only came later, after he had completed *A Princess of Mars*.[1] With later books he learned two things that helped him pace his stories for maximum excitement. These devices can be employed by any writer who gives thought to the shape of a story.

---

1. Lupoff 1968:48.

The first technique, which we saw used by W. Somerset Maugham, is to introduce a dramatic pause after a fast-moving scene because a "dramatic pause or contrast" makes for effective pacing.[2] Unlike Maugham, however, in many novels Burroughs doesn't slow pace down, instead he shifts *away* from one line of narrative to another equally exciting story line, forcing readers to wait to resume the action of the first scene. An effective time to do this is at a chapter break. For example, in his Caspak and Pellucidar series Burroughs employs this device numerous times. By leaving one character in danger, the reader is forced to worry about him and the peril he faces until his story is rejoined. This enhances suspense and helps pace a story, even though it doesn't always *slow* the action down.

Another technique, and the one most commonly encountered in literature, is to speed up the action for certain sections and then pause and slow things down. In this way, manipulating the tempo of the narrative, Burroughs keeps the reader involved but not exhausted. By making everything run at top speed and by staying with one story line, some writers fail to pace themselves. Just as a runner cannot win a race by running full out the entire time, a writer will want to vary the pace to achieve maximum effect. For example, in *A Fighting Man of Mars* (1931) there are extended scenes where Hadron of Hastor is searching on the Red Planet for a missing princess. These slower-moving sections allow Burroughs to build up tension. Such scenes also vary the intensity of the story and contrast with the exciting fights, battles, and near-death escapes that occur in other sections. While Somerset Maugham also used this device for pacing control, Burroughs's use is easier to notice because his works are more action-oriented; therefore, when the pace is changed it's usually a rather obvious *physical* slowing that occurs. In Maugham, on the other hand, more often than not the slowing of pace is accomplished by changing the *psychological* intensity of a scene. It is interesting to compare these two methods of varying pace. Both are effective and both can be used in all kinds of stories, although Burroughs's approach is more suited to the action tale.

2. Williams 1998:84.

WHY CONFLICT IS NECESSARY

Burroughs was a prolific writer. He often wrote quickly and, as John Taliaferro points out in a highly readable biography, he relied on a handful of time-tested devices to get him through his stories:

- There is usually a "stranger in a strange land—Tarzan in the jungle, John Carter on Mars, David Innes in the Inner World, Carson Napier on Venus."
- The hero "is a warrior by both breeding and training."
- "Repeatedly he is chased, outnumbered by savage hordes, and thrown into a 'Stygian' cell."
- "[O]ptimism is shared by all Burroughs protagonists."
- "By application of brawn, brains, and valor, he eventually prevails over his adversaries and either makes his way home or else finds a new and better home."
- "Always, too, the leading man is called on to rescue a damsel in distress with whom he inevitably falls in love. ... In most instances the object of the hero's affection is well-born, beautiful, and often provocatively clad."
- Many battles, fights, and close escapes from death.
- No sex, but the threat of rape: "sooner or later in nearly every Burroughs story, the heroine must confront a 'fate worse than death.'"[3]

This summary of the plot devices Burroughs relied upon clearly puts the spotlight on conflict. For example, in *Beyond the Farthest Star* (1964), which incidentally was written in seventeen days, there is conflict before the reader has turned more than two pages. A fighter pilot is transported 450,000 light-years from Earth and finds himself naked on the planet Poloda. He is captured by a group of men wearing red sequins and black boots. As the novel unfolds more conflict develops. The Earthman is put on trial for being a spy. Then the conflict escalates

---

3. These formula items are from Taliaferro 1999:18-20, 65.

and he discovers that the entire world he has arrived on is at war, with Kapar and Unis fighting for the past 101 years.

In *The Land of Hidden Men* (1932) Gordon King ventures into the jungle and conflict begins on page one in the form of man versus man. His Cambodian guide refuses to take him further, citing fear of the jungle. Gordon decides to go the rest of the way alone. Of course, readers know that this will be a mistake. Then we have conflict in the form of man versus himself, as Gordon feels he has done the wrong thing by venturing into the unknown wilderness. Before long we encounter additional conflict in the form of man versus beast as Gordon is charged by a wild boar. Then there is man versus man again as he fights the Leper King.

Pick up any Burroughs novel and you'll find it filled with conflict. It's not unusual for the hero to be chased by six-limbed giants, pursued by flying men, captured by warring tribes, menaced by unevolved proto-humans, or attacked by wild beasts and dinosaurs. The woman he loves is almost always captured by an evil tribe led by a lustful and vicious leader who threatens to dishonor her. The conflict continues and often erupts into wars between tribes, nations, and even worlds.

A final example will illustrate how to keep a hero in peril by pitting him against immense odds. In *Thuvia, Maid of Mars* (1920) the hero is Carthoris, an honorable noble of high birth and a fine warrior. He attempts to rescue Thuvia, who has been captured by soldiers from Dusar. When he finds her he must fight with three men simultaneously. Meanwhile the girl is removed from the scene by another warrior. Carthoris kills two of his adversaries and sets off to find the woman he loves. After a number of adventures he sees her in the power of Hortan Gur, Jeddak of Torquas. At this point he must confront not only her captors but also her suspicion of him. She mistakenly believes that he has engineered her abduction. Numerous complications ensue until the pair are finally brought together—on the last page.

This high level of conflict is not, strictly speaking, necessary in a mainstream novel, but Burroughs's method of keeping the hero in peril is instructive. From his example a writer can learn the essential secret of strong plotting. Conflict is the engine that drives a story forward, and if you find a tale flagging you may discover that upping the ante and increasing the stakes by putting the hero in conflict with someone will bring the story back to life. If you can achieve even one tenth the conflict Burroughs piles into his stories and resolve the romantic entanglements in the last chapter (let alone the last page!)—consider yourself a master storyteller ... and give thanks to the lessons taught by Burroughs.

HOW TO ADD ROMANCE TO YOUR STORY

As we have mentioned, romance is at the heart of most Burroughs stories. In chapter five of *The Land of Hidden Men*, for instance, Gordon King is enchanted by the jungle girl, Fou-tan. "Every movement of her lithe body, every gesture of her graceful arms and hands, each changing expression of her beautiful face and eyes were provocative. She radiated magnetism. He sensed it in the reaction of his skin, his eyes, his nostrils." The descriptions of the leading ladies in other Burroughs novels are equally alluring and often poetic. "Boy meets girl was hardly a new motif by the time Burroughs got around to employing it, though remarkably, he was the first to introduce it to science fiction."[4] The use of romance in adventures set on other planets served to make the stories retain an element of believability despite the otherworldly settings. The hero and heroine may be on Mars and wandering through vast dead sea bottoms—"Far out across the ochre sea-bottoms beyond the twin cities of Helium raced the swift flier of Tara of Helium." (*The Chessmen of Mars*, 1922)—but the universal appeal of romantic love ensures that the stories rise above the level of mere fantasy. Romance lends believability to Burroughs's tales and interjects a device that has appeared in all of world literature.

When incorporating romance into your stories, of course you won't simply have a boy meets girl, boy gets girl plot. You'll need obstacles to

---

4. Taliaferro 1999:19. The motif would be picked up and used successfully by other space opera writers, such as E.E. "Doc" Smith and Robert Heinlein.

love.[5] In *The Moon Maid* an Earthman named Julian travels to the inside of the moon and meets an alluring beauty, with whom he falls in love. He and the girl, Nah-ee-lah, are captured by ferocious creatures that are half-man, half-horse, and he tries to protect her from harm. There is, along the way, some hint that the girl may return his feelings. But Burroughs keeps the potential lovers apart throughout the book: first because they are prisoners and later because of a misunderstanding on her part about his intentions. (In order to see how *universal* obstacles to love are, consider how similar misunderstandings keep Elizabeth and Darcy apart in Jane Austen's *Pride and Prejudice*.) Julian tells us, "I saw that something was amiss, that she seemed to be angry with me, but the cause I could not imagine."[6] Some ten pages later their misunderstanding is cleared up, but they still cannot declare their love for one another because conditions are perilous for them and they are pursued by warriors who seek to kill them. As usual Burroughs prolongs their separation until the end of the novel, when all the loose ends are tied up and the hero and heroine can reveal their true feelings for one another.

There is no question that the effective introduction of a love story into science fiction made Burroughs's stories more interesting. His example should reinforce the message that romance can help almost any story, no matter how fantastic, have more reader appeal. Never hesitate to strengthen and work on characterizing your hero and heroine, and never shy from introducing romance into your story. If even so bleak a writer as Kafka could introduce romance into the heart of his fables, and if the master of fantasy and SF could do so, it stands to reason that there is hardly a story that can't be improved by bolstering the love interest.

---

5. *See* the article "Obstacles to Love" in Falk 1983:65-67. "No matter how strong the plot, the book won't work unless the obstacles to love are serious enough to keep the lovers apart."

6. Burroughs 1923:144.

CHAPTER 9

WRITE LIKE

Franz Kafka

Kafka baffles many people. They read him and admire his work but it never crosses their mind that they might be able to learn anything about *writing* from him. I admit that this is understandable in light of the fact that his style is so unique. In fact when I propose that there might be something to *imitate* in his work students say things like: "For heaven's sake, I don't want to write about people turning into bugs or faceless nonentities suffering in a bureaucracy!" Because Kafka is so unusual there are many who believe *nothing* can be learned from him. But his very *strange*ness may be his greatest strength for there are things *only* he can teach. Despite his oddness, or perhaps *because* of it, this may very well be the most important chapter in the book.

I'd like to start out by suggesting that writers will profit from reading Kafka with a certain sense of humor. Admittedly he is often thought of as a dark and brooding writer. His heroes try with all their might to accomplish some simple task—such as getting an appointment with an official or traveling to some nearby destination—and they fail. In *The Trial* (1925) the hero is arrested for no apparent reason and goes through endless unsuccessful machinations in an attempt to have his case resolved. In *The Castle* (1926) the hero spends the entire book trying to enter a castle and never even sets foot in it! In "The Metamorphosis" (1915) the hero is turned into an insect and never finds out why. Philip Roth, the Pulitzer Prize-winning author of *Portnoy's Complaint*, wasn't the only one who found this story tremendously funny; Kafka himself certainly *intended* it that way. "I was ... strongly influenced by a sit-down comic named Franz Kafka and a very funny bit he does called 'The Metamorphosis.' ... I had read somewhere that he used to giggle to himself while he worked. Of course! It was all so *funny*, this morbid preoccupation with punishment and guilt. Hideous, but funny."[1] Roth's comment contains a valuable insight. If we start with the understanding that behind the grimness there is a good deal of humor, I think we'll see that there is more to Kafka than meets the eye and that writers can learn a good deal from him, not only about how to be funny but about how to present stories in an allegorical style.

Born in 1883 in Prague, Kafka grew up with three younger sisters; however, he should probably be considered an "honorary laterborn" because of the severe conflict he experienced with his father.[2] Educated as a lawyer, he worked for an insurance company by day; his writing was usually done at night.[3] His most famous works include *The Trial, The Castle,* and the short story "The Metamorphosis." Most of his writing portrays heroes caught in a hopeless bureaucracy and the term Kafkaesque refers to situations that are "nightmarishly complex" or overly bureaucratic. It is sobering to realize that after Kafka's death, all three of his sisters were destroyed in Nazi concentration camps. While he could not have foreseen this catastrophe, his work certainly strikes many as presaging some of the worst aspects of modern man.

Before we go any further we must certainly concede that Kafka was a unique writer, a trailblazer in content, form, and style. His work is rather unlike anything that came before—or since. That being said, let's not forget that even the innovator Kafka was not working in a vacuum; yes, even *he* imitated. He was, in fact, heavily influenced by Dickens. "His known models include Russian, German, French, Czech,

---

1. Roth 1992:39-40.

2. This is a term coined by Frank Sulloway to describe firstborns who have lastborn traits (including creativity and affability) because of significant parental conflict (Sulloway 1996:123).

3. Citati 1990:100.

and American authors."[4] In order to situate Kafka properly in the web of intertextuality that influences all writers (and readers) and in order to illustrate how profound the notion of one text influencing another is as an analytical tool, it may be of interest to modern readers to know that J.D. Salinger was a tremendous fan of Kafka. Salinger devoured Kafka's diaries while living in Cornish, New Hampshire, and was probably influenced by him in writing *The Catcher in the Rye* (1951).[5]

THE SECRET OF KAFKA'S SUCCESS

Kafka was a literary and artistic success, his accomplishments inspiring countless modern writers. For example, Samuel Beckett was influenced by Kafka in writing his trilogy of novels. Dag Solstad copied Kafka's style in *Shyness and Dignity* (1944). Philip Roth was influenced by Kafka's style. One of the first things to note about Kafka is that, like a lawyer, he can concoct sentences and arguments that read like contracts at times. He does tend to go on in a rather plodding manner when describing the intentions of K. or the troubles he experiences. But this is all in good fun. The more interesting stylistic device is clarity and precision of language, especially notable in the openings of all his works. Certainly one of the reasons for his success was his famous opening sentences.

If you can begin a story like Kafka, what a dynamic start you'll have! If you can open with a bang-up introduction the way his novels and stories open, readers will drop their jaws in wonder, hooked from the get-go. Do you dare start as concisely and to the point as Kafka? "Someone must have slandered Josef K., for one morning, without having done anything truly wrong, he was arrested."[6] The opening sen-

---

4. Spilka 1963:39.

5."A parallel which emerges between Holden's adventures and the world of Joseph K. [from *The Trial*] is that he never makes real contact with any of the people he meets. . . . Like a psychotic, he is constantly divided between his contempt for almost everyone else in the world as irritating . . . phonies . . . and then, as if trying to make up for it, wanting to throw in an extravagant reference to how much he likes them or misses them after all." (Booker 2004:394).

6. Kafka 1925a:3.

tence of *The Trial* encapsulates the entire plot and conflict. There is no endless scene setting (like Balzac) or long character analysis (like Dickens) or convoluted prefatory scene (like Hardy). *Poof!* and we're right into it.

Anyone who has opened "The Metamorphosis" will have been struck by the first sentence, and indeed the premise of the story, which is set up by that opening, is strikingly original: "As Gregor Samsa awoke one morning from uneasy dreams he found himself transformed in his bed into a gigantic insect." It's one of the most famous sentences in all of literature. Quote it to an English major at any university and most of them will be able to tell you, "That's Kafka!" They may or may not like Kafka (it's the rare exception who doesn't) but they *will* know.

In both openings Kafka does something remarkable. He boils down the essence of his story and summarizes the entire conflict. Many writers fear to do this; they prefer holding back, waiting to reveal the major conflict and the premise later. But in some cases, as in horror stories, science fiction, or in even a mystery novel, the first sentence can jump right to the heart of things. If it sets the right tone it need not be considered too revealing.

THE CLUE TO KAFKA'S GREATNESS LIES IN HIS APPROACH TO PLOT

Kafka was a myth maker. Eleazar Meletinsky, an expert on myths and stories, suggests that myth was the guiding principle of his work.

> Kafka's plots and protagonists are ... beyond historical time. They have a universal meaning. The Kafkaesque 'everyman' represents all of humanity, and the world is described and explained in terms of the events that form the plot. [He] imparts a dream-like quality to the everyday life of his protagonist: the bright spots in the shadows, the labile quality of his protagonists' ability to focus and concentrate, their protean natures, action that is inappropriate to the locales of the narrative, and the spontaneous eruption of erotic motifs.[7]

7. Meletinsky 2000:317.

Tom Wolfe also suggested that Kafka was a myth maker, but he made this comment in a general discussion of the *worst* aspects of American fiction. Wolfe sees modern myth making as an error to be avoided. And yet, to the extent that myth *works* in a narrative, to the extent that a writer *can* succeed in creating the universal by stripping down factual realistic elements, and to the extent that a story might sometimes be more *powerful* with this bare-bones style of presentation, the way of Kafka is still valid. A short list of successful examples might include the novels of Beckett, Marguerite Duras, Dag Solstad, and Alain Robbe-Grillet.

The hero of a Kafka story is always caught in the plot and rarely makes the story go forward; he is, instead, buffeted about by the difficulties and requirements of his world. In this sense, no matter how he strives to accomplish something, he remains rather passive. He may try to be proactive, like the hero of "The Burrow," but he only succeeds in fortifying his hole in the ground. In *The Trial,* no matter how he exerts himself, K. "never meets the superior court judges who are orchestrating his fate."[8] This passivity goes against all the advice most writers receive today about making a protagonist a "doer," a veritable "mover and shaker." K. *would* be a doer if he could manage to accomplish anything, but his chief task is to survive in *The Trial* and to enter the castle in *The Castle.* In both books he can hardly creep forward an inch, like the hero of "The Burrow." In "The Metamorphosis" the protagonist can hardly move in his unwieldy body. Similarly in *Amerika* (1927), Kafka's first novel, the hero is "constantly seduced and abused" by other characters.[9]

All of this suggests the nightmarish quality of the dream. Indeed it has been observed that all Kafka's plots "retain a dream-like quality, recognized by Kafka as corresponding to his own dream-like inner life."[10] But his use of the elastic quality of dream landscapes (where one

---

8. Meletinsky 2000:322.

9. Kirsch 2009:BR23. The acclaimed new translation of *Amerika,* by Mark Harman, is a must-read for writers interested in Kafka's prose style and punctuation. It's the next best thing to reading it in the original German.

10. Reiss 1978:134.

FICTION WRITING *Master Class*

opens a door in a hallway only to find one has come into a courtroom, or where one cannot escape a pursuer, or where one cannot find the answer to a question)—all of this is used not only to portray his *own* authorial state but also to represent, in an expressionistic manner, the state of mankind. This is where his work becomes universal and this is why it has had such a wide appeal. The human mind operates like this: It functions in a nonlinear manner, a dreamlike manner. Freud *analyzed* this property of the mind in his work. Kafka *illustrated* it in his.

Kafka's approach to plot was expressionist. He did not embrace the formal terms of the movement known as German expressionism, considering it too flashy and "noisy," but his work nonetheless has the dreamlike qualities that make it similar to the work of Hamsun, childhood fables, and myths. In many ways it is similar to the allegorical *The Pilgrim's Progress* (1678) by John Bunyan, which is about a man's symbolic journey to heaven. But Kafka's novels aren't allegorical in the sense that one thing stands for another in a clear way, as the path in *The Pilgrim's Progress* stands for the way to God. Instead Kafka's allegory is fluid, changeable, and more open to personal reader interpretation. Certainly the world in which his heroes live is threatening, strange, and alien. The hero sinks deeper and deeper into this strange world, and he accepts it as the real world. As a result the reader is drawn into this dream through vicarious experience and sees it through the hero's eyes. In this way Kafka's plots manage to shepherd readers through a modern mythic landscape—one with powerful allegorical overtones.

HOW TO STRUCTURE STORIES LIKE KAFKA

Everyone knows that Kafka's novels and stories transport readers into alien nightmarish worlds. What few writer's realize, however, is that if your plot is similar it may be worth your while to study Kafka's methods in order to see whether you can learn anything to help shape your own work, especially if your story has a confining and alienating story line. As Beckett realized, to structure a story like Kafka you need to put your hero into a quandary: he must be perplexed in some way, must have entered strange new territory, and should be frustrated at every turn in his quest for understanding and completion. Flannery O'Connor's writing has been called Kafkaesque[11] because her heroes (for example, Hazel Motes in her first novel *Wise Blood* [1952], and Tarwater in *The Violent Bear It Away* [1960]) cannot come to terms with the strange world they feel they inhabit.[12]

George Orwell's *Nineteen Eighty-Four* is similar to Kafka in many ways because it pits man against unbeatable odds. In order to get a handle on how to structure a story like Kafka it may be helpful to contrast the Orwellian and Kafkaesque approaches. Both involve a hero at odds with the world and the society in which he lives. They differ in that *Orwellian* "may describe the way that language is twisted and corrupted in the service of power. ... Equally, the word may describe the nightmare world of repression and state violence."[13] The term "*Kafkaesque* can be used to describe a bleak and alienating city-scape just as easily as it can apply to an individual's struggles with bureaucracy, always 'faceless,' of course."[14] From this distinction, we can see that a plot structured like Kafka puts a hero at odds with the world and up against either a nightmarish twilight zone that baffles him, or a complex system of government and societal regulations that has the same effect.

For writers, a helpful way to understand what Kafka is doing is to analyze his work along the lines proposed by Christopher Booker in *The Seven Basic Plots* (2004). *The Trial* represents a dark version of the "voyage and return" plot. In this type of story a hero enters a puzzling world in which things become increasingly strange and more bizarre— another example would be Lewis Carroll's *Alice's Adventures in Wonderland* (1865)—until people and events in this bizarre new world loom menacing and threatening. In other words the strangeness and danger increase as the plot thickens. In the "light" version of this plot the hero

---

11. Davis 1953:24.

12. Another modern Kafkaesque novel is *Notable American Women* by Ben Marcus.

13. Gooden 2008:141.

14. Gooden 2008:101.

(for example, Alice) eventually returns home. In the "dark" version (for example, *The Trial*) the hero "remains trapped, never returning home."[15] Booker's analysis is similar to Northrop Frye's observation that Kafka focuses less on linear plot and more on "the psychological event"; Frye also characterizes *The Castle* as "an anxiety nightmare."[16]

Can a modern writer actually find anything of use in this plot type? The answer lies in the work of some of the most respected writers of the twentieth century. Flannery O'Connor, as we have observed, works with a Kafkaesque plot and her heroes are outsiders who see the world differently from almost everyone else. Saul Bellow's *The Victim* (1947) is also a "Kafkaesque novel" in which the hero feels trapped in New York City and put upon by the other characters and by his responsibilities for a sick nephew.[17] Philip Roth's *Portnoy's Complaint* (1969) incorporates a similar motif, and "does take the Kafkaesque preoccupation with victimization and guilt to its limits in an exaggeration."[18] Neil Gaiman's *Neverwhere* (1996) propels the hero into a strange world underneath London. The list of examples of contemporary writers who have successfully used Kafka's approach to plot extends far beyond this. The point is that modern fiction is ready for the dark version of the voyage and return plot, a type of story in which the hero finds himself in a world that becomes increasingly strange and threatening. If you're writing a story like this, or even one with a Kafkaesque element, there's no better model than the originator of the genre himself.

For example, you can clearly learn from Kafka how to thrust a hero into a bizarre and strange world, such as in *The Trial*. Kafka has his hero *worry* about the circumstances of his descent into this bizarre world just as Carroll makes Alice worry about her fall into Wonderland. If your protagonist is entering an alien landscape you can use the same technique by making him worry about the bizarre new world and why he has been thrust into it. What did he do to deserve such a fate? You

---

15. Booker 2004:393.

16. Frye 2003:40–41.

17. Bercovitch and Patell 1994:144.

18. Jones and Nance 1981:81.

must also address the question of whether your hero will ever emerge from the world he enters. If not, then like Kafka you will be writing a "dark version" of the story and your protagonist will remain forever trapped in the new world. Kafka shows you how to end such a story—at the conclusion of *The Trial* K. is executed. If you dare to give your main character a similarly severe fate you may find Kafka inspirational. Salinger's conclusion to *The Catcher in the Rye* is similarly Kafkaesque since Holden winds up insane. And the ending of Orwell's *Nineteen Eighty-Four* is just as bleak since Smith loses his mind and all his earlier convictions.

DISCOVER HOW KAFKA'S GREATEST WEAKNESS AS A WRITER CAN BE YOUR GREATEST STRENGTH

One of Kafka's weaknesses as a writer is his failure to provide background for his characters. Who is Joseph K., from *The Trial*, for example? We learn precious little about him. He is more an everyman than a specific realist personage. In Kafka "all objects exist only in relation to the central character. ...the textual richness of an individual past, an environment, even a specific set of psychological tensions—all this is what we do *not* find in Kafka."[19] This scanty background information runs counter to what writers are told in modern fiction books and courses. Developing character is urged on writers; they are even encouraged to do character development exercises.

Another glaring weakness is Kafka's failure to portray developed romantic relationships. There are no loving couples, as in D.H. Lawrence and George Eliot. There are no passionate love affairs such as we find in even the writers he admired: Dostoevsky (think of Raskalnikov and Sonia in *Crime and Punishment,* or Prince Myshkin and Nastasya in *The Idiot*), Dickens (think of Pip and Estella in *Great Expectations* or David and Dora in *David Copperfield*). "But," you may say, "Kafka never *intended* to include such romances!" Nonetheless, human relationships,

---

19. Rolleston 1986:28.

especially romantic relationships, and the capacity to sustain them, form a large part of literature. Their absence in Kafka, except in slight and minor form, is certainly one of the things that makes his work seem dreary to some. The erotic interludes are never sustained and relationships are fleeting, at best.

But perhaps Kafka's greatest failing is the absence of not only relationships but of connection between the central character and *any* other people. Joseph K. in *The Trial* has no friends. His brief flirtation with Leni is empty and leads nowhere because "he is later told she falls in love with any accused man."[20] No one helps him in any significant way. In *The Castle*, K. is also a loner. His two assistants are so perfunctory, the innkeepers so minor in their roles, and the women so unhelpful, that K. can be seen as living in his own world. Not only doesn't he have meaningful relationships, he doesn't even seek them out. When he does try to form a relationship with a woman it is usually for the ulterior purpose of advancing his move into the castle. Yet the women he meets do not even help him achieve that small goal. Likewise, in "The Metamorphosis" Gregor's own family abhors him and finds him disgusting and repulsive because he is a gigantic insect. His sister, the closest one to him, eventually comes to feel the same repugnance. Gregor, like the protagonists in most of Kafka, has no one he is close to and no relationship that means anything.

Christopher Booker even goes so far as to imply that the hero of a Kafka novel is akin to a psychotic because of his lack of relationships.[21] So how can these "faults" help you? The answer lies in your intention to write a story that is mythological or allegorical in nature. Such stories *can* work, as Kafka's stories certainly have, by reducing character background information, omitting romance, and cutting back on relationships to focus on the alienation of the hero. Samuel Beckett succeeded in using such an approach with *Molloy* (1951), *Malone Dies*

---

20. Booker 2004:393.
21. Booker 2004:394.

(1951), and *The Unnamable* (1953). Dag Solstad achieved similar success with *Shyness and Dignity*.

If you set out to tell a story in which a character is alienated in some significant way, in which the world the hero enters is strange and bizarre, and in which the menace become overwhelming as the plot progresses, then Kafka is a good guide. You might even wish to try tweaking the Kafka approach in some manner. Perhaps allow the protagonist to have one strong romance. Try fleshing out the background of the character who is the hero. Or maybe you will allow him to have an ally or friend who can help him or at least understand his plight and sympathize. In this way Kafka's greatest weakness as a writer, the lack of direct connection between characters, might become your greatest strength. You could, in effect, rewrite the Kafka mythos.

In *The Castle,* Joseph K. has an affair with a girl on the floor of a bar. Then he becomes involved with another girl and the first becomes jealous. He spends time trying to calm both girls down. These incidents don't usually receive attention because critics focus on the bureaucracy in Kafka's work. But a writer might decide to imitate his style, picking up where he left off and adding some Kafkaesque romance to an otherwise nightmarish work. Of course, neither Beckett nor Dag Solstad approached imitation of Kafka with exactly this goal, but the possibility still exists for some writer to pick up where Kafka left off and complete the story in a new way. This is what is meant by emulating and going one step further than the model you're using. In the same way that D.H. Lawrence imitated George Eliot but went one step further by focusing on details such as the eyes of the couples, you could imitate Kafka but increase the romance or add other elements that you find relevant. In this way imitation becomes a contest between you and your model in which you try to emulate or improve upon the writer you're studying.

In conclusion, all this is said not so much to urge you to strike out and rewrite Kafka or to copy him slavishly, but to show you that it is *possible* to learn from another writer. The important point is that imitation can take *one good thing* from a writer and bend and change the rest.

This is why Quintilian believed that we should always *emulate* the best, that is, try to improve upon it and outshine it rather than slavishly imitate, copy, and plagiarize. All who advocate imitation believe that we should try to better the model we are using, in other words, "imitate in such a way as we strive to overtake him; finally all our effort should be devoted to surpassing him once we have overtaken him. ... But emulation should always be joined to imitation."[22] If you don't start out imitating, you will never achieve the goal of emulating or surpassing your target. And that, quite clearly, should *always* be the goal.

---

22. Galbraith 2000:168n.77.

CHAPTER 10

WRITE LIKE

D.H. Lawrence

A warning may be in order as we consider one of the most controversial writers of the past century: Familiarity with the content of this man's work might encourage some to take immoderate risks, to wander into perilous territory, or even to adopt similar stylistic faults. Lawrence is a seductive writer, often excessive and uneven in his novels, but his rebellious venturing into new realms may ultimately be just what is needed to inspire and shake up a slumbering talent. Be forewarned, however, that discretion and good taste will be required every step of the way because those who follow in Lawrence's footsteps tread upon a narrow path, with pitfalls of unevenness, stylistic excess, and dangerous issues waiting like traps on all sides. For those who dare, however, the trek may well prove bracing and inspirational.

D.H. Lawrence was born in 1885, the middle child of a coal miner and a teacher. His family figured prominently in his early writing, and men were often portrayed as rather uneducated whereas women were paragons of intelligence, breeding, and beauty. *Sons and Lovers* (1913), his third novel, focuses on the close relationship he had with his mother. The coal mines also figure prominently in the story because Paul Morel's father works there. The character of Miriam (Paul's girlfriend) is based on Jessie Chambers, the girlfriend of Lawrence's youth. The novel offers a living portrait of the adolescent Lawrence. *Mr. Noon* (1920) offers a similar portrait of Lawrence's relationship with his wife,

Frieda Weekley.[1] Frieda left her husband and three young children to run off with Lawrence. Their elopement suggests some of the magnetic attraction he exerted on women. He certainly put all he knew about relationships into his books, and they're quite unlike anything else in modern literature.

Lady Chatterley's Lover (1928) was banned for many years in the United States, the U.K., and elsewhere. Lawrence believed sexuality should be discussed openly, and in that book his vocabulary was rather direct and shocking for its day. Continually harried by government agencies, Lawrence and his wife moved often, seeking political freedom as well as warmer climates in an attempt to deal with his tuberculosis. They lived for some time in Taos, New Mexico.

WHY NO ONE WRITES DIALOGUE LIKE LAWRENCE

In addition to understanding correct form, Lawrence also had a unique ability to translate what he knew intuitively about people onto the written page. These two conditions are essential to good dialogue, and understanding his approach can help even beginning writers craft lively, intelligent conversations.

The first thing one needs to master, of course, is correct form. This entails writing a line of speech and, in many cases, an attribution. Naturally Lawrence observes good form when writing dialogue, but he goes considerably beyond the norm by interjecting descriptions of the characters while reporting their speech. *Women in Love* (1920) is a supremely romantic novel about two couples, Gerald and Gudrun and Rupert and Ursula. Much of the novel's power results from Lawrence's command of dialogue. For instance, there is a scene in chapter six which illustrates Lawrence's mastery of adding telling details to exchanges between the main characters. Gerald and Rupert are in a

---

1. Maddox 1994:117-120. *See also* Meyers 1990:92. In addition to being a fictionalized account of his relationship with Frieda, *Mr. Noon* contains the most extended kissing scenes in English literature.

café talking with a Miss Darrington, whom Gerald finds attractive. The key to the dialogue is in Lawrence's descriptions of the participants.

> "How long are you staying?" she asked him.
>
> "A day or two," he replied. "But there is no particular hurry."
>
> Still, she stared into his face with that slow, full gaze which was so curious and so exciting to him. He was acutely and delightfully conscious of himself, of his own attractiveness. He felt full of strength, able to give off a sort of electric power. And he was aware of her blue, exposed-looking eyes upon him. She had beautiful eyes, flower-like, fully opened, naked in their looking at him. And on them there seemed to float a curious iridescence, a sort of film of disintegration, and sullenness, like oil on water.[2]

The extended description of Gerald's reaction to the girl and the loving attention given to the description of her eyes provides a world of detail not commonly found in dialogue. Lawrence is unique in his ability to find the right emotional language to describe eyes, looks, and expressions. He also knows what is relevant: Gerald's desire, the girl's staring at him, the prolonged gaze, the way they looked at one another. And he knows the words that will express their inner psychology. He displays a fine feeling for appropriate and suggestive language, and the words he chooses are full of connotation and emotion. Where could he have learned such a skill? Certainly it is not apparent in any other novelist, although there were descriptions of couples in the work of Hardy and George Eliot, both of whom he admired—and imitated.[3]

He told Jesse Chambers, his girlfriend, how he proposed to begin *The White Peacock* (1911).

> "The usual plan is to take two couples and develop their relationships," he said. "Most of George Eliot's are on that plan. Anyhow, I don't want a plot. I should be bored with it. I shall try two couples for a start."[4]

---

2. Lawrence 1920b:57.

3. "Lawrence began *The White Peacock* by trying to emulate George Eliot's style" (Krockel 2007:20).

4. Lawrence, quoted in Krockel 2007:20.

He adopted the same plan for *Women in Love*, where the two couples are the sisters Ursula and Gudrun and the two men they love, Rupert and Gerald. But Lawrence focused more attention on the relationships of the individuals than on the plot and as a result the story has a kind of episodic feel. He makes up for this by a terrific exploration of the hearts and minds of the individuals. One of the chief rewards of reading the novel is discovering how each chapter is filled with scenes depicting deep emotional relationships. Lawrence clearly picked up some structural skills from his predecessors but he developed the technique of good dialogue through his own invention.

PLOTTING AND WRITING DRAFTS

Like most successful and professional writers Lawrence wrote more than one draft and revised his work. But unlike most of these writers Lawrence was much more fastidious about the process of making revisions and his work was often done in an unconventional way. He would write a quick first draft. Then he would write a second draft, but it would not be a *revision* of the first, with mere reshuffling of pages like Faulkner or mere corrections of the text like Hemingway; instead it would be a rewrite from the ground floor up. "Lawrence did not merely revise, but frequently started a work from the beginning again."[5] Incredible as it may sound he would begin on page one with a blank page and write anew the entire story! Sometimes he did this to fix the relationships and motivation of major characters; for example, there are three published versions of *Lady Chatterley's Lover* and "in each version the motivation of the gamekeeper and Lady Chatterley are different."[6]

Women in Love had an even more checkered history. Indeed, "[t]hree decades of scholars have been looking at the textual history" of the book! In some sense this has to be seen as humorous, but it is also instructive for us as writers. The book was initially written in 1913

---

5. Poplawski 2001:31.
6. Madden 1988:106.

and titled *The Sisters*. Later that year he began anew but by the time he reached page 380 he stopped, unsatisfied with this second version. The third version was written in early 1914 and entitled *The Wedding Ring*. He actually sent it to his publisher but the outbreak of war prevented their publishing it immediately. So then he started again, going at the same material from 1914 to 1915, writing a huge manuscript which he titled *The Rainbow*. In 1916 he began yet again and wrote another manuscript, which he subsequently typed. He then revised this typescript. "Ten per cent of the novel was totally re-written ... and the other 90 per cent heavily revised."[7] In other words, *Lawrence wrote the book over more than five times.* Why this heavy cycle of revision and reworking? Critics feel that part of the reason was that he was working with material that was voluminous enough for two books. Another reason was that he wanted to alter certain relationships. "[T]he crucial relationships—especially those between Birkin and Gerald, and Birkin and Ursula—are enormously changed."[8]

One cardinal lesson to be gleaned from observing Lawrence's methods of producing books is that you may very well be surprised by what you have done when you have finished a first draft or by the time you are substantially through writing a second or third draft. In looking back upon what you have done you may feel quite dissatisfied. At that point you may decide to rework various character relationships or make other major changes. It may be easier for you to start anew, as Lawrence often did. Of course, you may find that making major revisions to a manuscript is easier; today, the use of computers usually makes the latter procedure quite simple. But one should not rule out using Lawrence's method of starting anew when that becomes necessary or expedient.

As one critic has noted, "In a story by Lawrence, plot is never the primary interest."[9] In fact, Lawrence pointedly told Jessie Chambers

---

7. I am indebted to Peter Preston and Peter Hoare for this chronology of the early versions of *Women in Love*, which I have somewhat simplified here (Preston and Hoare 1989:11–12).

8. Worthen and Vasey, "Introduction." In Lawrence 1998:liii.

9. Thornton 1993:5.

that he did not *want* a plot. Yet his books do employ classic plot devices (including conflicts and resolutions) that you may find enormously useful, especially if you're writing primarily about relationships. And yet it is certainly true that most of the time Lawrence worked in a free-form style, using characters and character pairs to get started and to inspire his storytelling throughout a book-length manuscript. His favorite method was to proceed without much of an outline, composing scenes and chapters to suit his fancy, after which he would look over his raw material and revise. This method, which succeeds for many novelists, can also work for you, provided you aren't made anxious by not knowing where your story will take you. There are many writers who begin a story not knowing what the climax or resolution will be. Lawrence used this same technique, called *character possession*, "during which the characters become so alive for the author they begin to assert themselves and say and do things the author had no idea they would say and do when he began to novel."[10] If you can relax and let your characters come alive as Lawrence did then you may find his freewheeling and unstructured approach highly satisfying. Plotting will become secondary and writing first drafts will become easier.

HOW LAWRENCE CREATED EXCITEMENT IN THE SIMPLEST OF SCENES

Writing about relationships instead of crafting big action scenes or gun battles, Lawrence nevertheless manages to create a tremendous deal of excitement. In *Sons and Lovers* he does this by introducing male-female flirtation into scenes where it might not be expected. For example, in chapter seven when Paul almost forces Miriam, his platonic friend, to learn algebra, they sit at a table and he begins the lesson. Before long, though, things develop into a situation like Heloise and Abelard, and the young man feels the attraction of this young girl. "It made his blood

---

10. Meredith and Fitzgerald 1972:35-36. William Faulkner is another novelist who used this technique. In fact he is famous for commenting on the fact that he did not know what his characters would do. *See* page 124.

rouse to see her there, as it were, at his mercy, her mouth open, her eyes dilated with laughter that was afraid, apologetic, ashamed." In chapter twelve Paul begins an affair with a married woman, Clara Dawes. The affair commences with innocent dates, after which he yearns for her. Following the train of Paul's thoughts is where Lawrence hits his stride as a writer for there is excitement in the description of Paul's emotional state. "He was in a delirium. He felt that he would go mad if Monday did not come at once. On Monday he would see her again. ... He could not bear it." Later in the chapter Paul cleans Clara's boots after a walk through the mud and she kisses him. "He kneeled at her feet, worked away with a stick and tufts of grass. She put her fingers in his hair, drew his head to her, and kissed it." Even the simplest acts are intensified by Lawrence's careful attention to the feelings of the boy during the budding affair. This same attentiveness to the intimate details of a man and woman's relationship would mark all Lawrence's subsequent work.

In *The Rainbow* (1915) he creates excitement by focusing in a similar way on the relationship of sixteen-year-old Ursula and her twenty-one-year-old lover Skrebensky. Now we see that Lawrence has acquired more confidence about dipping into the intimate feelings of his characters, and their inner monologues become much more intense. For example, in chapter eleven: "She kept still, helpless. Then his mouth drew near, pressing open her mouth, a hot, drenching surge rose within her, she opened her lips to him, in pained, poignant eddies she drew him nearer, she let him come further, his lips came and surging, surging, soft, oh soft, yet oh, like the powerful surge of water, irresistible, till with a little blind cry, she broke away." This passage reflects some of the excesses of repetition that Lawrence has been faulted for in his novels, and yet the use of interjections—"oh"—and the length and punctuation of the sentence add to the breathless quality he is striving after.

Lady Chatterley's Lover creates excitement by sexualizing the relationship of the protagonist and her lover, the gamekeeper. When Lady Chatterley thinks about the man she experiences a swoon of feeling and Lawrence utilizes all the descriptive skills he had developed in earlier works to portray her passion. For example, in chapter ten: "She was gone in her own soft rapture. ... And in herself, in all her veins, she felt him and his child. His child was in all her veins, like a twilight." Examples of this type of description of feeling—both creative and slightly repetitious, with that Lawrencian gift (some would say fault) for repeating the important word—examples of this kind of rather florid writing occur throughout the book and lend it a special power and intensity over and beyond what the simple facts of the plot could produce. It is, as numerous critics have observed, never the plot after all that is of primary concern with Lawrence; it is the people, their relationships, their inner feelings and desires in all their subtle shades of exhilaration and rapture.

And in *Women in Love* the excitement of relationships reaches its peak. Gudrun and Gerald are locked in a conflict that extends beyond romantic love and embraces the fundamental contest between man and woman. Ursula and Rupert enjoy a more placid, though decidedly tempestuous and passionate relationship. "Where the relationship between Rupert and Ursula appears to be advancing with mutual exploration, that between Gerald and Gudrun continues to evoke images and suggestions of violent opposition, as if one must always assume a dominant position over the other."[11] Descriptions such as the following, from chapter eight, abound throughout the story, sparkling like jewels to make the characters come alive: "And Birkin, watching like a hermit crab from its hole, had seen the brilliant frustration and helplessness of Ursula. She was rich, full of dangerous power. She was like a strange unconscious bud of powerful womanhood. He was unconsciously drawn to her. She was his future." Writing like this is not purple prose, instead it is a means of adding a certain romantic excitement to the simplest of scenes and it is one of the chief joys of reading Lawrence. After a few hours spent with his books all relationships become more meaningful and you feel that you, too, have this divine ability to see to the heart and soul of the people around you. Their eyes are suddenly complex and full of significance. A glance, a turn of the

---

11. Miller 2006:91.

head, the intonation of a voice—all of it becomes surprisingly illuminated and meaningful.

You can achieve similar excitement in the simplest of scenes by throwing light on the feelings and flirtations of characters. Especially if you're writing about relationships, use Lawrence's trick of delving into the minds of characters to reveal their deepest longings and half-hidden desires. It is highly advisable to read Lawrence with a highlighter so that you can see what percentage of a passage he allocates to male-female flirtation. Then try to make your own scenes match this percentage. Doing so will elevate your work above the average and put it into the stratosphere of delicate sensitivity that few writers other than Lawrence have ever entered.

SYMBOLISM

In *Lady Chatterley's Lover* we find both plenty of realistic action, most particularly the love affair between Oliver Mellors and Lady Chatterley, as well as a good amount of ambient symbolism.[12] We use the term ambient symbolism to refer to symbols that appear in the background of a story or that run throughout a work, recurring with such frequency that they may be said to surround and embrace the characters or the world in which they live. Examples of ambient symbolism include the gamekeeper's woods, the industrial village of Lady Chatterley's husband, and the manor house where Lady Chatterley lives. *The New York Times* acknowledged that the novel manages to portray "a searing indictment of post-World War I England, providing both a fierce, disturbing portrait of a sterile society undermined by industrialism and class-bound conventions and a plea for its regeneration through passion and a return to nature."[13] Much of this indictment was accomplished through the use of ambient symbolism, an indication of how powerful symbolism can be in a work of art.

---

12. *See,* for example, Humma 1983:77-86, which discusses the prevalence of pastoral imagery and symbolism throughout the novel.

13. Kakutani 1992.

Studying how Lawrence used symbolism can enable any writer to become more conscious of this literary device. Of course the specific symbols that Lawrence used need not appear in your own work; you will certainly find your own symbols. But examining his method of incorporating symbolism, especially throughout a novel and during high points of the story, should prove especially instructive and helpful. Regarding *Lady Chatterley's Lover*, Mark Schorer, the noted Lawrence scholar and biographer, has observed that it is filled with symbolism.

> [I]t is a novel in which everything is symbolic, in which 'every bush burns,' and which in itself finally forms one great symbol so that one can easily remember it as one remembers a picture. In the background of this picture black machinery looms cruelly against a darkening sky; in the foreground, hemmed in and yet separate, stands a green wood; in the wood, two naked human beings dance.[14]

Lawrence works with symbolism in such a way that one can learn technique from him more easily than from more subtle writers. It's not a question of his use of symbolism being blatant or overdone, but his choice of symbols is relatively clear and easy to follow. In *Lady Chatterley's Lover* the "structural method involves a simple juxtaposition" of two symbolic approaches: on the one hand, the "abstract, cerebral, unvital," and on the other hand, "concrete, physical, and organic."[15] The former symbology is associated with Lady Chatterley's husband, a crippled representative of all that Lawrence found distasteful in modern man, the latter with Connie (Lady Chatterley) and Mellors, her lover, the gamekeeper. As Rebecca West points out, in *Lady Chatterley's Lover* "the baronet and his impotence are a symbol of the impotent culture of his time, and the love affair with the gamekeeper [is] a return of the soul to a more intense life."[16] These themes were important to Lawrence, and his use of symbolism to support this aspect of the work is understandable.

---

14. Schorer, "Introduction." In Lawrence 1928b:24–25.
15. Moynahan 1959:66.
16. West, quoted in Levine 2003:121–122.

Because symbols are, by definition, people, places, and things that have significance that goes far beyond their literal meaning, pointing to larger ideas and values, they can add power to a work of art and give it a fuller, more weighty feel. Readers often refer to symbols as things that convey a message or that embody a work's theme. Indeed, reader satisfaction is almost always higher, and a work appears more literary, when symbolism is present and handled in a way that meshes well with the story. In the final analysis it is hard to see how Lawrence could have written as powerful a novel as *Lady Chatterley's Lover* without the use of the gamekeeper's woods as a symbol of the natural life and the manor house as a symbol of the stagnant life. The industrial world also functions symbolically. If its significance is not clear Lawrence virtually hits the reader over the head with the message by having Lady Chatterley accuse her husband of ruining lives with his "ugly industrial" coal mines.[17] "[W]ho has taken away from the people their natural life and manhood, and given them this industrial horror?"[18] Don't be afraid to occasionally nudge your readers into understanding, as Lawrence does, by having a character make an impassioned speech about how he feels, a speech that encompasses the symbols in your work. If done like this, in the heat of an argument or intense feeling, it will not be perceived as overly blatant even though it will be clear and easily understood. Bringing ambient symbols to the forefront now and then, as Lawrence does, can provide your work with a more serious and literary tone.

Certain symbols, such as vitality, the value of nature, and the regenerative power of sex, recur in Lawrence's writing. Animals were also important symbolically in his work. It was he who exclaimed, in *Apocalypse* (1931), "The horse, the horse! The symbol of surging potency and power of movement, of action." His short novel *The Fox* (1923) uses a fox to symbolize the predatory nature of Henry in his relationship with the two female protagonists. In *Women in Love* cat-

---

17. Cavitch 1969:198.
18. Lawrence 1928a:170.

tle symbolize sexuality and vitality. Gudrun taunts a herd of cattle in the same way she taunts Gerald, with contests of sex and power. Like other artists Lawrence often used the moon as a symbol of the feminine.[19] For example, in *Women in Love* when Rupert is throwing stones into the lake and destroying the image of the moon he is symbolically destroying his tie to Ursula, his potential other half. Perhaps this is why she is so shocked when she sees him: "Ursula was dazed, her mind was all gone." The moon symbolizes the woman, the feminine, the nebulous presence that circles Rupert and that tugs at his heart with its tide, threatening to disrupt his sense of self.

Studying Lawrence's use of symbols can help a writer become more confident about employing this important literary device. It would be a mistake to think that symbolism is beyond your ability. Keep in mind that you may already have incorporated symbolic elements into your stories without even knowing it. This is often how it is with writers. Images are often multidimensional, pointing to the literal thing in a narrative and also to a larger meaning. Not infrequently, becoming conscious of symbols is a process of unfolding your own work to yourself, a true process of self-discovery. As you learn what you have accomplished you will come to a greater appreciation of symbolism in the writing of others. And the more you understand how symbols work in literature, the more effectively you will be able to incorporate them appropriately. As a final note, beginning writers, indeed even experienced hands at the use of symbolism, might profit from obtaining a dictionary of symbolism or from reading the works of writers such as Joseph Campbell and Carl Jung. Particularly helpful and accessible for the layman is Jung's *Man and His Symbols* (1964) and Maurice Beebe's *Literary Symbolism: An Introduction to the Interpretation of Literature* (1960).

---

19. Young 1999:113.

CHAPTER 11

WRITE LIKE

William Faulkner

Some readers are actually afraid of Faulkner because of his reputation for complexity, but by holding fast to this view they're certainly selling Faulkner *and* themselves short, and in the process they're missing all the fun one can have with one of the most poetic writers of the twentieth century. There's no question in my mind that the perfect introduction to Faulkner is *Sanctuary*. The Nobel Prize winner's most accessible linguistic achievement, the novel is a fine way to become acquainted with the best of Faulkner without having to deal with the overwriting that mars many of his later novels.

Born in 1897, William Faulkner was the first of four sons. He wrote poetry as a young man and also joined the Canadian Air Force, claiming he was British. His knack for invention started young! In 1929 he married Estelle Oldham and together they lived in Rowan Oak, an estate in Oxford, Mississippi.[1] A heavy drinker, Faulkner worked for a time in Hollywood, where he also had an affair with Meta Carpenter, the secretary of legendary film director and producer Howard Hawks.[2] The location of many of Faulkner's novels is the fic-

---

1. I visited a small narrow apartment in New Orleans where Faulkner lived in 1925. While in the city, he met Sherwood Anderson. He said Anderson's life looked easy: working part of the day and having the rest of the day free to do whatever he wanted. "I decided that if that was the life of a writer, then becoming a writer was the thing for me. So I began to write my first book" (Faulkner 1956:18). That book, *Soldier's Pay*, was published in 1926.

2. Her memoir, *A Loving Gentleman*, is a revealing inside look at the writer and shows a rare romantic side to the man. *See* Wilde and Borsten:1976.

tional Yoknapatawpha County, Mississippi, and stylistically one of the writer's most notable achievements is the poetry in his work. "Language is my music," he said.[3] Known as an innovator in fiction, he claimed that he only became successful after he realized that he had to write to satisfy himself rather than other people. At its best, his style is filled with the beauty of sounds and allusions and the cadence of language; at its worst it is gothic, rococo, and convoluted, relying on a vast vocabulary tending toward the ornate. His love affair with words was well-known: His brother reported that Bill's dictionary was dog-eared from use, and Faulkner once criticized Hemingway for taking no risks with vocabulary. Popular at about the same time as Hemingway, Faulkner is in many ways the opposite type of writer; whereas Hemingway is spare and concise, Faulkner is often complex and prolix.

His first novel was *Soldier's Pay* (1926). His breakout novel was *Sanctuary* (1931), the story of a college girl who is raped by a gangster named Popeye. "[I]t was deliberately conceived to make money," said Faulkner in a "misleading" introduction; the novel is actually a carefully constructed and brilliant work that was certainly not written simply for the money.[4] His most famous novel, *The Sound and the Fury* (1929), is composed in four sections, one of which is from the point of view of a mentally stunted individual. The novel jumps around in time and uses italics to signal some of its time shifts. "I wanted to have it printed in different colors," Faulkner said. "Each color would indicate a different time." His creativity was boundless, and he learned to take risks with his work. A major theme in his novels is race relations. For example *Light in August* (1932) is about a black man accused of raping a white woman. Faulkner won the Nobel Prize for Literature in 1949.

Despite an occasionally ornate and often difficult style, there is nothing so beautiful as a good Faulkner story, and there is much that a writer can learn about language and the possibilities of prose from his

---

3. Faulkner, quoted in Rio-Jelliffe 2001:44.

4. Joseph Blotner's line page notes to the corrected edition of *Sanctuary* indicate that Faulkner didn't want the "misleading" introduction included with the Modern Library reprint in 1932 (Blotner 1987:337).

example. We will focus on how he worked and why his method can be successful for you, how to begin and end a story, characterization, and the use of mystery in mainstream fiction. The definitive biography of Faulkner is by Joseph Blotner, with a one-volume version containing all the essential Faulkner lore. If your work is too simple; if it's relatively unadorned or lacking in depth; if you desire to add significance and "place" to your stories; or if you simply yearn for the ability to craft prose with a lyrical and sonorous sound, then reading Faulkner may be exactly the kind of medicine that will inspire you to reach new heights; indeed, incorporating some elements of his style has helped a generation of writers enlarge the meaning and enhance the resonance of their work. Particularly Southern writers—Flannery O'Connor, Truman Capote, Robert Penn Warren, Cormac McCarthy—have understandably been influenced by his work; but his influence extends far beyond the South, even beyond the United States, to countless others, including Joyce Carol Oates, Toni Morrison, Sartre, and Albert Camus.[5] So you're in good company if you can admit that you too have been influenced by Faulkner.

WHY HIS METHOD CAN SUCCEED FOR YOU WHETHER YOU'RE WRITING FICTION OR NONFICTION

Faulkner worked for a time in a post office, but he was hardly attentive to his job responsibilities; instead he "would sit in a rocking chair with a writing arm attached, in the back of the post office, and was continuously writing. ... Faulkner would pay no attention to [customers]. They would rap on the counter with a coin to attract his attention, and finally he would begrudgingly get up to serve them."[6] This anecdote illustrates a small lesson for any writer who wants to be successful: Concentration is the key to getting work done. Let other cares pass you by when you write, for if you can forget other concerns and

---

5. Parini 2004:432.
6. Blotner 1984:110.

focus on your story the work will progress at a more rapid pace than if you fritter away your time with inconsequential details—such as fulfilling the obligations of your day-to-day job. Naturally there needs to be a source of income, but the dedicated writer always favors his writing and gives precedence to it whenever and wherever he can.

Faulkner took advantage of another method of making progress with his work, for he was not above imitating other writers to learn their compositional and stylistic secrets. In composing poetry he freely imitated A.E. Housman, Algernon Charles Swinburne, Tennyson, and T.S. Eliot. The poetic styles he learned were also incorporated into his fiction, where the beauty of language is evident in the choice of words, the cadence of phrases, and the meter of sentences. With his prose he also fell under the influence of Kipling, Conrad, Joyce, and Huxley, among others.[7] A great innovator himself, Faulkner claimed in later years that it was a mistake for writers to imitate anyone else; but his own practice belies that statement.

He worked in longhand, transcribing his work into a typescript, which he then revised as he reread his manuscript. Never satisfied with his own writing, he would often cut and paste, moving huge chunks of material to different sections of his stories.[8] His concentration on his career made him seem somewhat aloof, although he was polite and well-mannered. Friends and teachers remember him as a dreamy boy, uninterested in athletics or schoolwork. His main interest was in self-expression.

WHERE TO START A STORY

Sanctuary begins with Popeye and Horace looking at one another across a spring where Horace has stopped to drink. They contemplate each other and exchange tense words pregnant with threat and fear. *As I Lay Dying* begins with the making of a coffin for Addie Bundren. *The Sound and the Fury* begins with a confusing section told from the point

---

7. Blotner 1984: 49-50, 137-138, 144, 159.

8. Blotner 1984:137.

of view of Benjy, who is non compos mentis. *Light in August* begins with Lena Grove arriving in Mississippi from Alabama, a symbol of life and rebirth in a novel centered on violence and death.

As these examples suggest, the device of beginning in medias res is rarely used by Faulkner. Beginning in the middle of a story is a technique other writers have found appropriate and dramatic, but Faulkner's technique is more complex and worth noting, especially if you wish to write literary fiction. Faulkner usually begins not in the *middle* of a story but on its *periphery*. *Sanctuary* begins with Popeye meeting Horace well before the main action of the story: the kidnapping and rape of Temple Drake. Popeye and Horace are characters with a complex past and their interaction is a mystery to the reader, but a mystery which the reader will look forward to unraveling.[9] By beginning on the outskirts of the story and in an out-of-the way locale, Faulkner starts creating a dense world populated by gangsters, into which he will eventually thrust his antiheroine.

As I Lay Dying (1930) concerns attempts by the children of Addie Bundren to bring their mother's body to Jefferson, Mississippi, for a burial. Like much of Faulkner's other work, the book has "a complex multiplicity of points of view and a convoluted chronology."[10] The book begins at one point in time and jumps around, coming back repeatedly to the central images of the coffin and the trip to Jefferson. In this way it is like Marguerite Duras' *The Lover* (1984), which comes back repeatedly to the central image of the girl on the ferry. By starting with the coffin building rather than with an action scene, and by beginning from the vantage of one of numerous narrators, Faulkner builds curiosity about a complex world.

The Sound and the Fury is the most famous example of Faulkner's stream-of-consciousness technique and his most complex novel. It is

---

9. Often mistakenly seen as a simple gangster story, *Sanctuary* is actually a complex literary work that Faulkner heavily revised. He moved pages and sections around many times before he was satisfied. "Before page 11 would be permanently fixed in that sequence, it would bear seventeen other pages numbers. All but 34 of the 139 pages in the completed manuscript would be tried in more than one place" (Blotner 1984:236).

10. Anderson 2007:62.

as if he took a story told in strict chronological order, cut it up, shuffled the pages, and then renumbered them, forcing readers to immerse themselves in the facts and motifs of a tale told *out* of order. Actually there is a method to this madness, for the first section follows the logic of free association rather than the logic of chronological time. One sense impression or word, for example, will cause Benjy to think of something that happened at an earlier time. Often a shift in time will occur *more* than once on a single page, and although sometimes these scene shifts are indicated by a change of typeface from roman to italics, sometimes even this indication is lacking. "One time I thought of printing that first section in different colors," said Faulkner, "but that would have been too expensive."[11] Many readers might wish for such help even today, though there are numerous summaries available that straighten the chronology out; but by beginning from Benjy's peripheral point of view and making the story hard to follow, Faulkner deepens the reality of the world into which we enter.

Light in August also adopts a reshuffled chronology involving many flashbacks, telling the story of Joe Christmas. Half black and half white, he kills a white woman in self-defense and is lynched. Most of the tale is dreary and dark, uncovering the sordid past of the main characters: Joe Christmas suffered so much racism as a child that he feels a compulsion as an adult to lash out violently against those who discriminate against him, and as a result he kills his own lover, Joanna Burden, when she too treats him less than evenhandedly; Reverend Hightower suffers from the double burden of his wife's suicide and his grandfather's murder; Joe Brown escapes his paternal responsibilities and becomes a criminal. By starting with a relatively minor character, one who never even *meets* Joe Christmas, Faulkner gives us his usual off-center introduction to the story, coming at it from an unexpected angle and using the goodness of Lena to comment on the potential goodness of Joe Christmas.

Many books on craft urge writers to take the common approach and begin in medias res, that is, in the middle of the action. While this

---

11. Faulkner, quoted in Cowan 1968:15.

might work in some cases and can certainly provide a dramatic start to your tale, there is much to be said for Faulkner's peripheral beginning device. By taking his time to get a story going, and by building in backstory with great depth and complexity, Faulkner achieves the creation of worlds that are both three-dimensional and convincing. There is another kind of pleasure in striving, as a reader, to unravel the intricacies of a fully-realized fictional universe. Faulkner's approach, using a peripheral beginning, is also more likely to give your work literary qualities. While this approach does have its dangers—not the least of which are the confusion readers may experience and the slowness of the opening—it has its rewards and advantages as well since sophisticated readers will enjoy and appreciate the uncertainty and complexity of such a literary start.

HOW TO END SCENES, CHAPTERS, AND BOOKS

In addition to beginning stories in a rather unique way, Faulkner also worked to ensure that the conclusions of his stories were strikingly artistic. John Gardner calls this the "resonant close" in which "[w]hat moves us is not just that character, images, and events get some form of recapitulation or recall: We are moved by the increasing connectedness of things, ultimately a connectedness of values. Coleridge pointed out...that increasingly complex systems of association can give a literary work some it its power."[12] The conclusion of the scene in *Light in August* where Percy Grimm castrates Joe Christmas resonates with meaning. The men who helped lynch Joe will remember it forever, we are told. Anyone who reads the scene will also remember it, in part because of the cumulative power of repeated images and motifs, such as the evocation of the central theme of racism, and the linking of violence with the life and death of Joe Christmas.

The end of Jason's section in *The Sound and the Fury* is equally memorable and, incidentally, also has castration as a theme; Jason refers

---

12. Gardner 1983:192.

to his castrated brother as "the Great American Gelding" and adds, "I know at least two more that needed something like that." His coldness and callousness is unmatched in all of Faulkner's writing. The conclusion of the section resonates with meaning, illustrating how the Compson family has become corrupt from the inside in the person of its most reprehensible brother.

The conclusion of *Sanctuary* is both poetic and filled with significance. Temple Drake has falsely accused Goodwin of the murder of Tommy. Popeye has been executed for the death of a man he did not kill, and Goodwin is lynched. Finally Temple Drake, both victim and victimizer, is portrayed on the last page. "It had been a gray day, a gray summer, a gray year." So the penultimate paragraph begins. "Temple yawned behind her hand, then she took out a compact and opened it upon a face in miniature sullen and discontented and sad." Then, in the last sentence of the novel, she looks up into "the season of rain and death." The cumulative impact of life-and-death events; the evocative description of the ruined and guilty Temple Drake, and the final emphasis, ending the book with the word "death,"—all of these details pack a powerful punch and help make this novel one of Faulkner's most impressive achievements.

Faulkner's signature complexity is especially apparent in the way he concludes a scene, a chapter, and a book. Often employing the resonant close, he echoes previous events and links them together in a web of association that enhances meaning and impact. Giving his conclusions a hint of poetry, which might have seemed out of place earlier in a narrative, is another way Faulkner ensures that he has bought his stories to a satisfying artistic close.

You can employ Faulkner's powerful closing technique by repeating or echoing major themes in your conclusion. Think back on the various strands of your story and weave references to them into the final paragraphs. This is also the time to take risks with your language and reach for rhetorical structures and phrases—even poetry—that might have been considered excessive earlier in your work. Readers are much more willing to accept elevated prose in the final moments of a story. It's also a good idea to examine the scansion of your concluding sentences. This involves analyzing your writing for metrical patterns the same way a poet analyzes the lines of a poem. Believe it or not many readers memorize the conclusions of their favorite books. Can you imagine people committing your final paragraph to heart? If not, you may wish to revise it until it has the ring and rhythm of verse. This doesn't mean you need a singsong effect; instead simply avoid overly complex formulations and aim for a pleasing sound. One trick is to avoid using the word "but" in the concluding sentences—the word "and" is much more likely to lead to the kind of writing that makes for a strong finish.

CHARACTER CREATION AND THEME

William Faulkner created some of the most three-dimensional and well-rounded characters in modern fiction. Sometimes entire sections of chapters, as in *Light in August*, are devoted to telling us not what his characters are doing now but *who* they are, *where* they came from, *what* they did, and *why* they might do strange and unexpected things in the future. Is there anything you can learn from his methods? Actually there are three golden rules that Faulkner can offer any teller of stories. First, you need to think of character creation as one of the tools of the trade. This will inspire you to work at it and shape the character to fit your story's needs; but at the same time you may let them go, once you've conceived of them. "Once these people come to life, they … take off and so the writer is going at a dead run behind them trying to put down what they say and do in time. … They have taken charge of the story. … The writer has just got to keep up with them and put it down."[13]

Second, you need to learn observation. "A good creation is a real, three-dimensional character who stands up of his own accord and can 'cast a shadow,'" said Faulkner. In order to create him, you must observe people, listen to them, watch them interact with others. "There is," he

---

13. Faulkner, quoted in Gwynn and Blotner 1995:120.

said, "only one way in which to learn to write dialogue: listen when other people talk."[14]

Third, you need imagination—and the courage to follow your muse. As for imagination, Faulkner's comment on this element of creativity is in perfect alignment with modern right-brain thinking on the graphic nature of the brain and on how important *images* are for the unconscious. "With me, a story usually begins with a single idea or memory or mental picture," said Faulkner. "The writing of the story is simply a matter of working up to that moment, to explain why it happened or what it caused to follow."[15] Certainly in writing novels like *The Sound and the Fury* or *Light in August*, he put aside any thought of what a reader might like, and he worked toward his own self-defined goals. In order to follow your muse you need the same kind of self-confidence that can carry you through to the finish line. When he had read most of *Sanctuary* to his good friend Phil Stone, Stone told him, "Bill, ... this won't sell. The day of the shocker is past." As Joseph Blotner tells us, "Discouraged as he had every right to be, Faulkner characteristically trusted his own judgment and went on with the book."[16] It would take a strong sense of his own worth to continue with works like *The Sound and the Fury* and *Light in August*, but he had that kind of confidence. "The good artist believes that nobody is good enough to give him advice. He has supreme vanity. No matter how much he admires the old writer, he wants to beat him."[17]

In addition to character development, Faulkner also viewed *theme* as one more tool in the writer's toolkit. During a class discussion at the University of Virginia, where he spent two terms as writer in residence, Faulkner took questions from students about his working methods. Someone asked about theme. "The message would be one of the craftsman's tools," Faulkner said. "A message is one of his tools,

---

14. Faulkner, quoted in Inge 1999:77.

15. Faulkner 1956:17

16. Blotner 1984:237.

17. Faulkner 1956:11.

just like rhetoric, just like punctuation."[18] In a modest way, he often referred to his own work as a chicken coop and himself as a carpenter.[19] The basic idea that one needs to work at the craft, like a carpenter, with the suggestion that there be a period of apprenticeship, and that the tools can be mastered after study and practice, is inspiring, especially from a writer who accomplished so much and who was so innovative and creative.

MYSTERY STORY TECHNIQUE

One of the least understood tools of the writer's trade that Faulkner employed was the device of mystery. Like Dickens he introduced mystery into almost all his work, but unlike Dickens his mysteries were not usually the logical or ratiocinative kind; instead, his work was mysterious on another level, one that is eminently literary. An admirer of Joyce's *Ulysses* (1920), Faulkner believed that complexity itself was a virtue, and his books reflect that belief with complex characters, plots, and style. The first mystery that a reader encounters upon opening a Faulkner novel is the question of what is happening, and to whom. Who are these people? Where are they from? And what is their relationship? *Sanctuary* is perhaps the best example of how this mystery device ensnares a reader in the story, but *The Sound and the Fury* and *Light in August* both use the device, the latter to a lesser degree than the other two. There are few simple plots or stories in Faulkner's oeuvre. Even the deceptively simple *As I Lay Dying* is fraught with complexity and mystery. In it, Faulkner created "a complexity of tone that has proved difficult for some readers to cope with."[20] The relative value of complexity to Faulkner was that it allowed him to spin stories that fulfilled *his* particular vision, without having to worry much about reader reaction.

Today writers are told they must be clear, that readers won't give them more than five pages ... or five paragraphs, or five *sentences*

18. Faulkner, quoted in Gwynn and Blotner 1995:239.

19. Evans 2008:235.

20. Brooks 1963:141.

to hook their interest. Supermarket bookstalls are filled with mass-market page-turners claiming to be best-sellers and telling stories in a minimalist staccato style with a murder on page one and a car chase immediately following and a shooting and a stabbing in quick succession to grab interest. Faulkner, of course, wasn't above using violence, as the numerous murders, rapes, and castrations in his work clearly demonstrate; in fact, he believed that violence was one of the basic tools of the writer. But the modern style—filled with quick starts and unambiguous character relationships—is clearly not the *only* way to write. Depth of meaning, solid three-dimensional characterization, and a confidence that readers will follow into the thicket when your complex characters lead the way—all these virtues of the literary novel are the legacy of William Faulkner. Modern storytellers can have no better guide to some of the most universal problems, and solutions, of their craft. This isn't to say that you need to contrive plots that readers will get migraines trying to comprehend or that you must characterize with the complexity of Faulkner every time you introduce a hero. The point is simply that a little bit of his style goes a long way toward making a writer's work significantly deeper than the average novel, and there's no question that *that* might be a very good thing for modern American fiction.

CHAPTER 12

WRITE LIKE

Ernest Hemingway

Despite his reputation as the most imitated author of our time, not *every*one wants to write like Hemingway. J.D. Salinger, for instance, considered Hemingway's style too telegraphic and spare.[1] Salinger preferred more substance and emotion, and he didn't shy away from adjectives, adverbs, and complex punctuation. But contemporary writers owe a lot to Hemingway and probably no other writer has influenced American prose style more pervasively.[2]

So what exactly *is* the Hemingway style? And how can you use it to improve your writing?

Most critics agree that Hemingway's writing is notable for its short sentences, lack of subordination, reliance on nouns and verbs rather than adjectives and adverbs, and its heavy use—some would say overuse—of the word *and*. What isn't as well-known is the fact that Hemingway also employed traditional structural elements and character development techniques to good effect, especially in his later novels.[3]

---

1. According to A.E. Hotchner, who knew both Salinger and Hemingway, Salinger "would arrogantly condemn all the well-known writers from Dreiser to Hemingway" (Hotchner 1984:65-66). Salinger met Hemingway at least twice during the war and corresponded in a friendly way with him, but Salinger's ornate style, with its meticulously crafted long sentences, was the antithesis of Hemingway's spare and boiled down prose.

2. Lania 1961:5.

3. Young 1966:205-206.

HEMINGWAY'S CAREER

Born in 1899, Hemingway grew up in Oak Park, Illinois, with a sister eighteen months older as well as younger sisters and a much younger brother. He didn't want to go to college after high school, instead he began working as a newspaper reporter. His early work as a journalist left an indelible imprint upon his style.[4] "Use short sentences," commanded *The Kansas City Star's* style manual. "Use short first paragraphs. Use vigorous English. Be positive, not negative."

Hemingway quit this newspaper job after a few months and enlisted in the army. During World War I he served in the Red Cross Ambulance Corps in Italy. Three days before his nineteenth birthday he was wounded by an Austrian mortar explosion.[5] He spent the ensuing weeks in an Italian hospital attended by Agnes von Kurowsky, an American nurse six years his senior. It wasn't long before Hemingway fell in love with Agnes—in fact, he expected her to marry him—but when he returned to the states after the war she failed to join him and the blow to his pride became the impetus for *A Farewell to Arms* (1929).[6]

Back home Hemingway began writing for another newspaper and he continued this work even after he moved to Paris in 1921. While in Paris he met Gertrude Stein, who exerted a major influence on his style.[7, 8] She taught him how to connect clauses using *and* instead of employing more traditional subordination.[9] You'll learn how—and more importantly why—to do this yourself later in the chapter.

---

4. Hemingway was the first to admit that his newspaper work influenced his style (Lania 1961:27).

5. Anthony Burgess does a masterful job of romanticizing Hemingway's war injury (Burgess 1978:22).

6. Hemingway told A.E. Hotchner, about the novel, that "much of it was projected from my own experiences, but a lot of it…wasn't" (Hotchner 1966:51).

7. According to Anthony Burgess, Stein was seeking "a perhaps excessive simplification of language … Too much description for its own sake, she objected; too much decoration; compress, concentrate" (Burgess 1978:31).

8. Stein advised Hemingway to stop writing for newspapers because it would blunt his style (Lania 1961:47). *See also* Lynn 1987:197.

9. Another writing trick that she taught him was the idea of "living in the work as it goes along, letting each day make up its own action" which "allows for spontaneity" (Reynolds 1988:33).

Throughout his career Hemingway experimented with style and, like any professional writer, constantly learned new techniques. For example, his later writing has a more ornate sentence structure and delves more deeply into character than his early work. Despite these additional discoveries and experiments, however, the core Hemingway style persisted in most of his prose and today it is recognizable worldwide. When he was awarded the Nobel Prize for Literature in 1954 it was "for his mastery of the art of narrative, most recently demonstrated in *The Old Man and the Sea*, and for the influence that he has exerted on contemporary style."

SENTENCE LENGTH

True, Hemingway wrote short sentences. And true, he is known for simplified, direct prose.[10] But what most writers don't realize is that he worked hard for these effects and that there was a reason for them. Primary among those reasons was the issue of clarity. When he wrote for newspapers, clarity was the objective. Even today newspapers are known for their clear, direct style. Hemingway wrote sentences that were straightforward and clear so that readers could understand the points he made even if they were skimming quickly through his articles.[11] You can achieve a similar clarity by writing shorter, more direct sentences. This is especially helpful to keep in mind when rewriting your work. Don't hesitate to break up long complex thoughts into bite-size morsels for added readability. But clarity was not the only reason for Hemingway's brevity.

Another reason for short sentences is dramatic effect. In "The Snows of Kilimanjaro" (1936) when the protagonist is nearing death because of a gangrenous leg, Hemingway writes: "All right. Now he would not care for death. One thing he had always dreaded was the

---

10. Joyce Carol Oates calls Hemingway's writing "meiotic prose," highlighting its understated quality (Oates 1988:49). Hemingway worked hard for this effect, often revising a first draft and removing as much as two thirds of his words (Svoboda 1991:46).

11. In later years Hemingway was known for setting himself the goal of learning to write "one true sentence" (Scribner 1996:15).

pain." Here the short sentences have a cumulative effect, pounding home the idea that the hero is nearing death. Try to achieve a similar effect in your writing by stringing together a series of short sentences when you want to stress a point or add dramatic punch to your prose.

Still another use for short sentences is to add variety and music to your writing. Hemingway often mixes longer and shorter sentences for a euphonious effect. In *The Old Man and the Sea* (1952), for instance, he tells us the thoughts of the old fisherman: "Then he was sorry for the great fish that had nothing to eat and his determination to kill him never relaxed in his sorrow for him. How many people will he feed? he thought." The first sentence contains two conflicting thoughts: the old man's sorrow for the fish and, in contrast with this, his continued determination to kill it. The next sentence suggests the old man's motivation for fishing, namely to get food. The change in sentence length lends a musical quality to the writing and adds pleasing variety.

SENTENCE SPEED

One of Hemingway's most recognizable stylistic traits is a fast sentence speed. A writer's sentence speed refers to how quickly his sentences can be read, either aloud or silently. It's as if Hemingway's prose flies along at a rapid clip while the writing of other authors putters slowly in comparison. If you want to write like Hemingway, imitate this signature stylistic move. You'll be writing in the fast lane.

How does Hemingway manage to speed up his sentences? He uses two methods, the first of which involves choosing shorter words for simpler diction. We'll deal with that in a moment. The second method is to omit commas.[12]

Joseph Conrad used to retire to a room to write every day and he would have his wife lock him in so that he could concentrate. When he emerged for lunch one afternoon his wife asked what he had done. "I

---

12. Stein's influence is clearly at work here. Some of her writing uses so little punctuation, and employs so many other experimental stylistic devices, that it is "often unintelligible" (Lynn 1987:171). Hemingway was wise to use only *some* of what Stein suggested; his work is always intelligible and never suffers from the stylistic excesses of his mentor.

took out a comma," he said. After lunch she locked him in again and when he emerged for dinner she asked what he had done. He told her, "I put back the comma."[13] If Joseph Conrad struggled for an entire day over the placement of one comma, might it be worth your while to devote a few minutes to this mark of punctuation? Undoubtedly it would be time well spent. Hemingway waged a war against commas, and although he used them in his work he often achieved his greatest technical innovations by omitting them in compound sentences. A compound sentence contains two or more independent clauses. The clauses are usually joined by a comma and a coordinating conjunction, such as *and* or *but*. By far the most common coordinating conjunction is the word *and*.

Consider the sentence: "Often Miss Stein would have no guests, and she was always very friendly, and for a long time she was affectionate." It is composed of three independent clauses: *Often Miss Stein would have no guests. She was always very friendly. For a long time she was affectionate.* But the sentence plods along at a slow pace. The three commas slow it down and give it a choppy feel. Here's how Hemingway actually wrote the sentence in chapter three of *A Moveable Feast* (1964): "Often Miss Stein would have no guests and she was always very friendly and for a long time she was affectionate." Punctuated like this it zips along.

Let's look at another example, from *The Sun Also Rises* (1926). The narrator is hoping to see the bulls at Pamplona. Joining a crowd of spectators he rushes ahead with them to the bullring. At this point Hemingway speeds up the pace: "I heard the rocket and I knew I could not get into the ring in time to see the bulls come in, so I shoved through the crowd to the fence." The absence of a comma before the word *and* increases the tempo, conveying some of the feeling of being in the crowd.

Omitting commas can be a tricky business because such omissions can sometimes make sentences confusing, so this is a technique you don't want to overuse. But when you come to a section of your story where the action needs to move at a quicker pace, you may wish to

---

13. Smith 2005.

try Hemingway's trick of speeding up the sentences. You'll leave other writers in the dust.

DICTION

Diction refers to your choice of words. Hemingway typically uses simple Anglo-Saxon words, although he isn't averse to using a precise word, even an unusual word, on occasion. But more often than not he opts for the simpler vocabulary of spoken speech. Faulkner actually criticized him for this. "He has no courage, has never climbed out on a limb," said Faulkner, speaking informally to a college literature class. "He has never used a word where the reader might check his usage by a dictionary."[14]

Of course Faulkner's style was the exact opposite of Hemingway's and despite Faulkner's criticism, Hemingway had immense success with his blunt and direct word choice. Look at the first sentence of chapter twelve of *To Have and Have Not* (1937). "When he came in the house he did not turn on the light but took off his shoes in the hall and went up the bare stairs in his stocking feet." Every word but one is a monosyllable. Open any of Hemingway's stories or novels at random and you'll find similar passages.

Using a simplified vocabulary makes for highly readable writing. Rudolph Flesch developed a prescription for readability, which he outlined in *The Art of Readable Writing* (1949). Flesch suggests using short, common words. He recommends getting a copy of a dictionary of simple synonyms so that you can substitute simpler words for the big words that will inevitably appear in your first draft.[15] He also cautions writers to rely on verbs rather than nouns and adjectives. "The main problem with most current writing is that it consists of nothing but nouns and adjectives, glued together with prepositions or with *is, was, are* and *were*," says Flesch.[16] Of course the Hemingway style would have pleased him.

---

14. Blotner 1984:483.
15. Flesch 1949:142.
16. Flesch 1949:147.

If your writing sounds too technical or stuffy try Hemingway's approach. Get tough on adjectives and adverbs. Rely on verbs to do your work. Before you know it your writing will sound like speech and your readability score will improve. And if anyone says you sound too much like Hemingway … chances are they're jealous.

DETAIL AND COLOR

Another Hemingway trademark is the use of detail and color to paint pictures in the reader's mind. In the short story "Big Two-Hearted River" (1925) Hemingway chose to use a specific word, even though it is not a common word: "The river was there. It swirled against the log spiles of the bridge." *Spiles* adds the exact picture Hemingway wishes to convey. Many readers would have to look it up to be sure they understood it, but Hemingway is careful not to overdo this tactic. Once in a while he'll drop in a specific detail by using a word that is not ordinary, or a word from another language.

When he does use a word from a foreign language, he is often quick to define it, even in a novel. In chapter thirteen of *The Sun Also Rises* one of the characters uses the word *aficionado* and Hemingway tells us, "Aficion means passion. An aficionado is one who is passionate about the bull-fights." Defining the word doesn't distract from the story—there's a small pause and then the narrative picks right up where it left off.

In addition to selecting precise words for sensory detail, Hemingway makes very effective use of color. In fact, he uses color like a painter. He knows that if he mentions a color readers will see it—even if it's only one single color dabbed here and there a couple of times. Repetition tinges a scene with color and makes a setting come alive in the reader's mind. In *The Old Man and the Sea* he writes, "He was asleep in a short time and he dreamed of Africa when he was a boy and the long golden beaches and the white beaches, so white they hurt your eyes." The repetition of the word *white* splashes brilliance in the mind's eye.

In *A Moveable Feast* Hemingway contrasts white and black for an enhanced effect, describing Paris, where he lived in the 1920s. "There were no more tops to the high white houses as you walked but only the wet blackness of the street." The contrast with blackness makes the white stand out in stark relief. Hemingway may have learned this technique from the first generation of French Impressionist painters, who perfected the method of dabbing white paint in dark areas to show highlights or reveal light reflecting off a darker surface.

When using detail or color remember that the mind can only focus on a few things at a time. To make a scene come alive, sprinkle in a few concrete details. Reader imagination will take care of the rest. Don't hesitate to use a precise word now and then, even if it may be unfamiliar to most readers. And give a liberal sampling of color, repeating one color or contrasting two different colors for vivid effects.

USING "AND"

A good case can be made that Hemingway's favorite word was *and*.[17] Gertrude Stein's influence is apparent here, although reading her instructional manual *How to Write* (1931) might stymie even the most apt pupil. Sentences appear in it such as "Sentiment is awhile and weighed as a weight and romance is made to be authentic." That Hemingway could glean from her potpourri of maxims and advice something of value is a testament to his ability to sift the wheat from the chaff.

Stein's experimental style inspired Hemingway to use the word *and* to link independent clauses together, avoiding subordination. Subordination occurs when one or more clauses is dependent on the main clause, as in the sentence "When it rained, he went inside." The independent clause is *He went inside* and the dependent clause is *when it rained*. Rewriting this in a Hemingwayesque style would give us: "It rained and he went inside." This is more like speech and slightly easier on the eye since it omits the comma.

---

17. Even in revision Hemingway added more *ands. See, e.g.*, Donaldson 1990:235, where the various revisions of the short story "A Canary for One" are discussed.

Subordination isn't a bad thing, but it does tend to make some writing sound ponderous, especially when the technique is overused. Hemingway never wanted to sound ponderous.

If you wish to write like Hemingway, avoid a heavy-handed style and reduce the amount of subordination in your sentences.

The ending of *A Farewell to Arms* shows how to do this. Let's say your first draft reads: "When I went out after a while, I left the hospital and walked back to the hotel in the rain." This sentence uses subordination. The independent clause is *I left the hospital and walked back to the hotel in the rain.* The dependent clause is *When I went out after a while.* Notice that a dependent clause is an independent clause (*I went out after a while.*) that has been made dependent by tacking on a subordinating conjunction (*when*) so that it reads "When I went out after a while." The way to fix subordination is to begin by removing the subordinating conjunction, here the word *when.* This gives us: "I went out after a while, I left the hospital and walked back to the hotel in the rain." Next we remove the comma and substitute the word *and* which gives us: "I went out after a while and left the hospital and walked back to the hotel in the rain." We're getting there and the sentence is starting to sound like Hemingway. All we need to do now is shuffle the first two clauses so that we're left with: "After a while I went out and left the hospital and walked back to the hotel in the rain." Which is precisely how Hemingway ended the novel.

Like we said, subordination isn't a bad thing, but too much of it can make your writing sound old-fashioned and academic. And since the first step in reducing subordination is removing the subordinating conjunction, it would help to have a list of subordinating conjunctions. The major subordinating conjunctions, which when tacked onto an independent phrase can make it dependent, are:

after	so that
although	though
as	unless
because	until

before	when
how	where
if	while
since	

There's no rule saying *you shouldn't ever use these words*, but being aware that they can lead to subordination can help you spot problems that are easily fixed with a little Hemingwayesque rewriting.

THE LOOK OF YOUR PAGES

How often do you step back from your work and look at the pages you're writing? I mean actually look at them from a distance. "What good is that?" you say. "I wouldn't be able to read the words!" That's precisely the point. When you're far away you don't see the words, all you have is a sense of how the pages look—something that's actually more important than you might think.

One of Hemingway's little-known tricks of the trade was to be aware of the appearance of his pages. He didn't like fat paragraphs. Instead he relied heavily on dialogue, especially short lines of dialogue between two characters. This technique is actually more than two thousand years old and was invented by the ancient Greek dramatists, who called it stichomythia, literally short lines of poetry or dialogue. You'll find plenty of stichomythia in Euripides, Sophocles, Aristophanes, and other ancient Greek dramatists. Here's an example from Aeschylus' *The Choephori*.

> **Clytemnestra:** So, you plan to murder your own mother?
>
> **Orestes:** You are the one murdering yourself.
>
> **Clytemnestra:** Beware the fury of a mother's curse.
>
> **Orestes:** What of my father's fury if I don't avenge him?
>
> **Clytemnestra:** I gave birth to a snake not a son.

Notice that each line of dialogue is short and is answered by an equally short reply. This pattern was a standard with the Greek dramatists, who used it for pacing and intensity. What few people realize is that Hemingway used a similar technique when writing dialogue. His purpose in using stichomythia, however, was different from that of the ancient Greeks. The early dramatists conveyed parallelism and emotional intensity with their short alternating lines of dialogue; Hemingway's aim is to give the reader something pleasing to *look* at. Of course the content is also relevant and the pace is speedier with short lines of dialogue, but one of Hemingway's chief purposes was to make his pages look good. Incredible as it may sound, he was going after a visual appeal that was separate from the appeal of the content.

Hemingway's short story "The Killers" (1927) contains a modern example of stichomythia. The same pattern is at work in *A Farewell to Arms*, where much of the dialogue snakes down the page, leaving plenty of white space for visual appeal. The technique is also used by James M. Cain, most notably in *The Postman Always Rings Twice* (1934), and by Cormac McCarthy in all his novels.

Can you use the same technique in your writing? Of course you can.[18] Become aware of how your pages look and you'll be doing your readers a favor. They already care about what you're saying; that's a given since they're reading you. But they also care—if only unconsciously—about the way your pages look. If you doubt this, observe people in a bookstore. Although they may read a few words from the beginning or ending, they can often be seen flipping through the pages of a book before buying it, getting a sense of what the writing looks like without reading a word.

Consciously crafting the look of your pages is a relatively easy technique to employ in your work. One way to begin is to avoid overly long speeches and delete unnecessary words when rewriting dialogue. Consider getting rid of attributions. Once you start a conversation, you don't

18. As Philip Young points out, you don't have to agree with Hemingway's morality or adopt his themes (including a great deal of violence and many foreign settings) in your work; it's possible to copy just his style to give your writing a modern feel (Young 1966:211).

need all those *he said, she saids* cluttering things up. By trimming dialogue you'll make it sound better and you'll also ensure that it looks neater.

Instead of using too many long paragraphs, try inserting a short paragraph between them. Charles Dickens was a master of this technique, often breaking up a series of long paragraphs with a one- or two-sentence paragraph. That made his pages look good, and he was well aware of it. Many writers employ short paragraphs to break up a series of longer ones, and if you look for the pattern you'll notice it in both modern and classic prose. Whatever you do, keep in mind that when readers skim through your work the first thing that jumps out at them is the way the pages look. Too many long paragraphs can be intimidating.[19] ("Tell that to Kafka," you say? Well, there are exceptions to every rule!) But modern readers *do* love white space. It's inviting and it makes your book fun to read. This is one of Hemingway's little-known secrets that's easy to employ in your own work for a similar professional effect.

CHARACTERS BASED ON REAL PEOPLE

We already mentioned how Hemingway fell in love with Agnes von Kurowsky in Italy and how he used his romantic disappointment about their relationship in *A Farewell to Arms*.[20] In the Nick Adams stories the character of Nick is based on Hemingway. Most of the people in *To Have and Have Not* are based on Key West inhabitants whom Hemingway met while living and working in the town. *The Sun Also Rises* is a roman à clef which features many of the people Hemingway knew while living in Europe. In fact the first draft of the novel used their real names. The character of Jake Barnes is based on Hemingway, Brett Ashley is based on Lady Duff Twysden, Robert Cohn is based on novelist Harold Loeb, and the list goes on.

---

19. There are, of course, exceptions to this rule about the value of short paragraphs. Modern masters of style such as Beckett (especially in the trilogy *Molloy*, *Malone Dies*, and *The Unnamable*), Kafka, and Scandinavian wunderkind Dag Solstad (in *Shyness and Dignity*) use an opposite approach and embrace long paragraphs, sometimes to the point of parody and pastiche.

20. Hemingway was "stunned, sick, and angry" over the Agnes incident (Kert 1983:70).

Was Hemingway cheating by using real people as the basis of characters for his fiction? Or was he doing what all great artists do, including portrait painters like John Singer Sargent, N.C. Wyeth, and Norman Rockwell? How *you* answer this question reveals a lot about your maturity as a writer. If you think Hemingway was cheating by basing his characters on real people you may want to read a few literary biographies. Every great writer from Tolstoy to Flaubert to Hemingway to today's heavyweights uses real people as the model for fictional characters.[21]

Some beginning writers fear basing fictional characters on real people, afraid that they'll be sued for libel. They simply don't know how to change a detail here and there to make that unlikely. Some writers don't know how to base characters on real people. The technique is quite similar to the method used by portrait painters. You select a few features that are relevant to your story and focus on those characteristics that you are able to render in language, such as the sound of a voice, the look of a frown, or the curious way so-and-so slumps in a chair when talking with friends. Conjure up the person in your mind and then describe him in the context of your story. When you need to talk about a reaction, remember how your model reacted in real life. In this way your characters will have a vividness and lifelikeness that a totally fabricated character could never possess.

Don't write stories about totally made-up people.[22] Base characters on people you know and your stories will spring from an undercurrent of reality that can't fail to move readers. Sometimes it might even be prudent to base a character on more than one person. Hemingway used this technique on many occasions. The composite character is

---

21. Many writers claim that they don't base characters on real people, but this is often a ploy to prevent friends, relatives, and acquaintances from objecting to the portraits. For example, Ayn Rand claimed she didn't base major characters on real people but she admitted that she based the character Ellsworth Toohey from *The Fountainhead* (1943) on Harold Laski (Rand 2000:86-87).

22. In *A Farewell to Arms* and *For Whom the Bell Tolls* the main character is based on Hemingway and the secondary characters are based on people he knew. The love stories are particularly exceptional in both books, although Killinger believes the latter does a better job of portraying a "mature love relationship" (Killinger 1960:91).

one of the mainstays of literary fiction. To employ it in your own work simply think of two or more people whose traits and behavior you combine into a single fictional persona. If you do it correctly readers will never know that you're basing a character on two different people; instead, they'll have the experience of meeting a living person who has come to life on your pages. In fact, the composite character is often a richer, more fully realized three-dimensional portrait than one based on a single person.

STRUCTURE

The endings of Hemingway's stories are usually more memorable than the beginnings. This is remarkable since ending a story well is one of the chief challenges of the storyteller, or of any writer for that matter. That Hemingway's conclusions were so punchy and memorable says a lot about his attention to structure.

Isaac Asimov never began a story without knowing its conclusion. Other writers prefer to find their conclusion through the process of writing. Whatever method you use, once you have your first draft you can go back and do what Hemingway did, namely rewrite. I had an opportunity to examine some of his original manuscripts in the Ernest Hemingway Collection at the John F. Kennedy Library in Boston, and there are corrections and changes on nearly every page, sometimes so many that you'd find it difficult to read the original typescript. Clearly Hemingway worked hard to get the words right—and the structure of his plots.

The success of a story or novel depends to a large extent on the conclusion. The conclusion of Hemingway's novels and stories is almost always filled with significance. At the end of *A Farewell to Arms* one of the major characters, nurse Catherine Barkley, dies. This happens on the next to last page.[23] The significance of this event is driven home by the foreshadowing that occurs earlier in the book and by the narrator's

---

23. Robert Jordan dies on the last page of *For Whom the Bell Tolls.* Careful plotting, lifelike characterization, and suspending resolution until the final moments of the novel is the height of craft and rhetoric.

reaction to her death. Because Hemingway downplays the narrator's reaction, it sounds all the more realistic. At the end of *The Old Man and the Sea* the fisherman, Santiago, comes back with only the head of the huge fish. The rest of it has been eaten away by sharks. The symbolism of defeat is muted by the fact that the old man is at peace with himself and his world. He fought a good fight with the sharks, and that is what is important. The conclusion of "The Snows of Kilimanjaro" is prefigured by the narrator's knowledge throughout the story that he is nearing the end of his life. A hyena is used a number of times in the story to symbolize death. At the moment he dies the hero experiences a symbolic dream of rebirth into the temple of Mount Kilimanjaro, but the hyena cries a final time, echoing the theme of death and suggesting that the hero's dream of rebirth was no more than an illusion.

Like Hemingway, you can learn to emphasize your endings, imbue them with symbolic significance, and foreshadow final events. Drop subtle hints along the way to foreshadow your conclusion. Emphasize the ending by making other characters react to it or by having the central character gain insights at the last moment. Beef up your conclusions with added meaning by making universal or spiritual statements. You can also use symbolism to heighten the ending of your story, especially if your symbols have been planted earlier and mentioned a number of times, like the hyena in "The Snows of Kilimanjaro." By using these techniques your endings will have added meaning and impact and the overall structure of your work will give readers a more satisfactory experience.

There are good reasons why Hemingway is the most imitated writer of the past hundred years. He employed a modern style, one eminently suited to modern topics, ideas, and stories. Born in the newspapers of his day and perfected in the short stories and novels that entranced a generation, the Hemingway style has a lot to offer those who want to write modern prose.

CHAPTER 13

WRITE LIKE

Margaret Mitchell

Margaret Mitchell may not immediately come to mind when you think of the Western canon, yet she certainly wrote a classic; in fact, one of the most popular novels of all time, one of the best-selling books in the world. For this achievement alone she deserves serious investigation. She herself was quite a bit like her heroine, Scarlett O'Hara: both were beautiful and rebellious and both had numerous admirers. We may not be able to judge a book by its author's life, but certainly there is some relevance in looking at the biography of an author whose work so closely paralleled her own experiences, and it would be surprising if we could not glean some interesting tidbits and gain a few valuable insights by glancing, however briefly, at Mitchell's career.

Born to be wild would be an apt description of Margaret Mitchell. A hellion like her protagonist Scarlett O'Hara, Mitchell was born in 1900 and started telling stories from an early age. Her first was written when she was only six or seven, and more came soon thereafter.[1] A lastborn with a brother four years older, Mitchell had a creative and rebellious attitude that extended into her professional and social life. She was a newspaper reporter at a time when women were not usually found in such jobs. She went out with men her family disapproved of, and like Scarlett O'Hara was courted by two men at once.[2] Her first

---

1. Pryon 1991:49.

2. Pyron 1991:134-135.

husband (Berrien "Red" Upshaw) was a bootlegger who had the same kind of conflict with Margaret that Rhett had with Scarlett; in fact Red nearly caused the young author to have a nervous breakdown.[3] Their marriage was troubled and brief yet her first husband inspired a literary character that is now world-famous. Margaret married again, more successfully, but Rhett Butler was the legacy of her first husband.

MITCHELL'S MASTERY OF INTERNAL MONOLOGUE AND HOW YOU CAN USE THE SAME DEVICE

If there's one thing readers love about *Gone With the Wind* (1936) it's the voice of the heroine; indeed, Mitchell was a master of internal monologue. The way she wrote the book intrigued readers because although she occasionally followed the thoughts of other characters, the bulk of the novel is written in limited third-person viewpoint from Scarlett's perspective. This means that the greater part of the story is seen from the heroine's eyes and vantage point: We know more about her than about any other character, and essentially the book boils down to a plea for *her* point of view—her emotional, innocent, conniving persona at the focus of a chaotic and terrible time in human history.

Of course, the method of shifting viewpoint (third-person omniscient) often works best in a larger story like *Gone With the Wind*, but Mitchell actually resorts to such shifts in viewpoint very rarely. Most readers care for Scarlett above all the other characters and it is natural, therefore, for the author to reveal Scarlett's thoughts more than those of any other character. In fact, she dips into the heroine's mind at every step of the story, indicating what her protagonist feels and thinks about what is happening. Later we'll investigate how she transitions smoothly from far away to up close and personal, getting to the core of her character's feelings, but for now the point to be made is that the viewpoint of the heroine is the chief filter used to see the world of *Gone With the Wind*. Indeed, open the novel to

---

3. Pyron 1991:139-141.

any page at random and you will find that it almost always contains some of Scarlett's thoughts. These are not simply calm considerations, either, they're usually perturbed, emotional, pulse-pounding feelings and perceptions. She feels bad: "What a fool I am, she thought vehemently."[4] She feels pride seeing the Union soldiers: "Such handsome men, thought Scarlett, with a swell of pride in her heart."[5] She feels anger and violent emotions directed against Rhett: "Rage and hate flowed into her and stiffened her spine and with one wrench she tore herself loose from his arms."[6] This is just a sampling of the full spectrum of human emotions that run through Scarlett's heart as she goes from relationship to relationship and wends her way through the joys and sorrows of love found and lost.

The key point is that Mitchell filters what happens through the mind of her protagonist and by doing so ensures that readers are in close connection with her heroine throughout the story. George Orwell does the same thing in *Nineteen Eighty-Four* (1949), filtering events through Winston Smith's eyes. Ray Bradbury does it in *Fahrenheit 451* (1953), seeing the world through Guy Montag's eyes. And Maugham uses the same technique in *Of Human Bondage* (1915), filtering events through the perceptions of Philip Carey. All of these writers are employing a proven method of keeping readers oriented toward the world of their story and the consciousness of their chief character. With every change of emotion she feels, readers are drawn closer to Scarlett. The world of the protagonist of *Gone With the Wind* is a world dominated by love and relationships and by her *feelings* about these relationships; when she gains or loses a lover and when she loses her family estate, readers feel intense emotion along with her, and it is this emotional content that primarily drives the novel. For this reason Mitchell's use of internal monologue is a vital literary device that holds the story together and gives readers a close personal entrée into the world of her major character.

---

4. Mitchell 1936:569.

5. Mitchell 1936:168.

6. Mitchell 1936:384.

You can use the same technique in your own writing if you tell a story from limited third-person viewpoint. This means that you're limiting yourself to entering the mind of one central character. You'll sometimes tell what that character thinks, and other times you'll tell what that character does and says. The space you devote to character thoughts should only be about one-tenth of the story—which is about the percentage that Mitchell devotes to revealing Scarlett's thoughts. The rest of the time you'll be revealing what the character says and does and what other characters say and do. But this ten percent—when you reveal your protagonist's thoughts—will be enough to generate reader interest and empathy. And if you write about deep emotions and have your main character react passionately to what happens, you're sure to elicit some of the same reader identification that Mitchell enjoyed.

TWIST YOUR PLOTS LIKE MITCHELL

The plot of *Gone With the Wind* twists and turns in a way that keeps readers interested, and these plot twists are in large part a result of the fact that Mitchell's characters are unpredictable. For example, Scarlett loves Rhett yet she marries another man. Rhett loves Scarlett yet he leaves her a number of times, including at the end of the novel. They have a child, whom they love, but the child dies in a freak accident, causing a rift between them that eventually leads to divorce. The many changes that Mitchell introduces into the life of Scarlett contribute to the novel's reader appeal.

Plot twists, of course, must be unified by contributing to the overall rise in dramatic tension through a work of some length. In *Gone With the Wind* the events mount in intensity, going from the coming of war, to the burning of Georgia, to the marriage of Rhett and Scarlett, to the birth of their child, to the death of that child, to the final abandonment of Scarlett by Rhett. This mounting tension is one of the foundations of the novel, while the various plot twists and turns are like a scaffolding erected on top of that basic structure, contributing to enhanced reader interest. Once you have a skeleton plot, you can do permutations and variations on the theme: for example, there are numerous births in the book, there are numerous battles, and there are numerous marriages and breakups. All these plot twists dovetail nicely into the mounting tension of the main rising action, and they carry the story forward in a way that surprises readers and keeps them turning pages.

One of the chief methods Mitchell uses to twist plots, or change direction, is to have something catastrophic happen: a character dies, things need to change; a marriage breaks up, people need to change and a new man must be found; a battle occurs, society needs to change and people need to move; Georgia burns and Tara is lost, Scarlett must change and do something new, move somewhere else, and find new security and maturity. By constantly pushing your character to the limits—challenging her with disasters and making the plot twist in unexpected ways—you'll keep readers interested in your story just like Mitchell.

CHARM YOUR READERS

It may sound childish and somewhat insubstantial, but charming your readers is a valid technique that can sometimes work wonders for your writing because even *attempting* such a feat causes you to be aware of certain technical devices and how they impact on the flow and sound of narrative. So, it's not as silly as it might sound. And Mitchell was a master of charm, not only in her personal life but also in her fiction. Studying her secrets can unlock new doors for you and lead to more effective writing. But before we go there, it's important to contrast *this* method with the opposite technique, which we discuss elsewhere in this book (the chapters on Faulkner and Salinger, for example), which requires a writer to forget the audience and go with what you want to write. The two techniques may seem to be opposite, and in some sense they *are* contraries, but they're not mutually exclusive. The "charm school technique" requires a mindset which asks you to focus on the *effect* of your writing on others. The "Faulkner technique" of ignoring the audience requires a different mindset, one that frees you from the *chilling effect* of an audience. But both mindsets are necessary for writers, for ultimately you need to be inspired and to write what you love, but on the other hand you also need to have some sense of how the material will sound to others. Even Faulkner and Salinger, proponents of the "forget the audience" mindset, were acutely aware of audience, despite all their aversions to the contrary.

Mitchell was reportedly a very charming young woman. How, though, does she charm readers who, of course, won't have the pleasure of her physical company when reading her work? She achieves this through two primary techniques: First, through the use of feeling-charged language that will resonate with her readers as she shifts psychic distance and gets close to the heroine, and second, by thinking about the effect of her work on her audience and constructing scenes that will appeal to them psychologically.

The use of feeling-charged language is not unique to Mitchell, of course. Many of the best writers slip into this mode of narrative naturally and effortlessly, especially when they're reporting a scene through the emotional nervous system of one character at a time. In *Gone With the Wind* Mitchell keeps close to the viewpoint character of Scarlett throughout most of the story, and she uses her protagonist's emotions almost as a lens through which she presents events. But the use of feeling-charged language differs from viewpoint (discussed earlier) in that here we're concerned with the words used to express emotion rather than the point of view from which the emotion is expressed. As we'll see, this is a brilliant strategy and one that draws readers close to the events and makes them *feel* along with Scarlett. Over and over we're given access to her heartache, her joy, her despair.

> Scarlett sank to the stool, her breath coming so rapidly she feared the lacings of her stays would burst. Oh, what a terrible thing to happen! She had never thought to meet this man again.[7]

7. Mitchell 1936:180.

It's very important to notice *how* Mitchell gets deep into Scarlett's central nervous system. She uses a process of *gradual descent* into the hotbed of emotions, she doesn't just leap right in. This is known as a controlled shift in psychic distance: from distant to up close and personal. Psychic distance is "the distance the reader feels between himself and the events in the story."[8] Earlier in the chapter we're told that Scarlett is at a dance, and at that point the psychic distance is rather far off: "She sank down on one of the little stools behind the counter of the booth and looked up and down the long hall." When psychic distance is great, as in this sentence, it's like a long-shot in a movie: things are seen from afar. But in the passage quoted above, notice how Mitchell moves gradually closer. By closer we mean closer to the feelings of the character. "Scarlett sank to the stool, her breath coming so rapidly" is closer than a simple description of where she is sitting. By focusing on her quickened breath we get a sense of her emotional state. The language used is the key to psychic distance shifts. The next sentence moves even closer: "Oh, what a terrible thing to happen!" is as close as you can get. No longer are we receiving reportorial language from an objective narrator; instead, that sentence comes directly from the mind of the character. That "Oh" is Scarlett's "Oh" and the exclamation mark helps indicate that we are hearing her personal and most intimate feelings now. It's very important to move in slowly, without jumping from a long shot to a close up.[9] You can cut like that in the movies, but in fiction you want to lead the reader in *gradually* to the deeper emotions, as Mitchell has done here.

Let's look at another example, from the last chapter. Here Scarlett is coming to realize that Rhett is going to leave her for good. Of course, Mitchell is going to show us how upset Scarlett is, but notice that

---

8. Gardner 1983:111.

9. Lajos Egri provides a very instructive discussion of "jumping" in playwriting, which is analogous to moving in too quickly with psychic distance in fiction. He recommends avoiding jumping, that is, shifting a character's position or feelings too quickly. He suggests moving in small *steps* from one position to another, for example from honor to dishonor, making a character go through all the intervening stages and steps (Egri 1960:146-152). So too in moving up close with psychic distance we need to move closer gradually in a process of steps.

she doesn't begin with an exclamation or a direct thought from deep within her heart or mind, instead she begins by describing the *physical* setup of the scene with their eyes meeting. My explanatory comments are in brackets in the following passage.

> As his tired eyes met hers, she broke off in embarrassment, shy as a girl with her first beau. [This first sentence begins in a medium-shot by describing the physical setup of the scene, but it moves slightly closer at the end of the sentence, comparing her to a shy girl.] If he'd only make it easier for her! [This sentence is the deepest penetration into Scarlett's central nervous system and these words are her own thoughts. The exclamation mark indicates that we are deep in her personal thoughts and feelings.] If only he would hold out his arms, so she could crawl thankfully into his lap and lay her head on his chest. [This sentence is still close, but without the exclamation mark we are beginning to move back ever so slightly.] Her lips on his could tell him better than all her stumbling words. [This sentence is still close but again without an exclamation mark it is holding steady at a slightly removed distance.] But as she looked at him she realized that he was not holding her off just to be mean. [We have moved back to the medium-shot distance again with her looking at him.] He looked drained and as though nothing she had said was of any moment. [We have moved back slightly more for a medium-shot with a physical description of Rhett.][10]

By pushing in slowly and gradually and then getting up close with the exclamation, Mitchell shifts psychic distance in a controlled manner; she is neither clumsy nor abrupt. And then, after she hits us with the punch line,—"If he'd only make it easier for her!"—she gradually pulls back again to orient the reader in the scene. In this manner she shifts psychic distance in a gradual way through the controlled use of language, and she doesn't jar readers. This technique assures her that the reader will follow where she leads. Readers like it when they're led in close to a character who feels deep emotion. They believe it, too, when it's done gradually and skillfully like this.

---

10. Mitchell 1936:1015.

In addition to controlling the shifts in psychic distance, Mitchell also charms readers, making them like her presentation, by thinking about what *types* of events they'd like to encounter. Knowing that mostly female readers will be drawn to the book, she is careful to include plot points that appeal to this group. Tanya Modleski points out, in analyzing fiction geared for women, that many women psychologically have difficulty understanding the opposite sex and like reading about characters who have similar difficulty. For this purpose, a writer of works that will appeal to women will include scenes that deal with the issue of "the puzzling behavior of the hero: why does he constantly mock the heroine? Why is he so often angry with her?"[11] Mitchell certainly charms readers by giving them the goods. Throughout the book Rhett is alternately nice and mocking, and most of the time Scarlett can't figure him out. When he leaves her she wonders why, why, why?

> Why had he gone, stepping off into the dark, into the war, into a Cause that was lost, into a world that was mad? Why had he gone, Rhett who loved the pleasures of women and liquor, the comfort of good food and soft beds, the feel of fine linen and good leather, who hated the South and jeered at the fools who fought for it?

Knowing what readers will enjoy—either through research or through some artistic inner sense or through looking into her own heart and knowing what she enjoyed—Mitchell caters to those wishes by giving them what they will like to experience vicariously.

There are many ways to charm your readers. The two methods that Mitchell mastered include using feeling-charged language as she closes the psychic distance and gets deep within Scarlett's mind, and showing how women are puzzled by the men in their lives. You could also charm readers by including fascinating events, by discussing topics of universal interest (romance, love, sex, death), by using language that is poetic (like Vladimir Nabokov, Joseph Conrad, and William Faulkner, for example), by writing dialogue that sparkles, and by including

---

11. Modleski 1982:38-39.

conflict. There are many ways of making readers happy. Thinking about how to accomplish this is not wrong, it is not catering to the market, it is not selling out, and it is not inartistic. It is one of the tools used by writers to craft stories.

Of course, it is not necessary to *constantly* think of methods of charming your readers. Sometimes, as Faulkner and Salinger teach, it's more appropriate to look within and focus on your story without worrying about the audience. But a writer also needs to be able to keep the audience in mind—at least *some* of the time. And Mitchell certainly shows us how to charm readers. Learning this skill, learning to look at your work objectively—from a reader's perspective—is a valid writer's skill, one worth perfecting should you, at least occasionally, wish to charm *your* readers.

CREATE BELIEVABLE BACKGROUNDS

Despite its Civil War setting this is not a war novel in the conventional sense, as *From Here to Eternity* (1951), *The Naked and the Dead* (1948), or even *Catch-22* (1961) were. Mitchell sets the scene in war-torn Georgia but her focus is almost always on the love theme: the relationships, couples, and most of all Scarlett and her dreams of happiness. Nevertheless, Mitchell is noted for her competence in creating a believable background for the novel. She did a good deal of historical research about the Civil War while laid up in bed with a foot injury, and her voluminous reading enabled her to paint vivid pictures of battle-torn Georgia. Against the rich canvas of war she set the action of her human drama, a story of love, marriage, and child-rearing that rises to the level of importance of the war itself.

One way to create believable backgrounds is to use Mitchell's technique of describing a war scene and then putting characters into the picture like a painter sketching characters on the foreground of a landscape. For example, one scene has Rhett meeting Scarlett while Georgia burns in the background. In chapter twenty-three Scarlett notices that the city is aflame, and Mitchell sets the scene based on historical facts:

The Yankees had come! She knew they had come and they were burning the town. The flames seemed to be off to the east of the center of town. They shot higher and higher and widened rapidly into a broad expanse of red before her terrified eyes.[12]

Against the backdrop of this fire Mitchell introduces the image of Rhett, who has come to join Scarlett. "She saw him dimly as he climbed down from the seat of a small wagon." Notice that Mitchell starts with a long-shot. Then she brings him closer so that he seems to emerge from the backdrop of flames that she has already sketched. "He came up the walk with the springy stride of a savage." Finally, when he is close enough to touch, Mitchell reminds us of the fire in the background by including the word "glare" in the description: "His black eyes danced as though amused by the whole affair, as though the earth-splitting sounds and the horrid glare were merely things to frighten children." Later in the scene, Mitchell brings the setting right into the dialogue itself, having Scarlett pointedly ask Rhett: "Must—must we go through the fire?" Interjecting the setting into dialogue is a sophisticated technique, one ignored by many beginning writers. But it is certainly appropriate to incorporate bits of your setting into comments characters make, as Mitchell does here.

By thinking graphically, as Mitchell apparently has done in this and many other instances, you'll be proceeding the way most successful writers have. Faulkner and Bradbury, for example, admitted that they began stories, even novels, with the inspiration of a single image. Then writing the book was a matter of finding out what happened before and after that image. Put more simply, pictures inspire stories. Graphic imagination is too frequently downplayed by writers who conceive of their work as purely linear and verbal. It is not; as Mitchell teaches us, a large part of the work of fiction is actually graphic and is similar to the work involved in painting and drawing. The right side of the brain is graphic and picture-oriented, and thinking in terms of images can certainly help a writer set the scene realistically as he translates what

---

12. Mitchell 1936:368.

At Eaton he was taught by Aldous Huxley, whose *Brave New World* (1932) would have a profound influence on his work. "[T]his dystopian fantasy clearly struck a chord with him. However, as the thirties unfolded, he came to see Huxley's vision as a 'completely materialistic vulgar civilization based on hedonism'—'a danger past.' To him, a far more horrific future loomed with the rise of totalitarianism."[4] The issue of man against totalitarianism, or against other oppressive systems of social and political control, permeated much of his work, including *Animal Farm* (1945).

Orwell was employed for five years in Burma as a police officer and later in England as a teacher, but secretly he hated both jobs and yearned to become a writer. In "Why I Write" (1946) he explains that he learned partly by imitating other writers (such as Aristophanes) and that he "wanted to write enormous naturalistic novels with unhappy endings, full of detailed descriptions and arresting similes, and also full of purple passages in which words were used partly for the sake of their sound." The purple passages showed up in *Burmese Days* (1934).[5] Luckily the influence of W. Somerset Maugham's unadorned style eventually weaned him from this overindulgence and taught him to write clearly and directly. He also picked up style and plotting skills from Jack London, Zola, and Melville, and he actually copied "passages from Swift and Maugham, in an attempt to produce a prose devoid of adjectives."[6]

Although he was a soldier during the Spanish Civil War and was injured when a bullet hit his throat, he quickly returned to the writing life. Orwell's books, especially *Animal Farm* and *Nineteen Eighty-Four*, are often perceived as bleak and despairing, and there is evidence that Orwell was wrestling with inner demons of a peculiar nature in writing them. In a penetrating analysis of Orwell's life, D. J. Taylor concludes that although Orwell held himself out as strongly opposed to totalitarianism—and that is primarily how he is regarded today—he never-

---

4. Bowker 2003:133.

5. The book was influenced by W. Somerset Maugham "but decked with the most fantastic figurative garnishes" (Taylor 2003:80).

6. Bowker 2003:126, 144, 240G (caption 1).

theless had within himself a "conflict between his commitment to fair play and liberal principals and a latent authoritarianism."[7] There is no question that his work is rather unique, yet despite the fact that it falls into an unusual genre, with not many books sharing a similar plot and approach, the techniques that Orwell used in that work can readily be employed by the modern writer of mainstream and literary stories.

WHY *NINETEEN EIGHTY-FOUR* IS SUCH A POWERFUL BOOK

The power of *Nineteen Eighty-Four* is due in large part to its focus on one fascinating character. Less concerned with characterization than Maugham,[8] Orwell nevertheless approached the creation of Winston Smith with a degree of passion that made the book compelling. Employing the third-person limited point of view, seeing everything from the paranoid mind of Winston Smith, Orwell gives the reader an intimate view into this bizarre world. The first thing to note is that the novel gets inside the hero's mind in the first paragraph and never lets up with its relentless portrayal of the future from this privileged vantage point. The danger Winston Smith feels is made apparent early on, especially when he opens his secret diary. The very act of doing so, "if detected ... would be punished by death, or at least by twenty-five years in a forced labor-camp." How could a reader fail to sympathize with someone who lives under such a harsh regime! But this is just the beginning of the methods that Orwell uses to make the book riveting.

An unexpected pleasure, and a relief from the stress of life in this dystopia, is the love story between Winston and Julia. Her note to him, containing the simple words "I love you" propels them into a number of secret rendezvous that afford them both a brief respite from the horror of life in their totalitarian world. But it is their love, ironically and tragically, that leads to their eventual destruction at the hands of the

---

7. Taylor 2003:83.
8. Howarth 1973:163.

state. Nevertheless, the counterpoint of this subplot provides added intensity to the horror of the repression under which they suffer.

Many find the third section, focusing on the torture and confession of Winston Smith, too horrific to read. But the great length that Orwell devotes to showing us the crumbling of his resistance is artistically appropriate since it demonstrates how relentless the state is in quashing all dissent, and reading it is like a tonic for the mind, hammering home the philosophical message that we are all susceptible to a kind of brainwashing, and forced to accept beliefs and world views against our conscious will. As Huxley pointed out in *Brave New World Revisited* (1958), today "the propagandist has been able ... to convey his messages to virtually every adult in every civilized country."[9] The reach of the state in *Nineteen Eighty-Four* is just as merciless, and this is another reason the book possesses such power: We realize that we are being warned about a peril of monstrous proportions. When understood as a message and a warning the story takes on added significance, and this kind of meaning usually results in greater reader satisfaction.

HOW ORWELL CHARACTERIZES

The portrait of Winston is the most complete in the book since the entire novel is told from his viewpoint. It is no coincidence that Orwell was seriously ill with tuberculosis during the time he wrote the novel, and his illness is transferred to the frailty of Winston Smith, who suffers from "a varicose ulcer above his right ankle" which afflicts him throughout the entire story. Even when he is being tortured, the ulcer is mentioned ... until finally, after he has been brainwashed, the state treats his ulcer and bandages it. The fact that Orwell gave Winston his illness, albeit in a transformed manifestation, illustrates one of the cardinal principles of good characterization: Base your hero's traits on real traits that people have, including yourself, but *change* those things that need to be changed in order to suit the story you're telling. Here Orwell changed the disease from tuberculosis to an ulcer, making the

9. Huxley 1932:44.

disease more visible and therefore more likely to be useful for his story, especially for the section where the state bandages and covers the ulcer. The fact that the state *helped* him with his illness indicates that Winston is being co-opted by the totalitarian government.

In addition to making his hero frail and human, Orwell uses clearly demarcated dreams and flashbacks to fill in detail about the early life of his protagonist. In employing this device he is like Faulkner and Dostoevsky; but he uses flashbacks in a much clearer and more easily imitated manner than either of his predecessors. Sometimes Winston will have a dream that reveals his early life, such as when he dreams about his mother and sister. In fact, Orwell is quite direct when he introduces these dreams. For example, part one, chapter three begins with a simple one-sentence paragraph: "Winston was dreaming of his mother." The use of dreams helps characterize Winston in *Nineteen Eighty-Four* and fills in details about his state of mind, his relation with his relatives, the loss of his mother and his eventual sense of isolation from others and the world in which he lives.[10] The important point is that Orwell employs this device in a more discrete and clear manner than many other writers: His use is almost as obvious as flicking a light switch: *click!* the dream begins ... *click!* the dream ends; there is no ambiguity or confusion about when the character is dreaming or imagining an earlier time, as there is in Hamsun, for instance, or Faulkner.

Orwell also characterizes with an unusual but highly effective penumbra approach. A penumbra is a lighter shadow; in characterization it is a less direct and more ambiguous suggestion about a person than a positive assertion, and its very indistinctness makes it more powerful because it provokes curiosity on the part of the reader and prompts the reader to complete the gestalt and fill in the gaps. Like a cartoonish image, similar to what Marshall McLuhan calls a "cool" medium, the very indistinctness of the penumbra portrayal demands more reader involvement.[11] The penumbra works by creating a little *mystery* about

10. Lefort 2000:8-14.
11. McLuhan 1964:24-25.

a character: Is the fact true, or isn't it? The reader wonders ... and the mind spins off all sorts of possibilities.

One way the penumbra technique comes into play is when any character talks or thinks about another. For example, after Winston receives the love note from Julia he fantasizes about her, and as he thinks about her and wonders about the girl's motives, his conflicting thoughts serve to characterize—but in "low definition," to use McLuhan's term. At one point we are told: "The idea had even crossed his mind that she might be an agent of the Thought Police. That, it was true, was very unlikely. Still, he continued to feel a peculiar uneasiness, which had fear mixed up in it as well as hostility, whenever she was anywhere near him." The fact that Winston's thoughts hit their target like buckshot, not nailing it down with one single dominant trait, but instead with the possibility of *many* (she might be bad, she might be good)—all of this uncertainty serves ironically and almost paradoxically to characterize even *more* completely than a simple straightforward statement about her inner qualities. Of course, in real life we always wonder about other people—we never know. Here Orwell causes his reader to wonder ... and in wondering the reader *participates* actively in fabricating the story and conjures up a real person. Similarly, Winston has always wondered about O'Brien "because of a secretly held belief— or perhaps not even a belief, merely a hope—that O'Brien's political orthodoxy was not perfect." Winston doesn't *know*, and *we* don't know. But now we're curious, and this draws us into the story and makes the character of O'Brien more real than a simple statement such as "He despised the Party." When Winston is invited to visit O'Brien he wonders about him some more, which further serves to characterize O'Brien. Yes, Winston and Julia are *wrong* about O'Brien, but Winston's initial thoughts and musings do paint a picture of one side of O'Brien's assumed persona: his false nice side. When the truth is revealed it is as much a shock to Winston and Julia as it is to us. "They sprang apart. Winston's entrails seemed to have turned to ice. He could see the white all round the irises of Julia's eyes. Her face had turned a milky yellow." Their very surprise indicates that sometimes the penumbra technique paints a *false* portrait, just as in life we sometimes make erroneous assumptions about certain people.

Although Orwell is more well-known for his political views and themes than he is for his characterization, it is clear that he mastered effective techniques that can aid any storyteller. The third-person limited viewpoint can help make a central character vivid. In *Nineteen Eighty-Four* this is a critical accomplishment because Winston is pitted against the all-powerful state, so seeing the story from his viewpoint is almost necessary if he is to hold his own, even for a while, in this titanic yet hopeless struggle. Dreams and flashbacks can also help characterize, as can the penumbra technique, where you hint at things about people and make the reader wonder whether those things are true.

HOW TO PLOT LIKE ORWELL

The plot of *Nineteen Eighty-Four* is divided into three parts or sections, corresponding to the Aristotelian beginning, middle, and end of a story. The first part introduces the characters and their frightening world. The second part develops the story by showing how they plan to change that world, deepening the conflict by putting Julia and Winston together as co-conspirators, and hinting at the monumental forces they oppose as Winston reads from Goldstein's book. And the third part is the conclusion, where the two lovers are separated and Winston is thoroughly interrogated and brainwashed until the chilling final line: "He loved Big Brother."

But Orwell does much more than divide his story into three parts to ensure a plot that works. First, it must be noted that it is not a complex plot by any means; even its chief admirers refer to it as a "slender plot."[12] But this is to take nothing away from it; on the contrary, the simplicity of the story allows Orwell to embellish the philosophical and political analysis that is crucial to the full development of his theme. Simple plots sometimes are easier for an author to handle. Without the convoluted complexity of a book like *The Sound*

---

12. Lefort 2000:4. "The plot of *Nineteen Eighty-Four* is deceptively simple" (Bloom 2007:83).

and the Fury, for example, or the winding roads of a Dickensian tale, Orwell makes the story clear and then gets on with the characterization and the political commentary. Sometimes when dealing with plot less is more.

Anyone who fears tackling the complexities of plot should find Orwell an inspiration and a model for emulation. Unlike writers who favor complexity and plot twists galore, his stories adhere to an easy-to-follow path. If your material lends itself to this type of treatment you may find plotting like Orwell a relief: You'll always know what's happening and so will your readers. As in the works of W. Somerset Maugham the progression of events will always be clear. If you have political views, geographical details, or even philosophical notions (like Ayn Rand, for example) you'll have plenty of space for elaboration and explication while the bare bones architectural framework of your straightforward plot holds the whole shebang together. People won't need summaries to follow what happens in *your* story, although your ability to weave in fascinating and illuminating ancillary material (as Orwell does with large chunks of Goldstein's book) may make *your* work a classic some day too.

REPETITION IN ORWELL

Repetition is a key to the success of any novel-length story. In this regard it differs substantially from a short story because a novel needs to repeat certain major motifs, themes, and symbols numerous times. Characters come to realizations when they are forced into confrontations with people more than once. For instance, in *Nineteen Eighty-Four* there is a repetition of the notion that "Big Brother is Watching You." The repetition drives home the idea that this is a world dominated by a totalitarian regime. There is also a repetition and development in the meetings between Winston and O'Brien: First O'Brien is unknown, then he is falsely believed to be an ally, and finally he is seen as an enemy. There is a similar repetition and development in the meetings between Winston and Julia: First she is a stranger, then a lover, then a stranger again at the end.

On a more subtle level plot twists are also repeated. For example, Winston writes in his diary numerous times, and each time he does he fears that he will be destroyed, that it is all over, that the agents of the state will find him. These fears materialize from the first moment he opens the diary, and they are present even before he writes a word in it. "Whether he went on with the diary, or whether he did not go on with it, made no difference. The Thought Police would get him just the same." Another time when he opens the diary he has similar thoughts: "Nobody ever escaped detection, and nobody ever failed to confess. When once you had succumbed to thought-crime it was certain that by a given date you would be dead." The repetition of this pessimistic view is important for the message and the atmosphere of despair that permeates the novel.

The key point to remember is that when you repeat something—whether a theme, a character interaction, or an event—it should be integral to your story and the repetitions should help develop your plot and deepen it. A repeated idea or description is known as a motif. Motifs in literature help to establish a pattern, like a fugue in music, and these patterns should relate to the overall idea of your work. When Orwell repeats the writing in the diary, for instance, he hammers home the notion that Winston is one small man striking out against his dominating state. When he repeats the idea of inevitable death he foreshadows the eventual confession and breaking of Winston's will. And when he repeats the theme of Big Brother he is confirming the notion that this is a society where freedom is not possible because privacy is not allowed. All these repetitions work to add meaning to the book and support its central theme, "rebellion against 'the one.'"

HOW TO CREATE A VILLAIN

The chief trick to creating a villain is not making him *all* bad; to do so is to deprive your reader of a sense of reality and satisfaction. The trick is to ensure that he has some good qualities. A perfect example of this is the way Orwell masks O'Brien's true nature during the first two-thirds of the book. Winston and Julia are led to believe that O'Brien is good, that he is on their side, that he is a secret revolutionary. There are subtle hints that he is thoughtful, intelligent, unorthodox. At first, though, Winston is totally in the dark about the man, who is described as holding a Party post "so important and remote that Winston had only a dim idea of its nature." Winston "felt deeply drawn to him" and he fantasizes that perhaps "O'Brien's political orthodoxy was not perfect. Something in his face suggested it irresistibly." But "Winston had not made the smallest effort to verify this guess; indeed, there was no way of doing so." By making Winston wonder about O'Brien, Orwell ensures that the reader does the same; but more importantly, the reader is given hope that the man is good. In this way, the villain is painted with the same kind of uncertain brushstrokes that we have already seen bring about three-dimensional characters. More to the point, O'Brien *does* have some redeeming qualities: He is intelligent, he does express some fondness for Winston (even as he tortures him), and he is well-spoken and highly educated. He is a devil, to be sure, but he's not *all* bad.

Sometimes the most believable way to create a villainous character is to mix some elements of unconscious goodness into their nature. "[T]he most memorable, fascinating characters tend to have not only a conscious but an unconscious desire [and] these complex [characters] are unaware of their subconscious need."[13] Readers, however, sense that a character has inner conflicting feelings. The fact that O'Brien has a dual nature (is sometimes kind to Winston, other times administers electric shocks) suggests that he is the type of man who has a three-dimensional character. This villain is not all evil; or at least he has some intelligence and some aspects of caring in his personality. This makes him all the more sinister because he tries, in a way, to seduce Winston to his point of view, administering shocks almost like a protective parent might discipline a child for its own good.

In creating your villain, strive for this same effect. Don't make him all mean and nasty. Instead, give him some good qualities. By dividing

---

13. McKee 1997:138.

his personality, in the same way you'd flesh out a protagonist, you will be creating a more believable—and ultimately a more sinister—bad guy.

WHY THEME IS SO IMPORTANT

The "central Orwellian theme," according to one critic, is "personal alienation," and in Orwell's novels "the central character, seeking to liberate himself, undergoes a metamorphosis which involves the substitution of a new persona for an old self."[14] This certainly applies to *Nineteen Eighty-Four* in which Winston is alienated from his society and everyone around him, and in which he undergoes the most brutal torture in part three, resulting in a heartbreaking metamorphosis that destroys his spirit. Christopher Booker observes that Orwell's theme is the crushing of the Self by the dark forces. It is a story in which Winston "represented that Self, that core of individual human identity, which can never be wholly suppressed."[15] In the novel, "one of the darkest stories ever conceived," Winston is crushed down and annihilated when he renounces Julia. "He has committed the ultimate betrayal. He has disowned his *anima*."[16] We see then that the theme of the individual against the dark power controls the logic of the work.

Theme is important because it gives meaning to a work and meaning is what moves us: "*Meaning Produces Emotion*."[17] Because theme is central to a work, one can use a theme to measure a work's success. Orwell's novel embodies its theme on every page. The fact that Big Brother is *everywhere* reinforces the power of the dark force, the oppressive state, the faceless enemy. The fact that Winston writes in a secret diary illuminates the spark of life and goodness that he holds up, like a feeble candle in the wind, a finally useless gesture which is stamped out. The love he feels for Julia is part of his life and the good that is within him. But the theme of

---

14. Woodcock 1966:84.
15. Booker 2004:501-503.
16. Booker 2004:501.
17. McKee 1997:309.

the novel—man against all-powerful dark force—guides the conclusion to that story, too, and destroys even their love.

Your theme or controlling idea can be used as a tool, a powerful lens, through which to view your work and revise it, polish it, and make it stronger. When you have events that support the theme and embody it, milk them for all they're worth; when you spot patches of dialogue or scenes that go astray and do not embody your theme, prune them mercilessly. As Paul Mills points out, "Other words for theme are attitude, aim, drive, purpose. If in your view your writing lacks this quality, [you can, during editing] see why and take some steps to find what its theme might be."[18] It is relatively easy to see how thoroughly theme permeates *Nineteen Eighty-Four* and how Orwell uses it as a touchstone to ensure that the book holds together. The same use can be made of theme in your own work. Be prepared, however, for the fact that your theme or message might not be apparent to you at the outset of a project; in most cases it will emerge out of the work and become clearer as you mull over what you have created. Despite the fact that theme often emerges late in the writing process, it is an invaluable tool for editing and fixing structural flaws. It is also a powerful force for moving readers, and while it may never be stated in so many words, its cumulative impact cannot be denied.

---

18. Mills 1996:65.

CHAPTER 15

WRITE LIKE
Ian Fleming

Ian Fleming did more than create a fictional character named James Bond; he was the creative spark that ignited an industry of films, songs, and spy culture that has spread around the globe. The Bond stories captured the imagination of a generation and have continued to inspire readers and movie makers alike. In fact, today 007 is one of the most recognized symbols in the world.

Fleming was born in 1908 to patrician parents in England. His father died when he was nine. Young Fleming grew up with three brothers: one a year older, two younger by three and five years. He also had a half-sister, seventeen years younger.[1] A whiz at foreign languages, Fleming served in the secret service during the Second World War. Married late in life (in 1952), he indulged in many affairs, with a penchant for sadism during romantic escapades. Living a luxurious life was important, and he smoked and drank whiskey on his deathbed, against doctors orders.[2]

The success of Fleming's books is due, in part, to the suspense and the exciting subject matter; but another large part of Fleming's genius is his often overlooked fondness for sumptuous detail. Not only was Fleming passionate about getting the details right, but more often than not the details he included are those that excite

---

1. She was the illegitimate daughter of painter Augustus John and Ian Fleming's mother, whose husband had died years earlier (Lycett 1995:19-20).
2. Lycett 1995:441.

the senses and reflect a world in which pleasure for the sake of pleasure is the goal of life. As a matter of fact Fleming was a sybarite, a writer devoted to luxury and good times. He retired to a hideaway on Jamaica's North Coast after the Second World War, and there he wrote the books that made his reputation. *Casino Royale* (1953) was the first, followed by eleven more Bond novels. While in Jamaica, Fleming used a gold-plated Royal de Luxe typewriter, smoked Morland Specials incessantly and drank to excess. His appreciation of the pleasures of life was mirrored in his literary style, which relied on generous descriptive passages, exotic settings, and colorful characters. The Fleming style, which he consciously adopted and employed in all his work, includes details calculated to excite the senses and give readers a taste of luxury and hedonism.

Modern writers enamored of Fleming's style have sought to emulate his success, but if they have fallen somewhat short of the mark it is usually for one simple reason: They haven't taken the time to properly analyze his writing to find out what makes it so appealing to readers. Only by doing so can anyone hope to learn its deeper secrets. Very often a would-be author is so in love with another writer's work that he simply cannot see it objectively. In such a case, it helps to examine a few works of criticism because these analyses come at the work from a different perspective and they frequently point out precisely those elusive highlights of a writer's style that you're seeking to isolate. For example, one critic observes that Fleming's style is "characterized by an almost arid order and efficiency. At times, character and suspense literally give way to textbook-like displays of professional knowledge—decisively non-narrative lists, definitions, and reports."[3] Another critic notes that Fleming's books "were written for the total stimulation of the reader, encouraging the reader to share by proxy in Bond's sexual encounters and expensive lifestyle."[4] These critics have unlocked an important secret for writers. Once you become

---

3. Comentale 2005:20.

4. Chapman 2000:37.

aware of these element's of Fleming's style, you suddenly see them everywhere; in fact, you may ask yourself, "How could I have missed it myself?" The short answer, of course, is that in the midst of all the suspense and action these subtle devices (which were right in front of you all along) slip by unnoticed. But once you think about it, the inclusion of stimulating detail is certainly a key element of Fleming's magic. How else could we explain the opening of the second Bond novel, *Live and Let Die* (1954): "There are moments of great luxury in the life of a secret service agent. There are assignments in which he is required to act the part of a very rich man; occasions when he takes refuge in good living to efface the memory of danger and the shadow of death."[5] The book opens with this life-of-luxury motif, thrusting the reader at once into a fantasyland in which opulence and high living are juxtaposed with the kind of violent death and sinister antagonists that are common in spy novels.

ATTENTION TO DETAIL

In order to develop the same kind of reader appeal that Ian Fleming was famous for, you might try using some of the same techniques that he found so effective:

- Describe food in detail; but make sure it's *good* food.
- Have characters drink plenty of *quality* alcohol.
- Include sensuous details about clothes.
- Let your characters take time to relax and enjoy themselves.
- Sprinkle your book with sexual innuendo and references.
- Mention specific brands, expensive cars, and exotic locations.

These techniques are evident on almost every page of Fleming's novels. For example in *From Russia With Love* (1957) Bond is sitting in Darko Kerim Bey's office in Istanbul. "There was a knock on the door and

5. Fleming 1954:7.

the head clerk put *a china eggshell, enclosed in gold filigree,* in front of each of them and went out. Bond sipped his coffee and put it down. *It was good, but thick with grains.*"[6] The italicized passages contain the kind of sensuous detail that Fleming is famous for. Little touches like this add a realistic feel to every scene—but this is more than simple realism in the style of Zola or Sinclair Lewis, writers who drag us down into the mire of life at its worst. Fleming's sensuous details elevate the mood, stimulate the senses and invite us, vicariously, to taste life at its best. You can use the same technique in your fiction and nonfiction to add vitality to your work. You may not be writing about James Bond, but your characters can certainly live the sensuous life—to their benefit and to the delight of your readers.

It might be amusing to follow the vagaries of James Bond's diet from a health perspective, but examining his culinary proclivities from a writer's perspective is even more illuminating. He often drank alcohol and coffee, his signature drink a dry martini "shaken not stirred." In *From Russia With Love* he consumes eggs, which are healthful, and large amounts of coffee, the health effects of which are more dubious. In chapter two of *Goldfinger* (1959) he dines on crabs, melted butter, and champagne. In chapter five of *Doctor No* (1958), while thinking about the murder of Strangways, Bond enjoys a "delicious breakfast." Later, when he finally meets Doctor No, Bond and Honey realize that they're facing the real possibility of torture and death, but they first sit with their arch-nemesis, eating and drinking an elaborate meal consisting of three types of soup, cutlets, and champagne. All this good food serves a literary purpose. Fleming introduced the device of having Bond eat quality food in the first Bond novel. In chapter nine of *Casino Royale*, while discussing tactics in a restaurant with Vesper, we learn that "The caviar was heaped on to their plates." The propensity of Bond to live high on the hog and in the lap of luxury was a lifestyle choice that Fleming consciously selected for his protagonist because he knew that if Bond enjoyed himself then read-

---

6. Fleming 1957:96 (emphasis supplied).

ers would live vicariously in the same royal manner. This vicarious pleasure is a large part of the fun of entering the Bond universe. Of course, this indulgence in the senses also included Bond's smorgasbord of young women, featuring such memorable partners as Honeychile Rider in *Doctor No*, Tatiana Romanova in *From Russian With Love*, Pussy Galore in *Goldfinger*, Tracy (whom Bond marries) in *On Her Majesty's Secret Service*, and Kissy Suzuki in *You Only Live Twice*.

The obvious lesson to be taken away from this Fleming stylistic motif of luxury is to have your characters drink, dine, and love well. But the lesson goes beyond this ... to the very heart of the fictional process. As John Gardner[7] was fond of pointing out, detail is the life-blood of the creation of a fictional world: "the importance of physical detail is that it creates for us a kind of rich and vivid play in the mind."[8] When creating your fictional world, you might want to take Fleming's lesson to heart and present the kind of detail that will color the story as a lifelike dream. Bond's women were beautiful, his cars fast, the places he visited exotic. Of course, you need not copy these specific choices; once you understand how readers vicariously put themselves in the world of your hero, you'll understand how to make that fictional world serve your needs with the specific details that are applicable and relevant to your story.

Countless other examples of the use of sensual detail can be found in the pages of Fleming's novels, and they will show you how Fleming employed the device to good effect. In studying his technique you'll also discover a highly effective method of improving your own writing. It's important to realize, though, that not all of these brilliant detailed passages came straight from the pen of Fleming in one take, so to speak. Many passages were edited for added detail. I discovered this by accident while examining the original typescript of *You Only Live Twice*, which is contained in the Lilly Library at the University of Indiana.

---

7. John Gardner the novelist and critic, not to be confused with John Gardner the thriller writer who wrote many James Bond novels after Fleming's death.

8. Gardner 1985:30. Throughout *The Art of Fiction*, Gardner makes the point that fiction creates a dream in the reader's mind through the presentation of vivid details.

My perusal of that typescript revealed that Fleming often went back to what he had written *in order to add more vivid and sensual detail*. For example, when Bond and Tiger, his teacher and guide, board a ship for the islands, Fleming adds details about the suicide whirlpools that Bond will encounter later on Blofeld's estate.[9] Sometimes the details Fleming added bordered on the shocking or sexual. For example, in chapter eleven Fleming added details to the section where Tiger tells Bond how certain Japanese fighters have trained their muscles to retract their testicles up into their abdomen so that they will be immune to kicks to the groin.[10] On other occasions details are added because they give not only a more vivid picture but also tie in more closely with the *theme* of a book. For instance, when Bond at last comes upon Blofeld's castle, Fleming originally wrote: "Close to, the soaring black-and-gold pile was awe-inspiring"; but he changed this rather mundane description with handwritten insertions to read: "Close to, the soaring black-and-gold pile reared monstrously over him."[11] The addition of the word *monstrously* is not only more vivid, it's also in perfect alignment with the novel's theme, namely that Blofeld is a monster and that by defeating him Bond is a heroic "monster slayer."[12]

The essential secret that can be taken away from this examination of Fleming's working method should inspire any writer to add more vivid detail to passages of description and narration. The added detail might include things that relate to luxury, to the high life, or to bodily comforts. In this way readers will experience vicarious pleasure as they immerse themselves in *your* fictional world. The details can also verge on the shocking and sensual, even the sexual aspects of your characters, a technique that Fleming used, of course, in describing the Bond girls. More specifically and artistically, the details you add can also relate to

---

9. Fleming's original typescript, page 80.

10. Fleming's original typescript, page 82.

11. Fleming's original typescript, page 119.

12. I am indebted to Christopher Booker for this insight. "The success of Ian Fleming's James Bond novels, and the films they subsequently inspired, lay precisely in the extent to which they managed to create a hero who, while wholly contemporary, nevertheless seemed to act out the archetypal role of the monster slayers of yore down to the tiniest detail" (Booker 2004:380).

the theme of your work, buttressing your concept for the story and reinforcing the major symbolic elements you wish to communicate to your audience.

But without doubt the most important point to take away from this analysis of Fleming's working method is that the addition of telling and thematic detail need not spring from your mind in one burst of writing or during the first, or even the second, draft. If you reread your work and find that certain passages sound flat or lifeless there's no need to throw up your hands in despair and cry, "I'm not a writer after all because *my* descriptions don't come close to the vividness or brilliance of Fleming's!" Remember that, like most experienced writers, Fleming went back over his work and inserted additional details in the form of words and phrases to make his prose more effective and to lend vitality and sumptuousness to his stories. Ever since Hemingway burst on the scene with his pared-down prose, modern writers have been warned to go back through their work and strip it down to the bones, *removing* excess fat. While this undoubtedly has its advantages, especially with passages that are overwritten, the conscious *insertion and addition* of appropriate detail, as Fleming teaches us by his own stunning example, is a highly appropriate exercise and one which readers will thank you for with praise, loyalty, and increased sales.

USING ARCHETYPES LIKE FLEMING

Another secret of the Fleming style is the undergirding matrix which helps structure the conflict in his stories and which ultimately leads to a satisfying resolution. The plots of Fleming's books are constructed on an archetypical framework that resonates strongly with readers in the same way that fairy tales and myths do; in fact, it may very well be that all story writing makes use of these archetypes.[13] As you'll discover, the same archetypes can be incorporated into your own writing to

---

13. "Whenever any of us tries to create a story in our own imagination, we will find that these are the basic figures and situations around which it takes shape. We cannot get away from them because they are archetypes" (Booker 2004:215-216).

boost its power and effectiveness. Let's take a closer look at archetypal structure to see how Fleming uses it and how it can be employed in your own work. The Bond novels rely on four primary archetypes.[14] First and foremost is the superhero protagonist, James Bond. Although the hero in most fiction prior to the nineteenth century underwent a profound psychological and emotional change, learning things and maturing as a person along the way, in modern novels the hero often remains static.[15] James Bond, for example, never develops inner qualities of strength, never learns anything life-changing, and never grows as a man or a human being; he is the same at the beginning of each novel as he is at the end, except that he has had some electrifying escapades. The key to his character is his strength, his moral sense of righteousness about good and bad, and his mastery of the physical world, which allows him to prevail in the face of superhuman opponents.

The second archetype is the monster. This is the evil spy that must be overcome. Whether in the form of Ernst Stavro Blofeld, Goldfinger, Doctor No, Mr. Big, Le Chiffre, or any other opponent, the odds are always stacked against Bond. This evil man, the antagonist, is bad to the core. He has an ego that seeks to make everything his own. He represents the other side of the protagonist, the underbelly of human depravity, the ultimate evil. In the Jungian system this would correspond to the Shadow. It is a projection of the negative qualities that we all harbor inside us, the egocentric qualities that seek to aggrandize the Self and that have no consideration for others.

The Anima figure is the third archetype, and it is represented by the good female characters, which have been discussed elsewhere and which today are called Bond girls. Collectively they personify the feminine elements of the personality, the subtle considerateness that is largely absent from Bond's male-dominated character. The Anima

---

14. *See*, for example, the discussion of *You Only Live Twice*, a novel that uses four archetypes: the superhero (Bond), the monster (Blofeld), the Anima (Kissy Suzuki), and the Wise Old Man (a Shinto priest) (Booker 2004:410-411).

15. Some examples of modern novels in which the hero remains essentially unchanged psychologically include *The Catcher in the Rye*, *Père Goriot*, *Moby-Dick*, and *The Red and the Black*.

characters are attractive not only in the physical sense but also because they represent this other side of the personality which the hero must put himself in alignment with in order to reach true maturity.[16]

The fourth archetype is the helper, often personified as the Wise Old Man. M is the chief, Q is the props man, Miss Moneypenny is the secretary who loves Bond, Felix Leiter is the American C.I.A. operative who collaborates with Bond when he is in the States. These figures are friends and their function is dual: They listen to the problems of the hero (and in the process help *us* to understand him), and they aid him in his quest. While the aforementioned helpers appear in more than one Bond novel, there are numerous other helper figures specific to individual stories. In *You Only Live Twice*, for example, the Wise Old Man is personified by a Shinto priest, and Bond is also helped at the beginning of the novel by Tiger Tanaka from the Japanese secret service.

These four Jungian archetypes appear in the vast bulk of world literature. We can simplify this scheme even further by noting that most stories revolve around a conflict between just two of these archetypes: the good and bad forces represented by the first two archetypes, the superhero and the monster. Usually those good and bad forces are personified in separate persons, and the resolution of the conflict occurs when the monster (or evil genius) is overcome by the superhero with the help of his friends and the Anima, a resolution which allows Bond to finally unite with the Anima figure, as at the end of *Doctor No*—at least until the next episode.

You can employ archetypes in your own work, but the best way to do this is not to sit down and say, "I need a superhero, a monster, a Wise Old Man, and an Anima character." Instead, work on your story elements first, and then when you have a first draft or a plot outline, look it over to see if you have included any of these figures. Often you'll find that you have included at least a hero and an Anima figure. Then you may notice that there is a helper or friend (which sometimes appears as a Wise Old Man and sometimes is personified by a younger sage or

---

16. Booker 2004:298-299.

friendly associate). You'll almost always be able to identify someone or some group functioning as the evil forces or the monster. The fact is that your outline or first draft may very well have all these archetypes in one form or another. If you can identify the archetypal role of your major characters, you can enhance those mythical qualities in these characters as you rewrite. Sometimes, for example, you will need to increase the participation of the helper characters so that they fulfill their role of guiding the hero and listening to his problems. You may also have to fix the ending so that the hero and the Anima get together in a satisfactory way at the conclusion, arranging the happy resolution that mythical stories frequently provide. In this way, your knowledge of archetypes might be more helpful in editing your story rather than in creating it from the ground floor up.

POINT OF VIEW

The first chapter of *Doctor No* tells the story of the murder of Commander Strangways and Mary Trueblood. Written from a third-person objective point of view, the chapter reveals what happens from a "fly on the wall" perspective, but never do we find out what anyone is *thinking*. The rest of the book is narrated from a third-person subjective point of view, presenting a look at the story mostly from the mind of James Bond, but occasionally also offering the thoughts of other characters. By focusing on Bond, Fleming creates intimacy with the hero and allows readers to vicariously experience the world from his point of view. And this is exactly what readers want when they open a Bond novel: They want to *be* James Bond ... at least for a day. Fleming gives them that vicarious experience and all the thrills that go along with the ride. For example, Bond has a license to kill, he drives fast cars and he makes love to beautiful women. True, there may be men who are trying to kill him, and he invariably experiences some difficult moments, but that makes it all the more fun, for he always wins in the end; in fact, he usually winds up saving the world. That, too, is part of the thrill of being Bond for a day.

Fleming used the same approach to viewpoint in most of his novels. But in *From Russia With Love* he varied the pattern by staying away from Bond for an extended time. Indeed, the first ten chapters keep us in the world of the bad guys. First the counterspy Red Grant is described and we enter his mind, as well as the minds of various minor characters. Eventually we learn of a plot that has been concocted to attack James Bond ... but still Bond does not enter the story. We are then introduced to the Russian beauty Tatiana Romanova, who is to be used to lure Bond to his death. Fleming lets us see into her mind as well, and we feel a pang of sympathy for her: She is young and innocent and is being used as a pawn in a treacherous game of war between superpowers. By the time we meet Bond, in chapter eleven, the suspense has mounted to an overwhelming degree, and for the rest of the novel we are in his viewpoint as we watch him come face-to-face with the girl and then with the killer, Red Grant.

You needn't be writing thrillers or even detective stories to profit from the writing lesson taught by Fleming's mastery of point of view. Anyone who chooses to write in third-person viewpoint can benefit from studying how Fleming handles the technique. For example, Fleming's delay in entering into the central character's consciousness is particularly instructive in both *Doctor No* and *From Russia With Love*, where we do not see into Bond's mind right at the outset. In this respect, the novels are similar to *Hamlet*, for the hero of Shakespeare's masterpiece also does not appear onstage until an exciting prefatory scene involving a ghost is played out before the audience. When Hamlet does appear, just as when Bond appears, the focus instantly shifts to him, and the preliminary suspense makes us all the more keen to learn what he will say and do.

You can also profit from studying how *often* Fleming reveals the thoughts of James Bond once he is onstage. There are extensive passages where *none* of Bond's thoughts are revealed. These are usually passages of exposition, such as when Bond is learning about Japan from Tiger in *You Only Live Twice*. Other times, the reader learns *everything* that is happening filtered through Bond's consciousness. This is where

Fleming brings us close to the action, immersing us in the fictional world, such as when the superspy is crawling through the ventilation duct at the end of *Doctor No*.

Mastery of point of view is one of the hallmarks of a professional writer. Fleming's work can help even experienced novelists make better use of this all-important device. Especially if you're writing in the very popular third-person point of view and focusing on a central hero, you might find studying Fleming's work quite instructive. You can employ the same balanced approach, sometimes staying in the mind of your hero, other times moving away for a more objective presentation. By varying the psychic distance like this (see page 150) you can move from "far out and objective" to "up close and personal," giving readers a breather when you're distant and providing them with heart-pounding excitement when you're close.[17] In this way, you'll be using point of view to do more than simply tell a tale. This artistic manipulation of psychic distance can allow you to ratchet up the excitement for those moments when your story hits the highlights.

To write in the style of Fleming is to achieve technical mastery with various tried-and-true devices, most notably the use of detail and vivid luxurious descriptions. The use of archetypes is also important for it gives your story structure and provides for satisfactory resolutions. And the manipulation of point of view to create suspense and interest in a central character is something all good writers must master along the way toward becoming effective storytellers. It is no wonder that Fleming's work is known the world over. No matter what *you* decide to write about, if you use some of his stylistic techniques your work is certain to have added impact and appeal.

---

17. John Gardner discusses psychic distance in a very helpful commentary in *The Art of Fiction*, warning writers not to move from *distant* to *close* too quickly, but rather to move slowly from a long shot to a close-up (Gardner 1985:111).

CHAPTER 16

WRITE LIKE
J.D. Salinger

You don't know about J.D. Salinger unless you've read some of the more lurid biographies that have appeared in recent years, but there's much more to the author of *The Catcher in the Rye* than being America's most famous recluse. ... Of course this biographical angle is only *one* approach to his work; still, once you discover the story behind the story you might become even *more* interested in the prose style that prompted Hemingway to exclaim, "Jesus, he has a helluva talent."

Born in 1919 Salinger grew up on the Upper West Side of New York City, a town he would grow to despise. As a young man he experienced significant conflict with his father, who sent him to Europe to work in the family meat-and-cheese business; but Salinger was not at all impressed with his "grand tour" and returned totally opposed to the idea of working in a factory. He ran into difficulty in school and was sent to Valley Forge Military Academy where he did much better; some say he thrived, finally in his element. Shortly thereafter he enrolled at Columbia University, for no credit, in a short story course taught by Whit Burnett, famed editor of *Story* magazine. Before long Salinger had sold his first story to Burnett. While working on a number of other stories (some about a character named Holden) Salinger was drafted and sent to Europe, where he participated in the Allied D-Day invasion. He saw many of his comrades killed during the four months he served in Europe, and as a result he suffered a nervous breakdown.[1] While in France he married a German spy, but they divorced almost as soon as he returned to the States. Back home, he collected his Holden stories and completed *The Catcher in the Rye* (1951), which was an immediate success. After its publication he moved to Cornish, New Hampshire, to get away from New York City. There, at the age of thirty-six, he married Claire Douglas, who was nineteen. They had two children and eventually became disaffected because Salinger built a small concrete bunker a quarter mile from his house where he would retreat for weeks at a time to write. His wife became so displeased with his absences that she divorced him, citing "mental cruelty" as the reason. In 1972, at the age of fifty-three, Salinger began an affair with Joyce Maynard, who was eighteen; the relationship lasted ten months. Around 1977 Salinger met a nurse nearly forty years his junior, Colleen O'Neill, whom he corresponded with over a number of years and eventually married in the late 1980s.

It is a well-known fact that many writers are eccentric, but as Lawrence Kubie points out in *Neurotic Distortion of the Creative Process* (1958), it isn't necessary to be eccentric to be creative. In fact, he argues, eccentricity actually *diminishes* and *distorts* creativity. Great artists are great not *because* they are eccentric but *in spite of* their eccentricity. If they were *less* eccentric and neurotic, Kubie argues, they would be even more creative and productive. This intriguing theory runs counter to the popular view that artists are somewhat mad and that their eccentricities are a prerequisite to creative work. Kubie's theory seems to be supported by the case of J.D. Salinger; in fact, eccentricity may have done more than *distort* his work; it may actually have curtailed his career.[2] One of America's most promising young writers, affectionately referred to in literary circles as "the most private man in America," Salinger stopped publishing in 1965 and retreated to a remote New England town to escape from city life and from his fans. And yet despite

---

1. Alexander 1999:107-108.

2. His eccentricity is detailed in four recent books: Ian Hamilton's *In Search of J.D. Salinger* (1988) (the most reserved of them all), Joyce Maynard's *At Home in the World* (1998), Margaret A. Salinger's *Dream Catcher* (2000) and Paul Alexander's fascinating *Salinger: A Biography* (1999).

his eccentricity there are many important things we can learn from J.D. Salinger about how to write modern stories.

VOICE LESSONS FROM A MASTER STYLIST

Salinger was able to retire to Cornish, New Hampshire, and live in comfort on a large estate, including a hundred acres of rolling hills, meadows, and a brook—all because of his early writing efforts. Was this what Salinger had wanted all along? Perhaps so, for in *The Catcher in the Rye* Holden begs Sally to run away with him to New England, where they would live in a cabin, "somewhere with a brook," and he would chop wood in the winter, and they would live in solitude.[3] Salinger put so much of himself into the creation of Holden, including the psychological breakdown, that readers connected with the character as if they were reading about themselves.

Holden Caulfield is certainly like young people we all know: He has difficulty relating to his parents and he is alienated from all his friends and school associates. Not that young people don't have friends; on the contrary, they have on average more friends than their parents and adults in general; but the fact is that young people often feel alienated from their world and from the older generation. They often move through adolescence feeling that no one understands them, even their best friends. This may be one reason why Holden appeals so strongly to young people. On analysis it's clear that he has no deep relationships, no real friends, and no personal connection with anyone other than his little sister, Phoebe. He is, as Christopher Booker has pointed out, a man who wanders from person to person without making any significant connection. For many young people, this is precisely what adolescence feels like.

Another characteristic that makes Holden Caulfield come alive for readers of all generations is his unique and facetious voice. In fiction

---

3. Salinger 1951:132, 134. There are numerous similarities between Holden and Salinger, including the fact that both had a nervous breakdown, both lived in New York, and both went to prep schools and had discipline problems.

and nonfiction, voice refers to the feeling and tone of writing, a certain flavor determined by word choice and phrasing that gives a text dimension and makes it distinctly and peculiarly human. The voice of a writer is usually easier to hear in first-person texts because third-person narratives so often mimic the "beige voice" of an objective reporter. With first-person it's usually easier to be intimate, unique, and quirky; indeed, open any page of *The Catcher in the Rye* and you'll hear Holden's voice loud and clear. Salinger makes use of teen barbarisms, and he employs numerous leitmotifs, that is, words or phrases that recur with a character and lend him personality. F. Scott Fitzgerald used the same technique in *The Great Gatsby* (1925) (one of Salinger's favorite books) where an effective leitmotif was Gatsby's habit of calling people "old sport"—a phrase that did more to characterize *him* as affected upper crust than it did to describe the people he addressed. Similarly in *The Catcher in the Rye* we have the often repeated *goddamn*, *madman*, and *phoney*. Such words characterize Holden more than the people he describes. The use of leitmotifs is one way Salinger achieves a unique voice for his protagonist. The frequent use of italics, careful attention to diction (general word choice), and repetition all add to the sound of Holden's voice. For example, "The terrible part, though, is that I *meant* it when I asked her. That's the terrible part. I swear to God I'm a madman." This passage from the end of chapter seventeen illustrates the use of italics, careful word choice, and repetition, helping maintain the intimate and unique sound of Holden's voice. No one used voice better than Salinger, and if you pay attention to the way he captures the voice of his main character in *The Catcher in the Rye*—as consistently and saliently as Twain does in *Huckleberry Finn*—you'll surely be learning the technique from a master.

WHY SALINGER IGNORED HIS OWN ADVICE FOR WRITERS, AND WHAT HIS ADVICE CAN AND SHOULD MEAN FOR YOU

Many writers dream of receiving mentoring or advice from a writer like J.D. Salinger. Just imagine if you could drive up to Cornish, New

Hampshire, and talk with him and ask him to look at your work! What if you could ask him, "Mr. Salinger, what's your best advice for the beginning author?" Many writers have actually made the pilgrimage, but in most cases they failed to meet him or were unable to find his house because the locals are reticent about divulging that information. But one writer *did* get to ask him, and in fact she got to go *inside* his house and live with him for ten months. Her name, of course, is Joyce Maynard, and her memoir about her experience, *At Home in the World* (1998), is an eye-opener, to say the least. In that book she explains how Salinger advised her to do something he *himself* never did.

You must have a clear *purpose* in writing, he told her, and having an honorable purpose is much better than being motivated by purely materialistic desires. Put more simply, it's best if you have a message for people, something that will actually help them.[4] "Sooner or later you need to soberly consider whether what you write is serving any purpose but to serve your own ego," he told her.[5] The more heartfelt your purpose, the better your writing. Sounds a little like the conclusion to *Zooey*—doesn't it?—the part where Franny's brother tells her to be funny for "the Fat Lady"; after which we learn that the Fat Lady is *every*one—"There isn't anyone *any*where who isn't Seymour's Fat Lady."—and we learn that the Fat Lady is an analogue for Christ. ... All very altruistic, of course. But it gets even *better*. ...

"Suppose you made your subject something you loved and admired," Salinger told young Joyce Maynard. "Something you held precious and dear. *There* would be your challenge as a writer." Then he told her that he didn't like her article about her relationships with her mom and dad; although it was well written, that was just surface veneer. He criticized it severely for avoiding the harsh facts of her own private life, most notably her father's alcoholism. Then he predicted that someday

---

4. This should be contrasted with George Orwell's admission that at least one of the universal purposes of writing is "sheer egoism." "Desire to be clever, to be talked about, to be remembered after death. ... It is humbug to pretend that this is not a motive, and a strong one." Other motives for writing include "aesthetic enthusiasm. Perception of beauty in ... words and their right arrangement"; "historical purpose"; and "political purpose" (Orwell 2005:4-5).

5. Maynard 1998:139.

she would want to write about something important to her and that she would no longer care what others thought of her ideas. At that point, he told her, you will "finally produce the work you're capable of."[6] That was his message to her ... and to *all* writers. It sounds just like Faulkner, doesn't it, when he claimed he did his best work after he forgot about the audience and wrote just for himself. The ironic point, however, is that this is advice Salinger dished out *but never followed himself.* He never put into his books anything about his poor relationship with his father. None of his angst from World War II ever made it into print. He never talked about his relationship with the young women in his life, either: Claire and Joyce and Colleen and the others. He wrote about young people, true enough, but not about the relationships that were central to *his* life. Nothing about Sylvia either, his first wife, who he met in France during the war. Probably those topics hit too close to home. So although Salinger never took his *own* advice, can a writer rely on it in hope of producing good work?

Chances are you can. At heart it's sound advice for a writer. It apparently worked for William Faulkner, who stopped caring about his audience and went on to write books that won the Nobel Prize. Ironically it also worked for Joyce Maynard: Her memoir *At Home in the World*, with its exposé of Salinger's life in Cornish, received a lot of flack when it came out in 1998, but it's probably her best work;,and it follows Salinger's advice to a tee. In it she tells what she really cares about—her relationship with him and how she got over him. And she doesn't pull her punches or worry about what people might think. So probably Salinger's advice *will* work for most writers, especially those who have something deep inside that they want to say. The way to put his advice to work is to care passionately about something or someone. Then you have to get beyond the chilling effect of worrying about your audience. At that point, according to Salinger, you should theoretically be able to hit your stride and do your best writing.

---

6. Maynard 1998:140-141.

HOW TO FOCUS ON CHARACTER RATHER THAN PLOT

Salinger's characters are important even in his early stories, but as time went on his fiction became even *more* character focused and less plot driven. At least in *The Catcher in the Rye* something happens: Holden travels from prep school to New York City, and there is some plot development as he visits various girlfriends and teachers. In *Franny and Zooey* (1961), however, profluence, or forward plot movement, is virtually halted and things are rather static. By the time we reach *Seymour: An Introduction* (1963) we're simply investigating character. This shift to character focus annoyed some readers and puzzled others, but die-hard Salinger fans enjoyed his work, in part because of the language, in part because they relished reading about *his* people.

In order to focus on character like Salinger, two things are essential. First, you need characters who, like Salinger's, are idiosyncratic and who have a history that holds up under scrutiny. Second, you need to do your research about those people, to think about them and imagine them in their fictional world. According to Joyce Maynard, Salinger had an archive comprised of numerous notebooks filled with character notes, and this is how he kept developing characters above and beyond what we find in his published work. In other words, he had written a volume about each of the members of the Glass family, his major focus in his final works. This unpublished character analysis is so detailed that, according to Margaret Salinger, her father lived more intimately with these fictional people than he did with his own family. His monomania, his almost delusional focus on fictional people, is not, strictly speaking, *necessary* for the creation of character; however, Salinger's method certainly *does* suggest a fruitful exercise for any writer: Develop your characters *beyond* what is needed for the immediate story; this way, when you sit down to write, you'll have *more* in your mind than you can ever put down on paper. Even Hemingway suggested that this was his preferred way of working; it's his famous *iceberg theory* "that you could omit anything if you knew that you omitted and the omitted part would strengthen the story and make people feel something more than they understood."[7] A little later we'll see how Salinger used this iceberg technique to good effect with the ending of his short story "Teddy."

HOW TO CREATE FEMALE CHARACTERS THAT READERS REMEMBER

The work of J.D. Salinger is remarkable for its inclusion of some very interesting female characters, the first and foremost of whom is undoubtedly Phoebe Caulfield. She's remarkable because she represents the Anima, or the female side of the male protagonist.[8] Whereas Holden has difficulty relating to adults and almost everyone else in the book, considering them all phonies ("I was surrounded by phonies"), he *does* cherish his little sister. To him, she represents all that is good and fine in human relationships. In essence, the character of Phoebe represents an *absent* and conspicuously *missing* part of Holden's personality: the part of his personality that *can* relate to other people. Significantly, Phoebe can relate to her parents, to Holden, and to others, but this ability is something that Holden has yet to integrate into his own persona.[9]

Another female character that Salinger created, in part, to represent the spiritual side of himself, was Franny Glass. She is one of the Glass children in the fictional world Salinger invented, a world that carries over into a number of stories and novellas. The family figures prominently in *Franny and Zooey* and *Seymour: An Introduction*. Franny, the youngest of seven children (as explained in a footnote in *Zooey*), is on a quest to find spiritual knowledge. Paul Alexander's biography of Salinger offers insights into how Franny's spiritual quest mirrors the author's own spiritual journey: Salinger himself had been on a spiritual

---

7. Hemingway, quoted in Beegel 1992:61.

8. In Jung's psychology, the *Anima* is the female psychological characteristics that all males possess, just as the *Animus* is the male part of a woman's psyche.

9. Even the name Phoebe supports the notion that she is an *Anima* figure. Phoebe is one of the moons of Saturn. The moon, in Jung's psychology, is a symbol of the feminine, the *Anima*.

quest ever since he came back from the war, and the character of Franny pursues a goal similar to Salinger's quest for spiritual enlightenment. In the novella *Franny*, she has a conflict with her materialistic boyfriend Lane Coutell, and in the companion novella *Zooey* she has a nervous breakdown and is talked out of a delirious crying jag by her brother Zooey. His comment that "There isn't anyone out there who isn't Seymour's Fat Lady" suggests that her attempt to reach enlightenment cannot be confined to reading her Jesus Prayer book; she must go outside the prayers and engage the world in dialogue by *acting* and *doing*. Zooey's message, which Franny "gets" in the concluding words of the story (causing her to smile in the last sentence) is the classic message of Zen Buddhism: Adherents need to be detached from the emotional perturbations of life and to quench desire, and yet they still need to act and to be part of the day-to-day world. "You can say the Jesus Prayer from now till doomsday, but if you don't realize that the only thing that counts in the religious life is detachment, I don't see how you'll ever even move an inch," says Zooey. "The only thing you can do now, the only religious thing you can do is act." We know Franny receives the message on the last page of the book because she picks up where she left off. In fact, her calmness at the end indicates that she has found inner peace and enlightenment.

Knowing, as we do now, key biographical facts about Salinger— including his spiritual quest for enlightenment—some of his major female characters can be read and interpreted as parts of his persona, full-blown projections from the mind of the artist to the pages of his work. But what lesson can they teach a writer? The primary lesson might be that when creating female characters it's vital to get in contact with your own Anima. Try to avoid stereotypes and instead seek within yourself for key elements of your own personality that might be relevant to your story. The deeper you dig the stronger your female characters will be. This work was accomplished by D.H. Lawrence, Flaubert, and Salinger, to name but a few. Seek within yourself for the heart of the female personality, and your female characters will live and breathe like true people.

WHEN AND WHERE TO
WRITE FOR BEST RESULTS

A minor point, admittedly, but one which interests most writers, is the question of *where* to write for best results. By best results we mean, of course, not only your ability to produce quantity (which is certainly important) but also *quality* work. For our purposes, if you're going to be imitating with the intention of *emulating* your models, we want to investigate the best place to do this, whether that be a library, a beach, your study, or even a public café, the favorite writing haunt of Hemingway and Sartre.

The answer, according to J.D. Salinger, is to get as far away from the civilized world as possible; at least that was his *final* answer. He didn't write his *best* work there since he was still living in the midst of the most bustling metropolis while writing *The Catcher in the Rye* and *Franny and Zooey*, widely regarded as his most successful books.[10] Yet he longed for the peace and quiet that he could find only in isolation, and it's no secret that he moved to Cornish, New Hampshire, both to escape from the unwanted attention he had attracted as a result of *The Catcher in the Rye* and to find the kind of Zen-like isolation that would allow him to live and work in peace.

When in an isolated spot, away from distractions, it stands to reason that a writer can focus more intently on his work. As various biographers tell us, Salinger built a concrete bunker a quarter mile from his home and retreated for hours at a time to write. He extended his stay in this bunker for days ... and eventually weeks. The bunker was so small he could not stand up without hitting his head on the roof. He furnished the bunker with a desk, a typewriter, and a couch so that he could take naps. He also installed a green fiberglass roof, which admitted light during the day so that he could work. He and his wife, Claire, referred to the bunker as "the green house" because of its roof. It was this bunker that served as his hideaway for decades, and

---

10. Salinger wrote part of the novel in the offices of *The New Yorker*, and may have also written part of it in a New York hotel room and Westport, Connecticut (Alexander 1999:145).

professional writers will undoubtedly smile when they hear about it. They understand. It represents a concept familiar to them; it represents the kind of seclusion and isolation that allows an artist to concentrate. Stephen King calls it "writing with the door closed" and says it's especially important for first drafts. Call it what you will, Salinger found his seclusion in his concrete bunker, and as a result he may have left piles of books ready to be published ... someday. He admitted to numerous people, including Joyce Maynard, that he was still writing on a daily basis. He wrote, he said, for the pure joy of writing, with apparently no intention, however, of publishing anything further. But someday those manuscripts may come to light, and when they do they'll certainly be a testament to the value of writing in a place that is removed from distractions.[11]

HOW AND WHY TO SURPRISE READERS

Salinger is the consummate craftsman—and entertainer. He knows how, and why, to hold back crucial information until the most opportune moment. Why, you may wonder, should a writer withhold information from readers? The best answer is that withholding information can make your story significantly stronger and more impactful. Delay and suspense, two methods of heightening reader interest, both depend on waiting for the right moment to reveal certain crucial incidents and information. One of the best examples of how to surprise and withhold information is Salinger's controversial short story "Teddy." The controversy, as we'll see, centers on the interpretation of the ending.

But before we get to the technique itself and how Salinger uses it, a few words about *why* he resorts to this device should prove illuminating. The number one reason to surprise readers is that they *enjoy* the experience. They're more likely to remember and talk about your work if you throw in a few surprises. In "Teddy" the surprise revelation is

---

11. Virginia Woolf, in her essay "A Room of One's Own" (1929), makes the case that women, especially, need their solitude if they are to be creative—a solitude and isolation that is quite difficult, if not impossible, for them to find in modern society.

held back until the last paragraph, at which point it delivers a sublime punch line, one that caused controversy when it was first published in *The New Yorker* in 1953, and which people are still talking about to this day. The story focuses on Teddy, a ten-year-old prodigy, and Boo Boo, his six-year-old sister. Teddy has been chatting with a young man, Bob Nicholson, on board a yacht and has revealed that he might die. (The boy is able to predict the possible deaths of others.) Teddy says that later, when he goes to his swimming lesson, the pool *might* be empty and his sister *might* push him in, causing him to fracture his skull and die instantly. He mentions this as a mere hypothetical. The last paragraph of the story, however, tells what Bob Nicholson hears as he approaches the pool: "He was little more than halfway down the staircase when he heard an all-piercing, sustained scream—clearly coming from a small, female child." The scream suggests to the reader that Teddy's sister, Boo Boo, has seen her brother die "in a freak accident."[12]

This surprise ending is quite *memorable*, to be sure; yet there is another reason why a writer might want to withhold information until later in a story. By having a target, a specific end point, toward which you're aiming, you can often free your writer's imagination to elaborate all sorts of intermediate details that can intrigue a reader. "Teddy" is filled with such details, including the curious way the boy's father yells at him, the paternalistic way Teddy looks after his little sister, and the descriptions of Teddy's and Bob Nicholson's clothes. The section of the story where the little genius interacts with Ensign Mathewson is also intriguing, as are most of the boy's actions, up until his exit when he heads for his "swimming lesson."

Surprise works best when it's carefully planned and integrated into a story. It's rather inartful[13] and ineffective to simply have the floor fall out from under a character without any preparation or relation to the story you're telling. The effective use of surprise usually depends on

---

12. Yagoda 2000:284.

13. You won't find *inartful* in the dictionary, but William Safire defines it in the *New York Times*: "awkwardly expressed but not necessarily untrue; impolitic; ill-phrased; inexpedient; clumsy" (Safire 2008).

planting. A *plant* is an intentional mention, earlier in a story, of something which *explains* the significance of subsequent actions or events. In "Teddy," for example, Salinger carefully plants the boy's diary entry, having Teddy write: "It will either happen today or February 14, 1958 when I am sixteen." At the time the reader first encounters this diary entry it is quite puzzling and almost meaningless. Only at the end of the story do we learn that the word *it* refers to Teddy's death, which the boy has somehow foreseen. In addition, Salinger plants an amazingly graphic description of Teddy's death, having the boy tell Bob Nicholson that his (Teddy's) sister "might come up and sort of push me" into the empty pool. At which point, Teddy tells Bob, "I could fracture my skull and die instantaneously." By planting explanatory facts like this, a writer who uses a surprise ending sends a reader reeling back through the story to discover meaning, ultimately causing deeper involvement with a text and heightened reader satisfaction.

If you don't think that readers enjoy this kind of surprise and discovery, consider how often good writers use the technique. I'll leave you with one famous example, the surprising (yet in some way *not* surprising because it was carefully planned for) concluding sentence of George Orwell's *Nineteen Eighty-Four* (1949): "He loved Big Brother." Being surprised *in a meaningful way*—not by having a ton of bricks fall out of the blue—is actually one of the chief pleasures of reading good literature. So, go ahead and surprise your readers. It should come as no surprise to *you* that they'll probably love it.

CHAPTER 17

WRITE LIKE

Ray Bradbury

If there is magic in literature today and poetry, if there is fantasy and an unlocked doorway into another world ... it is perhaps in the pages of Ray Bradbury more than any other modern writer. From the time I was thirteen Bradbury opened those doors for me and my friends with stories and novels that invariably led into fantastic new worlds overflowing with possibilities. And, for my money, no writer conjures up a dreamlike reality better than Bradbury, no one plays with words so beautifully, and no one evokes the magic of childhood so consistently and with such genuine joie de vivre. Writing about the pleasures and pains of adolescence, Bradbury influenced a generation of writers, including Richard Mathesen, William F. Nolan, and Stephen King.

Born in 1920, Ray Bradbury was the second of two sons; his brother Leonard was four years older. A younger sister died when Ray was seven. As a young boy he grew up reading Edgar Rice Burroughs and other fantasy and science fiction. Although he skipped college and instead began writing and publishing at an early age, his work embodies the thoughtfulness of a philosopher and the savvy of a scientist.[1] Many of his stories have appeared on television and in films. A passionate man who believed in his ideas with a conviction that would shame a crusader, Bradbury's interest in playwriting led him to sink

---

1. Bradbury 1990:59.

$75,000 of his own money into a theatrical production. The venture was enough to make his wife temporarily leave him.[2]

WHY POETRY WILL HELP YOUR PROSE

Novice writers often think that they can obtain a prose style by dropping in metaphors now and then, by building a powerful vocabulary or by striving to write long convoluted sentences. These things are only likely to make your writing sound artificial and stilted. Instead, you might find more success with Ray Bradbury's time-tested approach: He believed reading and writing poetry could help you become a better *prose* writer.

"Read poetry every day of your life," he advises. "[P]oetry is compacted metaphor or simile. Such metaphors, like Japanese paper flowers, may expand outward into gigantic shapes."[3] There is no question that many of Bradbury's stories and novels expand ideas like metaphors and build a world around them. *Something Wicked This Way Comes* (1962) constructs a world around the idea that a strange and mysterious carnival gives two boys a chance to see into another world, one where magic *works* and time can speed forward and backward. *The Martian Chronicles* (1950) is a metaphorical exploration of colonization, with Mars symbolizing all the colonized countries that Europeans have conquered. *Fahrenheit 451* (1953) is built around the central premise that it is wrong to censor ideas and ban books. Each of these works, especially *Something Wicked This Way Comes*, is filled with poetry.

Many writers in addition to Bradbury have argued that writing poetry is good training for the production of prose. Faulkner, Hardy, and D.H. Lawrence, to name but a few, were also accomplished poets. Bradbury joined a poetry club in high school run by Snow Longley Housh, whom he thanked in the dedication to *Something Wicked This Way Comes*. He was embarrassed about being in the club because there were so many girls attending its meetings, but he developed a lifelong

---

2. Beley 2006:100.

3. Bradbury 1990:39.

love of poetry and even published a book of poetry, *When Elephants Last in the Dooryard Bloomed* (1973).

Bradbury's prose often contains poetry, as in this passage where he describes Mr. Electrico in chapter twenty-four of *Something Wicked This Way Comes*. "Somewhere, dynamos protested, skirled, shrilled, moaned a bestial energy. The light turned bottle-green. Dead, dead, thought Will. But live alive! cried machines, cried flame and fire, cried mouths of crowds of livid beasts on illustrated flesh." The key when including such passages in a story is making sure that the style doesn't get in the way of the story. "Finding the right word for poetry is a challenge," admits Bradbury. "My subconscious throws out a word and then tells me, 'Not that word, but this word.' I ask myself, 'Where did that come from?' I turn it into a game."[4] Readers may judge for themselves whether the poetry in his prose is overdone; in the opinion of most readers it adds to the enjoyment and the magic of his writing.

TRICKS THAT HELPED BRADBURY COMPLETE FIRST DRAFTS IN RECORD TIME

In writing a first draft many writers will admit that they achieve their best results by working quickly and not censoring their output. "Just get it all down," they'll tell you. Writers from Stephen King to Ernest Hemingway to William Faulkner wrote that way, then went back and revised. But probably no one else will ever tell you this little trick, one that served Ray Bradbury well over the years: When he wrote his first draft he didn't simply write quickly and without censoring himself, he actually purposefully overwrote, trying to come up with *multiple takes* on sentences and figures of speech, for instance, which he intended to prune and edit later. In 1960 when he sent the unedited manuscript of *Something Wicked This Way Comes* to his editor at Doubleday, he told him: "As you read, I know you will mentally cut some of the more florid metaphors which always encrust my first and second drafts. Sometimes I give myself, on a single page, 4, 5, or 6 similes which,

---

4. Bradbury, quoted in Beley 2006:168.

by the fifth draft, dwindle down to one or two really good ones, for proper emphasis."[5] As Bradbury explained to his editor, he typically *overwrote* so that later, when he was in "editing mode," he could choose the best phrase or the most apt figure of speech; in effect, during the first draft he was making his own thesaurus of words and phrases, from which he selected later while reviewing his work.

Of course, if you use this technique it will require some extra writing, but the beauty of this method is that it allows you to exercise your mind to its fullest capacity when it is at the peak of its performance; that is, when you're in the middle of the scene. This avoids the problem of coming back to an emotional section when your mental involvement has simmered down. If you get all the best words and phrases out during that first run-through, you're more likely to discover the words you want, words which might never occur to you when you're not as emotionally invested in the scene during the cooler and calmer editing process.

Another trick Bradbury "imposed" on himself was to press forward when working on a short story to complete the first draft in one day. "I believe first drafts, like life and living, must be immediate, quick, passionate. By writing a draft in a day I have a story with a skin around it."[6] In order to accomplish this daunting task, you may find that writing a more sketchy outline of the story works for you, allowing you to reach the conclusion and climax of the tale with all the intensity that is associated with a first draft. Later, when time permits, and when some of the energy and enthusiasm has subsided, you can flesh out the details, the descriptions, and the dialogue.

Yet another trick Bradbury used, which can work wonders for any writer, is to put a novel-length manuscript away for a year. Then when you take it out and read it the words will appear to have been written by someone else. This process allows you to get a new look at your own work. If you have the luxury of time, this method is highly

---

5. Eller and Touponce 2004:267.

6. Bradbury 2004:26.

recommended. It works best with writers who have multiple projects open at once and who can work on two or three books or stories at a time, in rotation. When one is completed, you can switch to working on another, and when that is completed you can go back to the one in your desk.[7]

Like many professional writers, Bradbury worked by a fixed routine every day: "I keep strict office hours, starting generally at nine every morning, five days a week. If I have had a good morning, I let myself out for a walk or a workout at the gym. In the afternoons I rewrite."[8] This regular working routine helps form the writing habit and keeps the words flowing. Finally, when revising, Bradbury had another trick up his sleeve; he went through each manuscript with the fixed intention of hunting for at least one word to change on each page. "My final drafts are always nit-picking surveys of the manuscript. I look to change one word on each page. When I go through the story and find that every word is perfect, it goes into the mail."[9]

HOW TO USE NOSTALGIA LIKE BRADBURY

"I write a book like *Dandelion Wine*, full of wonderful experiences I've had as a child growing up in this world."[10] Ray Bradbury's approach to writing—an optimistic one that sees the bright side of life—suffuses the pages of his work with something akin to a philosophy or a religious fervor. His approach manifests itself in the wonderful use of nostalgia, looking back at times that were rosy and warm and very good indeed, the way the best childhood memories always are remembered.

Sometimes, however, the nostalgia is tinged with darkness and remorse. After Bradbury lost his sister to a sudden and devastating bout of influenza in 1928, he felt guilt and depression. As critic Sam Weller

---

7. Tennessee Williams was known to work on more than one major project at a time like this.

8. Bradbury 2004:26

9. Ibid.

10. Bradbury, quoted in Beley 2006:3.

points out, there is no question that the deep emotions Bradbury felt have permeated his fiction with themes of loss and mortality.[11] The deaths and near-death experiences in *Something Wicked This Way Comes* and the deaths in *The Martian Chronicles* are just a few of the examples of how this motif has played itself out in his work. The point to be made, however, is not that a somber note need be present in your work; instead, it is vital to remember to keep in contact with *your* emotions, whatever they may be. If the past speaks to you in some significant way, then resurrect those memories, restructure them, and give them a new lease on life in fiction that embraces the past and transforms it into art.

Bradbury, of course, often writes about the childhood of boys. *Dandelion Wine* and *Something Wicked This Way Comes* are the two most obvious examples. These novels clearly spring from the wealth of experiences Bradbury had as a boy growing up. In fact, Bradbury's memory was terrific; he claimed he could even remember being born! Critic David Mogen calls Bradbury's approach a form of "autobiographical fantasy" because it is so heavily influenced by the places he knew as a child and the emotions he experienced growing up. But nostalgia can embrace *any* remembrance of things past that works for you as a writer; you could conceivably write about *girls* growing up, or schools you've attended, or places you've visited: As long as *emotion* is present, the people, places, and settings from your own life are the raw material you have to work with.[12] Unlike an artist who needs to buy paint, you've got all the "paint" you need in your memory. All you need to do is stir it up—and write.

WHY CHARACTER PAIRS WORK SO WELL

In *Dandelion Wine* (1957) Douglas Spaulding and his younger brother Tom experience the summer of 1928 with a rare intensity. It is during

---

11. Weller 2005:40-41.

12. Bradbury was an unabashedly emotional writer. He admitted to his biographer that he cried often, sometimes more than once a day. "Tears of joy. Tears of sorrow. He cries when watching the news; he cries when people say kind things to him; he cries when recalling fond memories. ... He is not afraid to express deep emotion" (Weller 2005:9).

this summer that Douglas realizes that old people were never children, that you can't depend on *things* because they fall apart and break, and you can't depend on *people* because "they go away" and die, and, finally, he comes to the stunning conclusion that he, too, must someday die. Together with his brother, Tom, he wants to obtain the Tarot Witch's help to live forever. But by the end of the book he has come to terms with his own mortality and he is a wiser boy, still able to enjoy life to its fullest.

Another close character pair animates *Something Wicked This Way Comes.* Will Halloway is thirteen years old and enchanted with the carnival that arrives in town. His friend Jim Nightshade, also thirteen, is a bit more daring and seeks to ride the magic carousel even at the risk of his sanity and his life. Together the two boys do battle with the dark forces in the carnival, and in the process they help Will's father realize that he *can* take action against the forces of evil as well.

These two books rely upon character pairs, a time-tested device in world literature and one that is skillfully and consciously employed by Bradbury to achieve two overarching purposes. On the one hand, the character pairs allow Bradbury to make comparisons and point out *similarities.* This enables him to characterize more deeply than one might be able to do with just a single boy to talk about. For instance, in *Dandelion Wine,* the brothers Doug and Tom are characterized as similar in their not getting along with their parents. "Doug, you hit it, you hit it!" cries Tom. "That's exactly why we don't get along with Mom or Dad. Trouble, trouble, from sunrise to supper! Boy, you're a genius!"[13] By showing how these two characters are *similar* in their opposition to their parents, Bradbury highlights a universal trait of children—the fact that they belong to different generations and must therefore see the world differently. We feel that Doug and Tom are allied in this realization, and we understand them better as people because we have all felt that generation gap.

---

13. Bradbury 1957:20.

At the same time, working with close character pairs allows Bradbury to highlight *differences*, even very subtle differences, in their personalities, which enables him to characterize very small psychological shades of character. For instance, in *Dandelion Wine*, we learn that Doug, who is older by two years, is more perceptive than Tom about the world and is questioning things that his younger brother simply cannot see yet. Doug realizes that "Grandpa and Dad don't know everything in the world" but Tom doesn't see this or rejects it outright.[14] This subtle difference in sensibility helps characterize the boys as wise (Doug) and childish (Tom).

Similarly, in *Something Wicked This Way Comes* a slight difference between the boys is used to characterize Jim as a risk taker, as brasher and more daring, and Will as more thoughtful, considerate, and introspective. For instance, at one point Will's father thinks:

> So there they go, Jim running slower to stay with Will, Will running faster to stay with Jim, Jim breaking two windows in a haunted house because Will's along, Will breaking one window instead of none, because Jim's watching. God, how we get our fingers in each other's clay. That's friendship, each playing the potter to see what shapes we can make of the other.

Bradbury notices the slight difference in running speed and impetuousness to highlight differences between the boys, and using a character pair allows him to get into the psyche of each boy more deeply than would be possible if there were just one central character. In limning the differences between Jim and Will, Bradbury goes on to make a further point about *their* friendship and about friendship *in general*, remarking that friends embrace differences and compensate for those differences in order to keep friendship alive. In this way the delineation of character works to strengthen one of the novel's recurring motifs, that of friendship and loyalty.

Remember this lesson from Bradbury when creating your own characters. If you have two characters who are similar, you can achieve

---

14. Bradbury 1957:19.

a great deal of characterization by comparing them and finding similarities. This technique of comparing characters in order to bring out their traits is used by many successful writers, from Plutarch (comparing numerous historical figures) to Shakespeare (contrasting Shylock and Portia, for instance) to Faulkner (comparing Joe Brown and Joe Christmas). At the same time you can enlarge the character portraits of two people by pointing out shades of differences between the two. They may both be thirteen-year-old boys, but the subtle differences between Jim and Will allow us to understand each one on a much deeper level.

The technique of comparison and contrast is one all writers learn in nonfiction writing classes. But as Bradbury's example demonstrates, it can also be used in the most accomplished fiction. Other novels that make prominent use of the device, comparing and contrasting character pairs, include Hermann Hesse's *Narcissus and Goldmund* (1930), Paul Auster's *Leviathan* (1992), and D.H. Lawrence's *Women in Love* (1920).

HOW TO WRITE ABOUT YOUNG PEOPLE

Mark Twain writes about young people, Charles Dickens writes about young people, J.D. Salinger writes about young people, but perhaps no one focuses on youngsters with as much nostalgia for the past and as much poetry in his soul as Ray Bradbury. While it may be tempting to speculate on what particular facts in his biography caused him to develop this focus, it is more apropos for our purposes to examine *how* he writes about young people. There are at least three themes that should be immediately apparent to any analytical reader: Bradbury relies upon a good amount of fantasy, he employs plenty of dialogue, and he thrusts his young heroes into magical settings.

When asked why he thought *Something Wicked This Way Comes* was so interesting to young readers, Bradbury explained that the fantasy element of the carousel—which could make people grow up—was the factor. "I think the merry-go-round is the center of people's interest. I think young people who want to grow up fast are fascinated with the merry-go-round, and when they read my story they fall in love with the carousel."[15] The lesson to be taken away from Bradbury's writing is that readers should be treated to magical elements and that characters should be allowed to experience magical transformations and experiences. There is some element of fantasy in all his work, and that is what takes it beyond the ordinary and commonplace. Young people, after all, have unfettered imaginations, and fantastic elements in stories will certainly resonate with audiences reading about young people.

The fact that Bradbury relies so heavily on dialogue when writing about young people is also instructive. Some writers may shy away from writing dialogue *for* and *by* young people, fearful that they won't get the vocabulary right, but listening to young people speak and thinking back to your own youth will certainly help cure that reticence. It would be a mistake to omit dialogue when writing stories about young people; how much better, instead, to do your best, like Bradbury, to capture in dialogue the quickness of youthful thinking, the emphasis on the important things in their lives, and the humor and wonder of childhood. Your readers will no doubt thank you for it. If you're unsure of your dialogue, you could run your manuscript by a few youthful eyes to test its efficacy, too, as Lewis Carroll did with *Alice's Adventures in Wonderland* (1865) and his other works for children.

Finally, Bradbury always manages to put his heroes into magical settings. In *Something Wicked This Way Comes* Will and Jim enter a carnival that, in itself, is an otherworldly adventure, but Bradbury ups the ante by making the carnival even more thrilling: It is run by devious and evil characters, Mr. Dark and Mr. Cooger, and it is filled with amazing dangers, including a house of mirrors, a magic carousel that can make people grow young or old, and Mr. Electrico, who may or may not be alive. A magical setting also propels *Dandelion Wine* out of the realm of the ordinary and charms readers old and young. The book is set in Green Town, Illinois, where the world of childhood comes alive: Things are never depressing (for long) or sordid (ever) in this

---

15. Bradbury interview by Colin Clark.

town because a twelve-year-old doesn't see the world that way. Bradbury himself manages to perceive the world through the eyes of a boy, and reading the book can make you see the world like a young child again. Remembering some of the magic *you* experienced as a child and incorporating that in your settings is sure to make your writing about children more vivid and effective.

THIRD-PERSON LIMITED POINT OF VIEW

When writing a story it is crucial to consider the device of point of view. Many successful books are written in multiple points of view; in fact, this is the perspective recommended by Al Zuckerman in *Writing a Blockbuster Novel* (1994). But this point of view is not *necessary* for a best-seller or for any other type of novel. There are numerous other points of view that are sometimes more appropriate. For instance, the point of view in *The Catcher in the Rye*, which was a phenomenal blockbuster, is first person. And the point of view in *Nineteen Eighty-Four*, another blockbuster, was third-person limited. The point of view of Bradbury's *Fahrenheit 451* is also third-person limited, and it, too, was a terrific success. Let's examine why you might want to adopt the third-person limited point of view.

Bradbury tells this story from the point of view of Guy Montag, the protagonist. He never deviates from this viewpoint, and consequently we never enter the mind of anyone else. His protagonist is a man who is an outsider. Like Winston Smith in *Nineteen Eighty-Four*, Montag thinks differently from other people, and in this futuristic society Montag knows that it is a crime to read books. That is why the government employs firefighters: to *burn* books. After talking with his open-minded neighbor, Clarisse McClellan, Montag begins to wonder whether burning books might be a mistake, and he slowly but surely begins to change. Indeed, before long he comes to believe the opposite of what he thought at the beginning of the novel: He begins to love books. He is then hunted and chased as a criminal, until at the end of the novel he meets a community of other people who also love books.

They have each dedicated their lives to memorizing one book, and in this way they can preserve the knowledge of that particular book for future generations.

The character of Montag, who begins to see the truth of his world, is the important focal point. Bradbury uses third-person limited viewpoint to focus on this central character to the exclusion of all others. In other words, seeing everything through Montag's eyes makes the story unified and tight and gives readers a vicarious experience that illustrates how a character comes to see the world in a new way. Like *Nineteen Eighty-Four*, the story works best by keeping to this limited viewpoint.

Despite the fact that it is called "limited," this viewpoint allows a writer to get very close to the inner thoughts of the hero. For example, when Montag is injured and on the run: "A shotgun blast went off in his leg every time he put it down and he thought, you're a fool, a damn fool, an awful fool, an idiot, an awful idiot, a damn idiot, and a fool, a damn fool."[16] This close investigation into the psyche of the central character is what makes the book so personal and moving; the reader is never distracted by thoughts from other characters, and since the entire story is seen from one limited viewpoint, Montag's, we are made to care for him by virtue of this close focus on his perceptions. The reason the device is called third-person *limited* is that we are limited to one character's viewpoint and are not distracted by the thoughts of other people in the story. This works particularly well when you wish your reader to see events from one character's point of view. In *Nineteen Eighty-Four* we never know what O'Brien or Julia are thinking. In *Fahrenheit 451* we never know what Montag's wife, Millie, or his friend Clarisse are thinking. Because of this sharp focus the story is almost claustrophobically tight and unified, and the central character's consciousness becomes *our* consciousness. It is for this reason that an intense novel, one with a strong point or theme, often succeeds in third-person limited point of view.

---

16. Bradbury 1953:121.

Bradbury's work is an open invitation to writers from all genres to stretch their imagination beyond science fiction and fantasy. His poetic language, his method of writing drafts, his employment of nostalgia, his comparing and contrasting of character pairs, and his mastery of viewpoint have encouraged and challenged numerous successful authors to take new risks with their own work. If you can divorce your attention from his fantastic stories long enough to examine the powerful techniques at their core, Bradbury will certainly prove to be a mentor of unparalleled inspiration for your work, too.

CHAPTER 18

WRITE LIKE

Flannery O'Connor

The down-home voice, the country locale, the grotesque characters, the violent plots twists—they're all there in Flannery O'Connor as they are in Southern fiction from writers like Faulkner, William Styron and Truman Capote.[1] Yet O'Connor shot them all to pieces with her unique blend of Southern Gothic, spirituality, and humor, a type of writing found only in her pages and employing a literary style that calls attention to itself for its freshness and bravura.

Born in Savannah, Georgia, in 1925, O'Connor was an only child, descended from generations of Irish Catholics.[2] Her father died of lupus when she was fifteen. She spoke with a very thick accent, which surprised Paul Engle, the professor in charge of the University of Iowa's graduate journalism program where O'Connor began her formal study of writing. She was a quiet student who seldom raised her hand in class but whose work, even then, was recognized by the faculty as superior.[3] After receiving her M.F.A. she began publishing short stories, a number of which served as chapters for her future novels.[4] At

---

1. Capote learned quite a bit from O'Connor about how to employ violence in his work (Hendin 1970:156). And yet O'Connor used violence in a significantly different way; usually to support a theme of spiritual awakening, with violence typically the result of a dim-witted approach to spiritual values. And while Capote admired O'Connor's work, she said his writing "makes me plumb sick" (O'Connor, quoted in Gentry 2006:42-43).

2. Simpson 2005:1.

3. Scott 2002:xv.

4. Scott 2002:xvi.

the age of twenty-five she contracted lupus and moved to her mother's dairy farm in Milledgeville.[5] It was here that she produced all of her major works, and it was here that she remained until her death at the age of thirty-nine.

HOW TO USE HUMOR IN SERIOUS WRITING

Few writers introduce humor into serious subjects as adroitly as O'Connor. Pick up *The Violent Bear It Away* (1960) and you'll be struck at once by the high tone and weighty subject matter but also by its darkly comic vision. The character Rayber, in particular, is a macabre gothic nightmare of a man, almost painted with elements of pastiche and parody. Once you examine how O'Connor accomplishes these effects, you'll find that the techniques she uses are not difficult to copy should you wish to add a touch of humor to a serious subject. In fact, she employs three primary techniques to add humor to her work: exaggeration, comic emphasis, and comic juxtaposition.

The Violent Bear It Away tells the story of a young boy, Tarwater, a fourteen-year-old orphan whose caretaker, his great-uncle Mason, has suddenly died. The great uncle was a religious fanatic, and Tarwater is afraid that he is going to become a religious fanatic too. His biggest struggle occurs within himself as he wrestles with his desire to baptize his cousin and his competing desire to prevent himself from becoming a clone of his fanatical great uncle.

O'Connor employs *exaggeration* when describing Rayber the first time Tarwater sees him with his hearing aid. "He was barefooted and in his pajamas. He came back almost at once, plugging something into his ear. He had thrust on the black-rimmed glasses and he was sticking a metal box into the waist-band of his pajamas. This was joined by a cord to the plug in his ear. For an instant the boy had the thought that his head ran by electricity."[6] All the major char-

---

5. Giannone 2000:8.

6. O'Connor 1960:175.

acters are drawn in caricature and are grotesque in some way: old Mason's fanaticism, Rayber's hearing problem, Tarwater's obsession with baptism. To use exaggeration effectively, consciously make use of O'Connor's own approach to the device and highlight those qualities of a character that define him and make a statement about him.[7] O'Connor was quite purposeful in her use of exaggeration because she believed that "it is the extreme situation that best reveals what we are essentially."[8] The focus on Rayber's hearing aid is blown out of proportion but the exaggeration in this portraiture communicates a powerful and unambiguous statement about what he is: That he relies so much on the hearing aid is symbolic of Rayber's mechanistic and Freudian approach to life, revealing that he is limited and cut off from the spiritual world.[9] When you select traits to emphasize, do so like O'Connor and make sure they embody your theme and strike a resonant cord in readers.[10]

Comic emphasis, or waiting until the end of a sentence to deliver a "punch line," is a device employed regularly by O'Connor. For example, when they check into a hotel, much attention is paid to the fact that the boy takes a pen and writes his own message on the registry, and at the end of the chapter the punch line comes: "'Francis Marion Tarwater,' he had written. 'Powderhead, Tennessee. NOT HIS SON.'" This is both serious and humorous: The boy wants to assert his identity and independence from Rayber, but his way of doing so is comical, and O'Connor's choice of communicating this information to us via comic emphasis is highly appropriate. O'Connor never tells jokes for the sake of joking, however, so that when the boy writes "NOT HIS SON" it

---

7. Every successful author exaggerates to focus attention on certain key conflicts and character traits. "For example, Flaubert in *Madame Bovary* exaggerates Emma's boredom and sense of emptiness to develop and sustain the basic conflict" (Meredith and Fitzgerald 1972:21).

8. O'Connor, quoted in Fodor 1996:42.

9. One critic observes that "even as a religious writer O'Connor accepted Freudian truths and understood Freudian symbols because she earnestly tried to come to grips with modern times and secular thinkers" (Rath 1996: 8).

10. O'Connor's exaggeration ensured that her message was delivered with uncommon clarity. As one critic observed, it is clear that "her theology holds nothing but scorn for everything human" (Bleikasten 1978:156).

is part and parcel of his self-definition; it is important to him, but it strikes the reader as grotesque, strange, and humorous.

Comic juxtaposition combines the technique of emphasis (or surprise) with the notion of novelty. Linking the unexpected or putting unlikely things together is one of the chief arts of the comic, and O'Connor uses the device repeatedly in her work. In a restaurant Rayber comes right out and tells the boy, "Until you get rid of that compulsion to baptize Bishop, you'll never make any progress toward being a normal person." The yoking together of baptism with psychosis is an unexpected combination. It is humorous on one level, dead serious on another. Another example occurs when the voice of the friend (which symbolizes the devil) tells Tarwater, "Be a man … be a man. It's only one dimwit you have to drown." Here the conjunction of being manly by drowning someone is bizarre and simultaneously darkly comic. Again it hits at the heart of O'Connor's theme of spiritual seeking, for drowning and baptism are symbolically linked through the use of water. Comic juxtaposition is the trickiest of the devices O'Connor employs to create humor. It is a gallows humor at times, but the effect is powerful. If at a loss for how to achieve a similar combination, try linking two improbable things in your story, always keeping a connection to your theme.

HOW SYMBOLS STRENGTHEN YOUR WORK

O'Connor's conspicuous introduction of symbols makes her a good artist to study to learn how to use this powerful device.[11] As one critic observed, her language may be "sparse and functional" and yet her work "is tightly unified by symbolism."[12] A devout Catholic, O'Connor

---

11. O'Connor also chooses names for their symbolic value. Tarwater = tar + water, two elements that don't mix, symbolic of the fact that his spiritual and material sides are in conflict. T. Fawcett Meeks's middle name ("faucet") reminds us that the copper flue salesman is grounded in the material, not the spiritual world. The old man, Mason, is linked with the cultlike brotherhood of freemasons. *See* Whitt 1995:93-94, 96, 99.

12. Hyman 1966: 20-21, 23.

employed Christian symbolism throughout her novels and stories, and yet as one critic eloquently remarked, "Flannery O'Connor was a Catholic. She was not a Catholic novelist. She was a writer, and as a writer she belongs to no other parish than literature."[13] Joyce Carol Oates, an admirer of her work, was of like mind: "Yet it is not finally necessary to share O'Connor's specific religious beliefs in order to appreciate her art."[14]

One of O'Connor's favorite symbols is the devil, and she wanted people to recognize the devil when he appeared in the form of Meeks and Rayber; she didn't want any mistake about it.[15] Meeks, the copper flue salesman, drives Tarwater to town and on the way is depicted as the devil.[16] O'Connor has set the story up so that whenever the boy hears a "stranger's" voice in his head (later referred to as a "friend") the devil is at work. When Meeks is introduced, O'Connor is careful to label him "his new friend," thus linking the man with the devil. The novel is about Tarwater's struggle with faith, and placing the symbol of the devil in his path strengthens the story by giving the boy someone dangerous to confront. Meeks may have a "meek" name and may appear friendly on the surface, but the devil lurks beneath.

Another symbol is the baptism of the cousin, Bishop, and this baptism is symbolic of acceptance of faith. But O'Connor doesn't simply tell us that the boy wanted to baptize his cousin; she makes Tarwater feel conflict over whether he should or shouldn't go through with the baptism. By making the symbol something the boy wrestles with, she ups the ante and underscores its importance to both Tarwater and to the theme of finding truth and faith.

---

13. Bleikasten 1978:157.

14. Oates 1973:49.

15. "I want to be certain that the Devil gets identified as the Devil and not simply taken for this or that psychological tendency" (O'Connor, quoted in Giannone 2000:6).

16. "Meeks is a tour de force for O'Connor the cartoonist. She makes him the flattest possible character, speaking in the flattest possible language and inhabiting the flattest possible moral setting. … His genial sales talk coats a despiritualizing cynicism that makes love and human contact mere commodities" (Giannone 1989:126).

O'Connor is a master of presenting people as symbolic. Rayber's mechanism, his reliance on psychology, and his deafness are all signs that he is not in contact with the truth. His obsession with psychology is another symbol of his rationality, an allegorical symbol of modern man. He cannot hear sounds well, but more importantly he cannot listen to the boy when he wants to talk with him. Significantly, we learn after they come out of the temple that "At any point along the way, he could have put his hand on the shoulder next to his and it would not have been withdrawn, but he made no gesture." We also learn that Rayber is afraid of love; not kindness or "love in general" but "love without reason" or unconditional spiritual love, the love that a person usually attributes to God. Rayber's link with the devil is solidified when we see that he is deaf to both sounds and to the feelings of the boy. More importantly he is deaf to the word of God and constantly tells the boy that his religious beliefs are nonsense.

The boy is a symbol of man on a quest, a projection of O'Connor's self, torn between the religious overkill of the great uncle and the forces (Rayber, Meeks, the stranger/friend, and the city itself) that attempt to *divert* him from his mission in life—"But just lemme ast you this: where is the voice of the Lord? I haven't heard it. Who's called you this morning? Or any morning?"[17] In chapter eight we are told directly that the boy's "mind had been engaged in a continual struggle with the silence that confronted him, that demanded he baptize the child and begin at once the life the old man had prepared him for." On its deepest level, the boy is a symbol of man's spiritual quest for wholeness and personal integration through the acceptance of faith or of a power higher than the material.

FREE INDIRECT DISCOURSE

If you've been wondering why Flannery O'Connor is such a fun author to read perhaps part of the answer is that she makes frequent use of the literary device known as *free indirect discourse (FID)*. A popular

---

17. This is the voice of the stranger (devil) jeering at Tarwater (O'Connor 1960:147).

technique with good writers, FID involves *narrating a scene in language that contains some elements from the lexicon of one of the characters.*[18] As a writer you're going to love this because employing FID can make your work sophisticated, powerful, and artistic.

Before we examine O'Connor's use of FID it might be helpful to mention the two more basic types of discourse that are found in fiction and nonfiction and from which FID ultimately springs. Direct discourse is simple dialogue, the speech of one of the characters directly quoted. Indirect discourse is dialogue *without* quotation marks, and it always uses a reporting verb, usually the word *said*: "Her parents and sister were going to a barbecue at an aunt's house and *Connie said no, she wasn't interested,* rolling her eyes to let her mother know just what she thought of it."[19] The italicized words are indirect discourse because they tell what a character said, but they're not enclosed in quotation marks. The author is *indirectly* telling the reader what Connie said.

Free indirect discourse is the same as indirect discourse except that it doesn't use a reporting verb (technically known as an orthographic marker) and it tells what a character said, thought, or felt in his mind, either consciously or unconsciously. It is "a linguistic combination of two voices,"[20] the voice of the narrator of the story and the voice of one of the characters. A helpful way to think of it is to conceptualize FID as narration *tinged* or colored with the voice of one of the characters. The word *tinged* is often used when describing how FID operates to color or affect a bit of narration, and this implied analogy with painting and color theory is quite useful in thinking about how FID works to add depth and shading to a narrative passage.[21] Because of the doubling of voices,

---

18. Rimmon-Kenan 1983:110. *See also* Atkinson 1990:124.

19. Oates 1966:823 (emphasis supplied).

20. Rimmon-Kenan 1983:110.

21. For example, one critic analyzing a short story by Katherine Mansfield comments that "a fair amount of the story consists of free indirect discourse ... heavily *tinged* with the idiom of the current reflector character" (emphasis supplied) (Fludernik 1996:198). Another critic says, "Joyce's method ... makes narration look like objective report, but in fact the narration is *tinged* with the idiom of the person described. A free indirect discourse of this kind provokes specific uncertainties about who is responsible for reported thoughts or speech" (emphasis supplied) (Barry 2001:75).

WRITE LIKE *Flannery O'Connor*

FID also allows a writer to achieve powerful polyphonic effects comparable to those achieved in music. Since FID uses words that the *character* would typically use, as opposed to words that the *narrator* would typically use, one critic emphasizes the fact that FID "reproduces verbatim the character's own mental language."[22] Another interesting aspect of FID is the fact that it "[f]ar more than in ordinary narrative passages … teems with questions, exclamations, repetitions, overstatements, colloquialisms" and it is narration for which "neither the content nor the style … can be plausibly attributed to their narrators."[23]

An example of FID from "Everything That Rises Must Converge"[24] (1961) occurs after the son, Julian, "raised his eyes to heaven" in regards to his mother's hat, for we are told, "It was a hideous hat." The word *hideous* doesn't sound like the narrator's type of word; it is a descriptive overstatement, clearly tinged with Julian's vocabulary and thinking. In the middle of the story we learn that Julian has "a kind of mental bubble" he retreats to, from which he can view the world.[25] We are then told "*he had turned out so well*. In spite of going to only a *third-rate* college … in spite of growing up dominated by a *small mind, he had ended up with a large one;* in spite of all her *foolish views, he was free of prejudice*" (emphasis supplied). The italicized words are those which we wouldn't typically expect from the third-person narrator; they're words tinged with Julian's mental outlook and prejudices.

Another example of FID occurs throughout *The Violent Bear It Away* when Tarwater's great uncle is referred to as "the old man," a term that sounds like it's from the viewpoint of the boy (and also from the viewpoint of Rayber). Also, in the middle of chapter two we are told: "The boy *had sense enough* to know that he had been betrayed by the schoolteacher" (emphasis supplied). The italicized words, tinged with

---

22. Cohn 1978:14. Throughout her fascinating book on narrative technique, Cohn refers to FID as "narrated monologue" (Cohn 1978:13).

23. Cohn 1978:102.

24. The title is derived from Teilhard de Chardin's belief that people on a spiritual quest rise and become similar as they approach enlightenment (Whitt 1995:111).

25. This is a good description of how an author uses FID to get into the "mental bubble" of a particular character's mind.

Tarwater's viewpoint, are FID. Later in the same chapter, when Meeks is using a telephone (a device which Tarwater had never seen before) we learn that "Meeks took the machine in two parts and held one part to his head while he circled with his finger on the other part." This entire sentence is shot through with Tarwater's language and sensibility.

To use FID in your own work, force yourself to jump into the mind of the character you wish to delineate. Be especially on the lookout for words or phrases that would not typically occur to *you* in this situation, but that *would* be in the mind or heart of the character in question; then blend these words and phrases into the narration. If done well, the result will be a more powerful presentation and will employ a voice closer to the character, maintaining a level of excitement that your typical "beige voice" narration can never convey.[26]

HOW TO PUNCH UP ENDINGS

As Robert McKee points out regarding screenwriting in an observation equally applicable to the novel: "The Climax of the last act is your great imaginative leap. Without it, you have no story. Until you have it, your characters wait like suffering patients praying for a cure."[27] O'Connor always provides the cure, punching up her conclusions and rescuing her characters from the doldrums of a lukewarm ending in three ways: first, by *echoing* what has gone before; second, by making sure that a *twist* occurs; and third, by leaving some *message* with the reader.

John Gardner talks about the need, in a novel-length work of fiction, to repeat themes, images, and symbols so that they take on greater significance. This is most important during the ending, where he suggests a "resonant close" is necessary. "What moves us is not just that characters, images, and events get some form of recapitulation or recall: We are moved by the increasing connectedness of things, ultimately a connectedness of values."[28] This literary resonance is similar to

---

26. Tom Wolfe is also a master of FID and it permeates all his best work.
27. McKee 1997:309.
28. Gardner 1985:192.

musical resonance and the repetition of a musical theme, and it may help to think of it that way. The ending of *The Violent Bear It Away* employs this device, echoing what has gone before, reiterating themes and phrases that were motifs in the novel: "The violent country," "the silence," "the truth," and other terms are woven into the concluding pages to provide a musical fuguelike resonance which connects Tarwater with the main theme of spiritual awakening that has followed him throughout the story.

There is also a plot twist, with the boy deciding, after all, to accept his destiny and follow in the footsteps of his great uncle. This was a decision that could not be predicted. As one critic points out, "*The Violent Bear It Away* delivers two symbolic alternatives for the reader: choose the way of Tarwater, which is less choice than a violence racked upon its chosen, or the way of Rayber, the ultimate torture because it yields only nothing disguised as free will."[29] The twist, or decision, lets everything fall into place, and we end the story knowing that Tarwater has chosen the difficult life of following in his great uncle's path.

The message of the novel is that to be a good person one must heed the call of destiny and faith and not reject it. Despite his wavering and vacillating throughout the story, at the end Tarwater comes home and realizes that he must fulfill his destiny. He has drowned Bishop and returned home to Powderhead, his ancestral home. Finding that his great uncle has been buried, he sees a vision of a burning bush and hears a voice telling him to do the work of God. In a symbolic gesture he grabs a handful of dirt from his great uncle's grave and smears it on his forehead. Then he marches back toward the city, ready to begin his life as a prophet. This ending is filled with overtones of meaning. Clearly O'Connor sides with Tarwater and, despite his faults, she presents him as the ideal man.[30]

You don't have to write Southern Gothic to learn from O'Connor. By using some of her sophisticated literary techniques you can improve

---

29. Whitt 1995:107.

30. The ending of her short story "A Good Man Is Hard to Find" (1955) also nicely illustrates how to use these three concluding techniques.

any story, even one that is not specifically about spiritual quests or a search for truth.[31] Adding humor to lighten overly serious work and employing symbols that strengthen stories, you can learn from O'Connor how to penetrate into the minds of characters with free indirect discourse and how to fashion endings that satisfy readers. If, however, you *are* writing Southern Gothic *and* you master these techniques ... you'll likely be considered another unstoppable literary force.

---

31. "Miss O'Connor wants her people to search for Truth" (Malin 1966:114).

CHAPTER 19

WRITE LIKE
Philip K. Dick

As man reaches out into the universe, heads for the stars, and discovers the wonders of the subatomic world, he experiences a million different stresses and shake-ups that conspire to make modern life uncertain. Science fiction helps us cope with the exponential growth of this technological change, and Philip K. Dick's work stands at the forefront of the genre. His lifelong goal was to combine SF and mainstream fiction and as a result his work has many literary qualities.[1] His biggest influences were L. Frank Baum, Alfred Bester, Flaubert, Stendhal, and Guy de Maupassant.[2]

Born in 1928, Philip K. Dick grew up an only child in a rather impoverished family. His parents divorced when he was five and he lived with his mother, developing a very close relationship with her. She encouraged him to pursue his writing despite the great financial difficulties he experienced throughout his life.[3] Like many male only children, he was intensely career focused. He married five times and always involved his wives in discussions of his work, demanding that they read his first drafts immediately. Like Aldous Huxley he experimented with psychedelic drugs, and his novels often focus

---

1. Sutin 1989:3. He also wrote about ten mainstream novels, including *Confessions of a Crap Artist* (1975). He pointed to *We Can Build You* (1972) as an example of what he was trying to do in combing SF and mainstream fiction (personal communication from David Gill).

2. Sutin 1989:3.

3. Sutin 1989:16.

on themes that include drug use, alternate realities, and doubt about what is real.

HOW TO WRITE QUICKLY YET POWERFULLY

The reality was that Dick knew he was a genius, he knew he was a brilliant writer and yet he was in so much financial trouble that he could not even pay his library fines. "I love science fiction, both to read it and to write it," he said. "We who write it do not get paid very much. This is the harsh and overwhelming truth: Writing SF does not pay."[4] As a result he was compelled to write quickly and to push himself to the limits, producing forty novels and two hundred short stories.[5] In this he was similar to Balzac; in fact, like Balzac he also used coffee (though not to the excess that Balzac did) and stimulants such as Semoxydrine.

One expert on writers and drugs remarked that Dick was "perhaps the greatest amphetamine-driven writer."[6] He was not a one-drug man, however:

> [He] took depressants, antidepressants, and various other psychiatric medications from the mid-1950s on and experimented with LSD in the early sixties. ... Dick used Semoxydrine, a brand of methamphetamine, both as a mood elevator and to crank out pulp science fiction novels and stories. ... In 1963-64, Dick wrote eleven science fiction novels, along with a number of essays, short stories, and plot treatments in an amphetamine-fueled frenzy that accompanied or precipitated the end of one of his marriages. The most remarkable of these novels is *The Three Stigmata of Palmer Eldritch* (1965).[7]

The Three Stigmata of Palmer Eldritch is a concisely written science fiction novel that explores a future in which colonists on Mars make

---

4. Dick 1995:18.

5. Sutin 1989:9.

6. Boon 2002:206.

7. Ibid.

life bearable by using hallucinogenic drugs. Characters suddenly find themselves in alternate realities and the reader is amazed at the shifting of foreground and background. John Lennon was so impressed he wanted to make it into a movie.[8]

Dick also experimented with megadoses of vitamins (including niacin, vitamin C, and the B vitamins) in an effort to get his brain to work better, faster, smarter.[9] But Dick's dependence on stimulants came at a frightening price: "Taking a thousand or more methedrine tabs a week, Dick developed various conspiracy theories about the CIA tapping his phone and breaking into his home, and was admitted to a series of psychiatric clinics, until, in 1972, after a suicide attempt, he was admitted to a Canadian rehabilitation clinic."[10]

Dick's usual speed of composition was two novels per year, "each novel taking six weeks for the first draft and another six weeks for the second (retyping and minor copy editing). Between each novel would be six months devoted to thinking out the next plot."[11] Thinking was important to Dick: "He warned [his wife] Anne never to interrupt him when it seemed that he was only sitting quietly."[12] He was usually thinking about a book and working on it mentally.

No one is recommending that you take amphetamines like Dick, although an occasional coffee might be justified in the same way that astronauts use drugs to boost performance during space missions.[13] Even more important is the idea that writers need periods of percolation time, during which the mind is free to ruminate over the ideas

---

8. Sutin 1989:129.

9. An article in *Psychology Today* convinced him to experiment with megadoses of vitamins to make the right and left hemispheres of his brain work together more effectively (Sutin 1989:212-213).

10. Boon 2002:207.

11. Sutin 1989:107.

12. Ibid.

13. The comparison with astronauts is apt since writers, like astronauts, have a task to perform and must have their wits about them to accomplish that task. Astronauts routinely take drugs, both hypnotics (sleep aids) and stimulants (usually dextroamphetamine). When a crucial mission task must be performed, astronauts are at liberty to take a stimulant to improve performance (Page 2004:415). *See also* Dinges 2001:337-338.

that you have come up with. Mental rehearsal can make the actual physical writing go more quickly and effortlessly.[14]

WHY IMAGINATION IS IMPORTANT

Not only did Dick possess an unusually good imagination, he also elevated imagination to a thematic element in many of his stories,[15] with characters in *The Three Stigmata of Palmer Eldritch*, for example, having to use their imagination to enter into an alternate world called the Perky Pat layouts. Of course the drugs Can-D and Chew-Z helped them "translate" into the sets, but once there they melded with the minds of others and enjoyed an exotic fantasy life until the drug wore off.

It may seem arch to ask why imagination is important to a writer, but the point is crucial to understanding creativity and how to boost your own ability to craft stories that will resonate with readers. There is considerable literature available now about the psychological abilities of the mind and how to enhance creativity. Dick was aware of research on right-brain and left-brain differences and wrote about the subject in his essay "Man, Android, and Machine."[16] He even tried to boost his own creative abilities by enhancing communication between his brain's hemispheres.[17] Like Nietzsche, who believed he was Dionysus at the end of his life, Dick's imagination was so fertile that it caused him to experience some psychological problems from 1974 until his death in 1982.[18] If Dick were less hampered by visions in the last eight years of his life we might not have had *VALIS* (1981),

---

14. This statement is based on both the working methods of many professional writers and on research demonstrating enhanced athletic performance as a result of mental rehearsal. *See,* e.g., Driskell, Copper, and Moran 1994:481-492, a meta-analysis of more than 70 studies.

15. Palmer 2003:86.

16. The philosophical essay appears in Dick 1995:211-232.

17. Sutin 1989:212.

18. In 1974 Dick began having delusions that he was living in the distant past (Pinsky 2003:159). Although he had some very strange psychological experiences, he was always able to come back to reality, and he was in relatively good psychological shape from around 1976-82. Writing *VALIS* was actually therapeutic (David Gill 2009 personal communication).

but we almost certainly would have had half a dozen other books of perhaps even greater significance.[19]

To develop creativity and imagination it is probably necessary to temporarily escape the censoring part of the mind—the editing side of the brain—which is critical and judgmental. One way to do this is to write quickly, like Dick did, getting that first draft down on paper before the editor can catch up with you and say, "Hey, slow down, and give me a chance to look this over." Some writers have found meditation increases imagination.[20] Others suggest that nootropics have a valid place in boosting creative thought.[21] If a genius like Philip K. Dick was interested in enhancing creativity, it stands to reason that the pursuit of *additional* creativity is a valid goal for any writer, and it's a sure bet that new methods of achieving this goal will be discovered in the not too distant future.

HOW TO DEVELOP A CONTEMPORARY STYLE

No writer had a more contemporary style than Dick. His lifelong ambition to combine SF with mainstream literature pushed him to develop narrative and descriptive talents that left other science fiction writers in the dust. For this reason, if you have any interest in science fiction you'll find his novels and stories helpful in developing a free-flowing modern writing style. But his technique is perfectly applicable to mainstream fiction and, indeed, is no different from the best you will find in Updike, Mailer or Styron. We'll examine three issues under the heading of style: motivation, sentence length, and character description.

---

19. *VALIS* is an important and highly regarded work, but it is also self-centered, convoluted, and marred by structural difficulties. The story is told from the first and third person, and the character Horselover Fat is an alter ego of Philip K. Dick. This kind of confusion between character and author is creative, funny, and revealing; but Lawrence Kubie argues that eccentricity that rises to the level of neurosis (which may be what we have here) can hamper the creative process (Kubie 1958).

20. Lynch 2006.

21. Pregnenolone and vinpocetine, for example, are nootropics that improve brain function (Kurzweil and Grossman 2004:276-277). Dr. Ray Sahelian, M.D., suggests that the former might boost creativity (Sahelian 1997:46).

In the eighteenth and nineteenth centuries, writers handled motivation by bringing in extended discussions of a character's past. Dickens, for example, goes on at length about Esther's parentage in *Bleak House* to illumine why Lady Dedlock, her mother, must never speak to her again;[22] Dostoevsky talks directly to the reader and explains that motivation is more complex than even *he* can reveal in *The Idiot*;[23] and in *Wuthering Heights* there is an extended discussion of Heathcliff's origins and how he came to be the person he is.[24] Dick cuts to the chase and brings in his character's motivation in an entirely different manner and an entirely modern way. In *The Three Stigmata of Palmer Eldritch* Richard Hnatt's motivation for seeking evolution therapy (which makes the brain more powerful) is sketched in deft touches with dialog and thought: "I'm up with the greats, he said to himself," indicating that he feels he'll be increasing his status, and later he tells his wife, "The farther we get away from them [our ancestors in caves] the better," indicating that he believes the therapy will be the next step in natural evolution and something that should be sought out.[25]

To use Dick's streamlined motivation technique, compress background facts and details to the barest minimum. Don't abbreviate them beyond what is needed to convey proper motives, but don't go on for pages like Dickens, Dostoevsky, or Brontë. A few lines of dialog or a few thoughts from a character will suffice to orient readers to that character's motivations. Readers will use their own imagination to take it from there. If the reasons for your characters' actions are truthful, it will suffice to limn them briefly. That's the modern way.

In the eighteenth and nineteenth centuries, sentences and paragraphs were longer, as a general rule, than they are in modern prose. You may find value in studying Thomas de Quincey's celebrated prose style, but his rolling meter and convoluted periodic sentences are not

---

22. Chapter thirty-six.

23. In chapter three of part four.

24. Heathcliff's childhood is described in chapter four, narrated as part of Nelly Dean's story about the past.

25. Dick 1965:66-67.

the norm in modern books. Dick enjoyed great literature and learned from it, but he didn't make the mistake of copying its dense sentence structure. Learn from the past, but keep in mind what needs to be trimmed to modern standards. Chapter four of *Do Androids Dream of Electric Sheep?* (1968) begins with the simple thoughts of the hero: "Maybe I'm worried, Rick Deckard conjectured, that what happened to Dave will happen to me. An andy smart enough to laser him could probably take me, too." Dick fleshes in the hero's motivation in two swift sentences. If your taste runs to prolixity, you may wish to curtail it somewhat for a more modern style.

Now Dickens—to whom we shall compare Dick, as though (how fortuitously!) the similarity in their names bespeaks a similarity in their approach—is sweet and oh so charming and oh so delightful and oh so at the top of his form when it comes to description that to cite a flaw in him is to court disaster; but at the risk of doing so, and to make an important point, we'll compare his introduction of a character to Dick's. Dickens introduces Lady Dedlock by describing her physically and, to a modern ear, at greater length than we're accustomed to:

> She has beauty still, and if it be not in its heyday, it is not yet in its autumn. She has a fine face—originally of a character that would be rather called very pretty than handsome, but improved into classicality by the acquired expression of her fashionable state. Her figure is elegant, and has the effect of being tall. Not that she is so, but that "the most is made," as the Honourable Bob Stables has frequently asserted upon oath, "of all her points." The same authority observes that she is perfectly got up; and remarks in commendation of her hair especially, that she is the best-groomed woman in the whole stud.

How can you fault this, really; it's witty and self-assured and at the same time gets the physical description across. The modern style, however, has abbreviated everything, most especially this kind of effusive physical description; today a sentence suffices where previously a paragraph or more was de rigueur.

When describing people Dick resorts to a similar Dickensian humor. In *Ubik* (1969), for example, he paints a droll portrait of Mrs. Frick, the secretary of Glen Runciter, an executive who runs a company staffed by anti-psis who can block psychic mindreading: "Withered, timorous Mrs. Frick, her face dabbed with spots of artificial color to compensate for her general ancient grayness. ..." He continues in the same whimsical manner Dickens so often employs: "She both advanced toward him and retreated, a difficult maneuver which Mrs. Frick alone could carry off. It had taken her ten decades of practice." Note that Dick has incorporated all the same Dickensian humor but in one fifth the space. Compression, compression, compression. It's the name of the game today. In chapter five he describes Fred Zafsky with one withering sentence from Runciter's viewpoint: "He fixed his gaze on a flabby, big-footed, middle-aged, unnatural-looking individual with pasted-down hair, muddy skin plus a peculiar protruding Adam's apple—clad, for this occasion, in a shift dress the color of a baboon's ass." Not only does Dick have men wearing dresses in his fantastical future, he has the panache to put a satirical description like that into the book. But the main point to note is that this is all done in the space of a single sentence; no paragraph is devoted to description like in our nineteenth-century masters. Go ahead and use some Dickensian humor yourself by incorporating satire into physical description, just remember to keep it short and to the point.

HOW TO WRITE ROMANTIC SCENES

It's a sign of his mainstream technique and competence as a writer that we can even learn how to write a *romantic* scene from Philip K. Dick. "Science fiction is considered to be something for adolescents, for just high-school kids and for disturbed people in general to read in America," said Dick, "so we are limited in our writing to books which have no sex, no violence and no deep ideas."[26] But Dick was a

---

26. Dick 1977b. This videotaped interview gives a rare glimpse of the writer talking freely to a French reporter about his work and his paranoia.

master of all forms of fiction and studied mainstream work to incorporate its ideas in his fiction. The love scene between Rick Deckard and the android Rachael Rosen illustrates how to craft an entire chapter around a romantic interlude. The scene includes three elements needed for a contemporary love scene: preparation, romantic banter, and the first kiss. The *preparation* includes any thoughts the characters might have about each other that include longing, love, or affection. Since this scene is written in limited third-person viewpoint, we enter Rick's mind alone. The description of the android is from his viewpoint, and he notices that "Rachael had been modeled on the Celtic type of build, anachronistic and attractive. Below the brief shorts her legs, slender, had a neutral, nonsexual quality, not much rounded off in nubile curves."[27] Like most of Dick's heroines, she is slender, young, and dark haired. The irony in the scene, and the science-fiction element par excellence, is the fact that Rick is finding himself attracted to a machine. Usually *romantic banter* precedes a first kiss, but here Dick almost completely transposes the elements. "I wonder what it's like to kiss an android, he said to himself. Leaning forward an inch he kissed her dry lips."[28] In the event your characters are both human, there will almost invariably be a response, which can be described to heighten the scene; in this case, the reaction is nonexistent because Rachael is an android. But apparently she *does* have feelings because shortly after *the first kiss* she tells him that she wants him to make love to her; in fact, she talks him into it when he gets cold feet. Again it is ironic that Rachael (an android) is the one to bring up the subject of love. There is additional irony in that Dick includes technical terms—such as the "Boneli Reflex-Arc Test" and discussion of specific types of androids, like the "Nexus-6 type"—in their romantic interchange. Nevertheless, despite the technical lingo and the transposition of the elements, their conversation has an undercurrent of romance, which is very appropriate, if not actually required, in a proper love scene.

---

27. Dick 1968:164.

28. Dick 1968:165.

A fourth element, *the fade out*, is optional. Technically a fade out only occurs in a film, but in a novel the term can be used to refer to the fact that an implied sexual encounter occurs between chapter breaks. Dick accomplishes this nicely by having Rachael demand that Rick get into bed in the next to last line of the chapter, the last line of which is "He got into bed."

To write a romantic scene one need only rearrange the elements so that the kiss occurs *after* the romantic banter, which is the more usual order. It is a matter of choice whether or not to include a description of the physical encounter. Sometimes, as in *Do Androids Dream of Electric Sheep?*, it's not integral to the plot and so is not included. Other times, such as in *Endless Love* (1979) by Scott Spencer, in which there is a twenty-two-page sex scene, the physical encounter reveals aspects of the characters and is necessary.

HOW TO MOVE DIALOGUE ALONG

Dick used his mainstream writing talents to produce dialogue that moves along much better than the typical fare we find in the pages of science fiction. Only two aspects of that dialog will be mentioned here because Dick used them to such good effect: The first is the technique of splitting a paragraph of dialogue to include the character attribution in the first sentence, and the second is known as tight focus, where two characters talk even though others are present.

An example of the first technique occurs in chapter four of *A Scanner Darkly* (1977) where Bob Arctor, a drug addict who is also an under-cover narcotics agent, is having a discussion with his friend Barris. Arctor is about to make a big speech in which he recounts what happened in a dream. To establish who is speaking, Dick begins the speech like this:

"'A dream awoke me,' Arctor said. 'A religious dream. In it there was this huge clap of thunder ...'" And the rest of the paragraph is Arctor's quoted speech. By mentioning the speaker's name briefly, without any character direction or any narration about what is happening, the identity of the speaker is quickly and effortlessly established. You can use the same technique to orient readers when writing dialogue that has large paragraphs of speech. Occasionally you can add little notes about what a character is doing, for example: "'Listen,' Barris said, rocking back and forth in agitation." These little snippets of information about what is happening keep the scene alive in a reader's mind and make it more than simply a transcript of what was said.

The second way to move dialog along is to keep *dialogue shifts* to a minimum in a scene. Even though a number of people are present, Dick often focuses on just two of them when rendering dialogue for a scene, as he does in chapter two of *A Scanner Darkly* when the master of ceremonies introduces Bob Arctor and Arctor makes his speech to the Anaheim Lions Club. By restricting speech to these two individuals, Dick effectively pulls the focus tight in the scene, and while the reader knows that there are many people present, the scene becomes manageable and understandable because of this limited focus. This is especially helpful in a medium like a novel where (unlike film) you cannot see a group and make sense of things visually but must compose the scene mentally. The same technique was used by the ancient Greek dramatists, who usually arranged for only two characters to speak even if more were onstage at the same time.

The novels of Philip K. Dick are doorways into alternative universes and for today's writers they're also doorways to some of the most helpful literary techniques of mainstream fiction. If you can adapt some of his techniques—such as writing quickly, using the full power of your imagination, concise character motivation and physical description, effective love scenes, and moving dialog along—your prose will sparkle with the same modern style that readers have come to expect from contemporary authors.

CHAPTER 20

WRITE LIKE
Tom Wolfe

The man in the white suit is one of the most innovative writers of the past four decades. His sparkle and wit, his embracing and defining of a new genre in journalism, and then his metamorphosis into one of the most accomplished novelists in America makes Tom Wolfe a man to keep your eye on if you wish to develop a writing style that speaks to contemporary readers—or any readers, for that matter. What Wolfe brings to the table is a smorgasbord of devices and techniques, some so dazzling and experimental that they have caused controversy.

Born in 1931 in Virginia, Wolfe is an only child. He went to Yale and graduated with a Ph.D. in American Studies. This has been his springboard to everything he has done and also the undergirding of his great critique of American fiction. According to Wolfe the biggest mistake writers are making today is failing to go out into the great vast cornucopia that is America.[1] There are not enough writers taking the challenge to report on the American scene the way Steinbeck did. Steinbeck, who wrote *The Grapes of Wrath* (1939) after making a trip to California and witnessing firsthand how the migrant farmers worked, was able to capture all the elements of the current American situation because he got his hands dirty, mingled with real people, and wasn't afraid to report what he had observed. By Wolfe's criteria, one of the best novels of recent time would be his own *A Man in Full* (1998), precisely because it is filled with realistic details about America today.

---

1. Wolfe's critique can be found in his essay "My Three Stooges" in *Hooking Up* (Wolfe 2000:145-171).

THE NEW JOURNALISM

The New Journalism is a style of writing nonfiction using fiction techniques. The fiction techniques include the use of scenes, character development, dialog, and penetrating into the central consciousness of characters to reveal their thoughts. In some cases the author will also put himself into the story.

The techniques of the New Journalists were borrowed from fiction writers, which is why Tom Wolfe's writing style—in books like *The Electric Kool-Aid Acid Test* (1968), *The Right Stuff* (1978), and *Hooking Up* (2000)—can easily be adopted by novelists. In fact Wolfe used all of the New Journalism techniques when he began writing fiction. *The Bonfire of the Vanities* (1987), for example, uses scenes, develops characters, and is filled with realistic dialog. In addition, Wolfe penetrates into the minds of his characters with the kind of internal monologues that make fiction so exciting. After Sherman McCoy has been questioned by two detectives, Wolfe goes into his mind to tell us his deepest thoughts, explaining that "he was swept by an overpowering dismay. His entire central nervous system told him he had just suffered a catastrophic defeat. ... He had been outrageously violated—but how had it happened? How had these two ... insolent ... Low Rent ... *animals* ... invaded his life?" Wolfe goes right into Sherman's innermost thoughts to reveal his feelings of crisis and catastrophe, including, along with the thoughts, details about the status of the contestants—Sherman is patrician and these two "Low Rent" animals are at the opposite end of the financial, and status, spectrum.

When rendering thoughts remember to hit the reader with serious material. For example, take a look at this shot into the mind of Sherman McCoy after he is arrested:

> Sherman reached around to his right to retrieve his jacket and pull it over the handcuffs. When he realized that he had to move both hands in order to pick up the coat, and when the effort caused the manacles to cut into his wrists, a flood of humiliation ... and shame! ... swept over him. This was himself, the very self who existed in a unique and

sacrosanct and impenetrable crucible at the center of his mind, who was now in manacles ... in the Bronx ... Surely this was a hallucination, a nightmare, a trick of the mind, and he would pull back a translucent layer ... and ...[2]

This excerpt from *The Bonfire of the Vanities* contains a description of what's happening and also zips into the mind of the hero. In fact, this little passage is somewhat self-referential and hints at exactly how Wolfe achieves his effects. It's a writer's "trick of the mind" in which he seems to open up the mental activity of a character and give us entrée into his consciousness. Moreover, Wolfe tells us just where the writer of fiction should aim his intracranial microscope—right into the "unique and sacrosanct and impenetrable crucible at the center of his mind"; a place which, when a writer sets his sights on it, actually isn't that impenetrable after all. That's one of the big joys of writing in the New Journalism style—you get to look into the soul of the boy sitting next to you, to use Woody Allen's phrase. In short, you get to see inside another person's mind.

I can think of no more important lesson to learn from the amazing Tom Wolfe. As he himself has told us (explaining his technique clearly so that anyone can use it), the goal is to penetrate into the central nervous system of the characters. The way to do this in nonfiction is to ask your subjects what they were thinking. For example, Wolfe interviewed some astronauts and asked them what they were thinking just before blastoff. Then he put their thoughts into *The Right Stuff.* In fiction, of course, it's easier because you don't have to ask, you simply have to make it up. Naturally, though, this involves substantial creative effort, and sometimes it also involves research.

Wolfe doesn't usually bother revealing the mundane thoughts his characters have; instead he sets his sights on bigger game, giving his readers a bird's-eye view into the minds of his characters when they're in the midst of some terrible quandary, when they're being psychologically pounded to a pulp by someone bigger and stronger, or when

2. Wolfe 1987:468.

they're suffering some anguish or mental turmoil. Not infrequently this mental angst is humiliation and shame; in this way he is like Dostoevsky. We've seen how Sherman felt humiliation in *The Bonfire of the Vanities*. Similarly, in *A Man in Full* Wolfe penetrates into the mind of Martha Croker in chapter twenty-one, where we learn that "She no longer had to articulate the thought in her mind to feel the pain and humiliation. She merely had to hear the name, and the *feeling*—which was in fact worse than pain and humiliation—which, at bottom, was *shame*—swept over her in a scalding wave."[3]

Nothing could be more exciting to readers than to delve into the mind of an interesting character. If you wish to adopt this technique in your own writing, follow Wolfe's advice and present the thoughts of your fictional characters by delving into their minds when they're in the midst of keen emotional turmoil and perplexity. Strong emotions like shame, anger, and humiliation will work best. And when writing nonfiction, remember to ask your subjects what was going through their minds during crucial moments in the story. You'll be surprised what they tell you—and so will your readers.

HOW TO CHARACTERIZE LIKE TOM WOLFE

Studying how Wolfe characterizes can be instructive for any modern writer. Like Dickens, whom he admires, Wolfe typically exaggerates a character's key traits, poking ironic fun at him and making his faults and foibles larger than life. For example, in portraying Charlie Croker, a real-estate developer who is crude, lewd, and rude, Wolfe doesn't focus on his strength (he's a former football player) or his wealth (he owns a plantation) as much as he does on his weaknesses. All throughout chapter twenty-one Croker is humiliated by the way a young football star, Fanon, ignores him. Then at the conclusion of the chapter, when Croker has been forced into promising to help Fanon (who has been accused of rape), Croker's angst is brought to a fever pitch: "So he was to be the lone

---

3. Wolfe 1998:541.

white person speaking out on behalf of this lout! ... It was impossible! Who could he look in the face after that? ... All that which comprised the great Cap'm Charlie—punctured, deflated, humiliated abjectly, pitied."[4] Again notice how Wolfe, at the highpoint of the chapter, zings us right to the humiliation of his hero. He makes him squirm and suffer. He takes off the gloves and punishes his hero.

If you want to write sizzling fiction, follow Wolfe's lead. Don't baby your characters, especially the hero. Don't let your sympathy for the hero (who usually represents a large part of your own unconscious psyche) stop you from making him suffer the way Wolfe makes Croker suffer. Pile on the shame, the humiliation, the angst, the turmoil, and the degradation. In this way you're bound to generate reader interest and reader identification. And the way to accomplish this, the way to pile on all this emotional suffering, the way to make your hero feel the slings and arrows of outrageous fortune is to penetrate into his consciousness and reveal his suffering firsthand, from the inside, from the core of his mind.

Once you learn to make your hero suffer ... and once you learn to follow him in his suffering by staying close to him, close to his interior mental activity—that's when you will have accomplished your best work as a novelist and a writer. Because to get to the heart of a character is the heart of writing. It is the one thing that writing does better than any other medium: music, theater, film. Getting to the heart of a character is getting to the heart of writing. And no one teaches this better than Wolfe.

MESMERIZING READERS WITH DEATH AND DESTRUCTION

In addition to delving into the minds of readers, Wolfe has a few other tricks up his sleeve that a fiction writer needs to know. In reading *The Right Stuff*, which employs all the best New Journalism scene structure, you might miss the device it's so adroitly used and so effortlessly woven

---

4. Wolfe 1998:628.

into the story: but one technique Wolfe makes use of over and over again is the technique of presenting the reader with vivid details about death and destruction.

Why, you may wonder, should this be of interest to you, especially if you're going to be writing emotionally pleasant tales about people who drink tea, go for outings in yachts, and vacation in Acapulco? The reason is that emotionally laden scenes (such as death scenes) fascinate readers. They always have and they always will. You may not have death scenes in your bucolic first novel, but studying how Wolfe uses the device will make you more aware of how to make your emotional highpoints higher and more effective.

In *The Right Stuff* there is a plethora of deaths as astronauts blow up in planes, crash-land to their death, parachute out of planes and have their parachute fail to open ... so that they fall to earth and hit it with a tremendous and reverberating ... splat! This theme of death and danger hangs heavy over the entire book. The astronauts have the "right stuff" precisely because they face this danger and yet do their job with courage and bravery. All around them men are buying it. "His Majesty the Baby of just twenty-odd years back, has been reduced to a charred hulk with wings and shanks sticking out of it."[5] But the astronauts persevere. They don't let another man's death scare them. Pete Conrad is sent on a mission to find one of his friends and discovers the bloody remains of the body "wound up there in the middle of a tree trunk."[6] Does that deter our boy from continuing his work as a test pilot and astronaut? Not on your life! It only gives him more determination, more machismo, more audacity. When Chuck Yeager learns that two test pilots coming in for a dangerous landing on an aircraft carrier narrowly missed death, one ejecting to safety at the last minute, and one staying in the malfunctioning jet and landing safely, he "was tremendously impressed by those two decisions by two men."[7] The smell of death,

---

5. Wolfe 1979:3.

6. Wolfe 1979:6.

7. Wolfe 1979:352.

the presence of death, and the specter of death haunts the book like a refrain.

Your own work will take a giant leap forward if you adopt this device. That doesn't mean you need to mop the floor with buckets of blood or strew the landscape with corpses the way Wolfe does in parts of *The Right Stuff*, but it does mean that you'll take every opportunity to hammer home a powerful emotion, one that is central to your theme. It might be destruction, but it might just as easily be love. It could be desire, or threat, or any number of other powerful feelings. Wolfe used death and destruction to good effect in *The Right Stuff*; other writers have used the danger element to keep a story moving along. Think of Jon Krakauer's *Into Thin Air* (1998) or the Ernest Shackleton saga, recounted in many heart-pounding books.[8]

INCORPORATING 'STATUS LIFE' INTO YOUR WRITING

Wolfe sees American fiction as being in a slump. It's anemic. It has been swamped by experimental novels. Realism is gone. The road back to reality can only be trod by those writers who stake out their territory in the great "carnival" of America and, piece by piece, enumerate its particulars—the long empty roads of *In Cold Blood*, the migrant workers of *The Grapes of Wrath*, the multimillionaires and blacks in *The Bonfire of the Vanities* and *A Man In Full*. This is the way back to reality ... and to success.

If you want to avoid the fate of writers who have "slipped off the face of the earth" because their books have not tackled American reality (writers as luminous as Mailer, Updike, and John Irving) then, Wolfe warns, you must take stock of America, go out into the wild of its lands, and—report! The way Hunter S. Thompson did with *Fear and Loathing in Las Vegas* (1971). The way journalists do. The way John

---

8. The best narrative account of Shackleton's Imperial Trans-Antarctic Expedition is *Endurance* (1959) by Alfred Lansing. The book reads like a novel but is based on diary accounts of the men who survived the two-year-long ordeal.

Sack did with *M* (1967). The way Michael Herr did with *Dispatches* (1977).[9] The way Tom Wolfe does in all his novels. This is the way of Balzac and Dickens and Zola, the way of naturalism and realism and writing that takes stock of America and reports what is real.

If Wolfe is right, a writer who does this is going to be much more successful than one who ponders the ineffable or tries to write a myth or a fairy tale.

But how is one to master this subject, the vastness of America? What kind of story should one write? Wolfe gives us liberty to select any subject from the vast canvass of America, as long as we keep to the reality of the story by including plenty of realistic people and accurate details. Wolfe is especially fond of the use of what he calls "status life," which he defines: "This is the recording of everyday gestures, habits, manners, customs, styles of furniture, clothing, decoration, styles of traveling, eating, keeping house, modes of behaving toward children, servants, superiors, inferiors, peers, plus the various looks, glances, poses, styles of walking and other symbolic details that might exist within a scene."[10] By recording all these details the writer will be creating a richly realistic scene that reflects the American way of life, or some aspect of the American way of life. That is the kind of reality that a writer needs to plunge the reader into in order to keep the interest of the reader today. In the process, you might also be revitalizing the anemic American fiction scene and writing the great American novel.

Examples of recording the status life include details about what people wear and the places they live. For instance in *The Bonfire of the Vanities* Kramer, an attorney who is rather down and out, sees one of his classmates: "[H]e was wearing a covert-cloth Chesterfield topcoat with a golden brown velvet collar and carrying one of those burgundy leather attaché cases that come from Mädler or T. Anthony on Park Avenue." Wolfe is a master of details of the high life. But he is able to

---

9. Two excellent books about the New Journalism are Marc Weingarten's *The Gang That Wouldn't Write Straight* (2006) and *The New New Journalism* (2005), edited by Robert S. Boynton. They're filled with tips on writing that can help modern storytellers of nonfiction as well as fiction.

10. Wolfe and Johnson 1973:32.

contrast it with the low life just as easily. When Kramer sees people on the D train wearing running sneakers, Wolfe contrasts those sneakers with the ones worn by the affluent midtown crowd:

> This [on the D train] was not for reasons of Young Fit & Firm Chic, the way it was downtown, where you saw a lot of well-dressed young white people going off to work in the morning wearing these sneakers. No, on the D train the reason was, they were cheap. On the D train these sneakers were like a sign around the neck reading SLUM or EL BARRIO.[11]

Other examples of status details include how Sherman walks his daughter, Campbell, to the bus stop in the morning. It's not just a bus stop. It's on Fifth Avenue and the bus is a private bus with a driver and chaperone sent from her private school.[12] There is hardly a page in *The Bonfire of the Vanities* that is not chock full of these status details. The same effect is at work in *A Man in Full* where Conrad Hensley's unemployed down-and-out furniture (including "a $9.95 folding aluminum chair from Price Club") is described in telling detail,[13] as is Charlie Croker's fleet of private aircraft (including the fact that he has "a *painting* installed on [one] airplane worth $190,000").[14]

When you set out to write about people it will help if you describe what they wear and the homes they live in, especially if these details will reflect on your characters' status vis-à-vis other people in the story. Like Wolfe, observe these details about people and record them, whether they reflect richness or poverty because the effort to get such details right will go a long way toward making your work come alive with readers.

USING CHARACTER VOCABULARY

Wolfe also believes it's important to get the *vocabulary* of the people you're writing about into the novel. This doesn't just mean using a Southern

---

11. Wolfe 1987:37.
12. Wolfe 1987:49-50.
13. Wolfe 1998:174.
14. Wolfe 1998:54-55 (emphasis in original).

accent when writing about Southerners or a Bronx accent when writing about certain New Yorkers. It also means incorporating these vocabulary details into the narrative itself.

In *The Right Stuff* he tells how Yeager and other pilots hate the publicity that reporters brought to them. They hate the way journalists open up the process of doing their job by exposing the very core of it to scrutiny and uttering words like "fear and bravery." Wolfe tells us about the pilots' dislike, using words the pilots themselves would use: "It was obscene!" he writes. And "It was repulsive!" These are not Wolfe's thoughts or the voice of Wolfe; instead it is the voice of the pilots that has crept into the narrative, tinging it with the thought patterns of the characters. In *The Bonfire of the Vanities* the same device is used throughout the book. For example, when Sherman tosses his jacket on the bed, we are told: "Cost a goddamned fortune." This isn't a line of dialog. It is simply a narrative statement from the point of view of one of the characters.

The device of using vocabulary that would be used by your people is part and parcel of writing from the point of view of the major characters. This, Wolfe insists, is one of the chief methods of the fiction writer and also one of the techniques that the New Journalists appropriated for their purposes.[15] When you write from a character's point of view you're more likely to engage readers, bringing them up close to the action and to the feelings of the people in the story. This vicarious thrill of living another life is what fiction is all about.

In order to detail this information you need to research people and their thoughts. To discover people in their natural habitat it is important to talk with them. Wolfe says it is crucial when doing research to be friendly and to associate with the people you hope to describe in your work. Eventually they'll open up and start telling you their secrets, their hopes, their fears. He spent three years researching the people in *The Bonfire of the Vanities*.[16] He spent eleven researching *A Man In Full*.

---

15. Wolfe and Johnson 1973:32.

16. Scura 1990:222.

While you needn't spend years doing research, the fact that one of the century's most successful novelists spends so much time doing research should suggest that there is value in the activity, value that will make your writing glitter with all the semblance of realism Wolfe claims is so essential to revitalizing the American novel. If *you* want to be part of that revitalization plan … you just might want to pay attention to the advice—and the example—of the man in the white suit.

CHAPTER 21

WRITE LIKE

Stephen King

Aside from the fact that no less an authority than William Faulkner recommends reading widely in different styles and genres, there's still another compelling reason why you might want to study Stephen King's novels no matter what kind of writing *you* do. King is the number one horror writer in America but you don't have to like horror to learn from him, you don't have to like thrillers, you don't even have to like modern American fiction. The key reason for reading Stephen King is suspense, and as we'll see in a moment suspense is one of the most important tools of the storyteller.

Born in 1947, a lastborn with one older brother, Stephen King grew up in a middle-class neighborhood in Maine. He was cared for by his mother since his father had left the family when Stephen was two. As a young boy his imagination was always strong, and when he started writing he immediately realized it was the most enjoyable way he could earn a living. Married in 1971 King worked for a time as a high school English teacher. He was also employed as a creative writing teacher at the University of Maine. The success of his novel *Carrie* (1974) changed all that, however, and once he started publishing he became an unstoppable force. To date he has published about a hundred short stories and forty novels, many of which have been translated to the silver screen. He even wrote a book on his craft, *On Writing* (2000). But despite using that forum to talk about his life and his approach to grammar and style, he left out what is probably the most important subject: the whole issue of suspense. Yes, the one thing that Stephen King is probably most famous for, the horrific buildup, the incremental *tick-tick-tick-tick* of the bomb, the gradual arrival of the monster, the slow but hinted-at materialization of the ghosts and ghouls that are festering underneath the normal world and inside normal-looking people like Randall Flagg ... this is omitted from *On Writing*, and it's pretty clear why. As he states in the introduction, "Fiction writers, present company included, don't understand very much about what they do."

I'm not suggesting that Stephen King doesn't *know* how to create suspense—far from it! In fact, suspense is so important to what he does that he actually refers to himself as "a suspense novelist."[1] I'm simply saying that he creates it almost intuitively, he doesn't use a magic formula. But as we'll see, even though Stephen King doesn't tell you how to create suspense in his writing book, he sure *does* tell you in his novels, and any analyst can see the pattern, which you'll understand fully by the end of this chapter.

"But I'm not writing a thriller," you say? "Why should suspense be so important *to me?*"

The answer to that question lies in the fact that no matter what type of story you're writing, suspense is integral to the process of storytelling. Shakespeare never considered structuring *Hamlet* so that the hero would be killed in the first act; the whole play builds suspense by making the audience eager to know whether the hero will discover the true killer of his father and whether Hamlet will try to avenge the murder himself. Your story may reveal information at a fast or slow pace, but no matter what pace you decide to adopt you'll never tell all in the first scene—or the second, or the third. Instead, you'll employ suspense in varying degrees, as all writers do, to move the story forward and engage reader interest and propel the plot to its conclusion.

---

1. King 2000:161.

WHAT EXACTLY IS SUSPENSE?

In its simplest terms suspense consists of making a reader anticipate some future event. Usually writers try to make readers experience a feeling of *apprehension* about what is going to happen next, but sometimes suspense consists merely in getting the reader to look forward to something with more or less eager anticipation or curiosity. That's the technical definition, and that being said it's important to note that Stephen King usually creates the kind of suspense that causes readers to *worry* about what's going to happen next. In other words in King's books suspense is writ large: It's not simple curiosity (as it might be in Shakespeare) or anticipation (as it might be in Jane Austen), it's usually nail-biting, sweat-producing, heart-pounding worry.

Suspense is so important to stories because almost all readers are inclined to *enjoy* the experience of suspense. Now, some critics claim that suspense is low art, the lowest form of all. In *Aspects of the Novel* (1927), E.M. Forster argues that suspense appeals to a caveman mentality: "The primitive audience was an audience of shock-heads, gaping around the campfire ... and only kept awake by suspense. What would happen next?"[2] In actuality the best literature, including Dickens, Dante, and Shakespeare, employs suspense and I doubt anyone would call them or their audience "primitive." Suspense is not something low or crude or anything you should be embarrassed about incorporating into your work. When you get right down to it, suspense lies at the heart of all storytelling and is an integral part of the best literature. There have even been book-length studies written about how authors like George Eliot, Charlotte Brontë, and Charles Dickens employ suspense.[3] But even though Shakespeare and Melville build suspense for particular narrative reasons,[4] there is no question that Stephen King

---

2. Forster 1927:26.

3. *See, e.g.*, Levine 2003:65-83 and Coolidge 1967.

4. Shakespeare makes good use of suspense in all his plays. For example, in *King Lear* after the king divides his realm, we worry about what will happen to him, especially after two of his daughters prove ungrateful. Melville employs suspense in many ways in *Moby-Dick*, including by building up to the voyage of the *Pequod* through an extensive introductory section in which we learn of the dangers to be expected on a sea voyage chasing whales.

FICTION WRITING *Master Class*

can rightly be called the master of modern suspense. His methods of creating suspense are relatively easy to see and, for that reason, will prove to be helpful for writers to study. This is not to say you shouldn't also learn to create suspense from Shakespeare, Dickens, or Melville; but the fact is that first lessons in suspense ought to be clear as a bell, and no writer is more clear about suspense than the King.

LITERARY SUSPENSE

Before we get to Stephen King, a little digression about literary suspense is in order to set the stage, so to speak, and to place King's use of suspense in context. I believe you'll say "Ah-ha!" when you see just how his use of suspense fits into the big literary picture and how it may be quite similar to, and also occasionally different from, the kind of suspense created by some of the most celebrated writers of all time. When Norman Mailer tells us in *The Armies of the Night* (1968) about his arrest on the steps of the Pentagon, he creates suspense by building up to the event in the same way that Stephen King builds up to the horror in Room 217, by talking about a danger (the possibility of getting arrested and killed by overeager police officers who are protecting the Pentagon) and by repeating references to this danger throughout the narrative.

Some readers may be thinking that simply because we're looking at Stephen King the technique must be reserved for popular fiction or thrillers or horror novels. Nothing could be further from the truth! The most elevated fiction, the most literary nonfiction, the most ambitious writing of any age—all of it relies upon the device of delay and suspense. Dostoevsky employed delay and suspense in building up to the murder of the two women by Raskolnikov and then in the unraveling of his confession. Melville employed delay and suspense in building up to the hunting of Moby Dick. Shakespeare employed delay and suspense in *Hamlet* so many times it would take a substantial digression to discuss all of the examples.[5]

---

5. One example will suffice: When the players are mentioned there is an extended discussion about them before they appear, heightening suspense, and audience interest (Clemen 1972:66).

But suspense is also a function of caring about characters who are in potential peril. In a Stephen King story that peril is usually the loss of life and limb. In a romantic comedy the peril more often takes the form of loss of love and fidelity. In a Dickens novel the peril is likely to be the revelation of a secret (about Lady Dedlock or Magwitch, for example). In *The Catcher in the Rye* the peril lies in the danger that Holden won't be taken seriously by people, something that for him would be a fate worse than death. The danger in your story could be any number of different things, but if you can name it and understand it, then you can heighten reader pleasure by withholding the resolution of that important issue for as long as possible, holding readers in suspense.

SUSPENSE, STEPHEN KING STYLE

Analysis reveals that there are three steps that Stephen King invariably employs to create suspense. First, he mentions or provides hints about something that can produce either reader curiosity, or a problem, or a *worry* somewhere down the line. Second, he mentions this worrisome thing or idea a number of times *after* he first introduces it, and before the payoff. I refer to this second step as a *callback* since it's similar to the way accomplished stage comedians refer to an earlier joke during the course of a set. Third, King brings suspense to a peak during the payoff, the section of the story where the horror is most intense.

Remember that in Stephen King's novels suspense is usually centered on creating reader worry. Put more simply, he wants the reader to feel that something bad is going to happen to some character the reader cares about. For example, the situational suspense in *Misery* (1987) is clear from the moment readers realize that Paul is imprisoned in Annie's house and is at her mercy. Much of the worry is created by the thoughts of our imprisoned hero: "She's going to go out now. She's going to go out and I'll hear her pouring the rinse-water down the sink and maybe she won't come back for hours because maybe she's not done punishing me yet." Paul's worrisome internal monologue continues throughout the entire book; whenever something bad *might* happen the hero worries about it and as a result (since readers sympathize with him) readers worry about it too.

The setup of the story in *Misery* is a device that creates a pattern of continued suspense. Of course the situation is revealed to us largely through the viewpoint character's thoughts, but the situation itself is a separate device used by King to create suspense. The physical confinement of the hero and the fact that he is partly paralyzed is, in itself, enough to create worry. Add to this the fact that his caretaker is a sadist and you have the setup of a situation that is highly fraught with danger. Anyone in (or reading about) such a situation would feel apprehension about what might happen next. The callback technique is brought into play whenever Annie says "Now I must rinse." The first time she says it she tortures Paul, and the recurrence of the phrase reminds readers that more punishment is on the way. The payoff and highpoint of the suspense occurs at the end of the novel when Paul finally attacks and burns Annie from his sickbed, managing through herculean effort to kill her at last.

In *The Stand* (1978) similar apprehension is created after the virus claims its first victims. The first part of the novel centers on the effects of the virus and during this introductory section it is partly through internal monologue that King lets us know how bad things might become. For example, Stu Redman thinks: "It hit you like the flu or a summer cold, only it kept on getting worse, presumably until you choked to death on your own snot or until the fever burned you down. It was highly contagious."[6] In the second part of the novel the suspense increases as a group of people struggle to save and rebuild the world after the destruction wrought by the virus. During these two sections, the virus itself functions as a callback, reminding readers that more destruction might occur at any moment. And the third part of the story provides the payoff as readers witness two political factions in a final apocalyptic confrontation.[7]

---

6. King 1978:65.

7. The character portrait of Randall Flagg adds to the suspense since he is obviously a bad man. His killing of Dayna invites readers to wonder what other mayhem he might be capable of committing.

Carrie, King's first novel, shows him already a master of suspense, using anticipatory hints, callbacks, and payoff to increase reader worry. Throughout the novel we wait in anticipation for the heroine to use her telekinetic powers to exact vengeance on a town for the humiliation and ostracism she has endured. Suspense is increased when the girl's overly pious mother reacts antagonistically after her daughter has been invited to the school ball: "Momma was staring at her with wide my-ears-are-deceiving-me eyes. Her nostrils flared like those of a horse that has heard the dry rattle of a snake." A moment later, in disgust, the girls' mother "threw her tea in Carrie's face." This is one in a series of humiliations that Carrie experiences. The reader expects there to be *some* reaction, but the rage that erupts during the payoff section, leaving many dead in town, is certainly the kind of overreaction that no one could predict.

By now it should be clear why King did not describe how to create suspense in *On Writing*: The method varies from book to book. What could he have said, after all—"Create suspense by having a character humiliated"? There's no way that such a specific direction could come close to explaining all the artistry that goes into making *Carrie* work. For example, the main character has to be sympathetic, the bullies have to be real, the mother has to be motivated to be mean, and the reaction of rage has to be deftly drawn and hammered home during the payoff. In truth, it's more helpful to be *less* specific and simply say you create suspense by making readers worry about something. It doesn't have to be humiliation they're worried about, either. The cause of worry, apprehension and anticipation will, of course, be unique to any particular story.

Cujo (1981), for example, builds suspense because readers know that once the dog begins to kill there will be more deaths; the question on everyone's mind is *who* will die next, and *how* will it happen. Among other devices, King uses *promissory words* to create suspense as early as the second page of the novel: "The monster never dies." As if that weren't clear enough: "It came back to Castle Rock again in the summer of 1980." Promissory words can be used anywhere in a novel to suggest that something bad will happen later. In effect, they *predict* bad things.

King's sure feel for suspense even affects his use of figurative language. For example, there is personification and foreboding in his metaphor about the moon being like a monster. "[T]he moon peered in Tad's window like the white and slitted eye of a dead man." Additional suspense is created when King enters the mind of the dog and reveals his thoughts as rabies begins to madden his brain. After the initial attack on Gary, King tells us that "Cujo was no longer sure if he wanted to attack or not. He hurt, he hurt so miserably, and the world was such a crazyquilt of sense and impression—" Because we have seen the dog attack once and then learned that Cujo is uncertain about wanting to attack again, we *worry* about the situation: What will the dog do? Here King has created suspense *by entering the mind of a dog!* In *your* novel you need to figure out what will cause reader curiosity, worry, or anticipation … then add *that* to *your* story.

The type of suspense we're talking about here is also referred to as delay. "Delay consists in not imparting information where it is 'due' in the text, but leaving it for a later stage."[8] *The Shining*, for instance, employs delay by making us wait for the resolution of certain character issues. King supplies a good deal of information in the early chapters about the three main characters: alcoholic Jack Torrance, his long-suffering wife, Wendy, and their psychic son, Danny. Before long we've learned enough about these characters to care about them. In this way, when King drops hints about things that might go wrong, we begin to worry about what it means in terms of their lives. For example, in chapter four King tells us: "[Danny] understood a great many things about his parents, and he knew that many times they didn't like his understandings and many other times refused to believe them. But someday they would have to believe. He was content to wait." This sets up a delay. The information held in reserve is information about two other characters and it is information that appears to be emotionally

8. Rimmon-Kenan 1983:125.

important to the third character, Danny. By delaying revelations and hinting at problems King creates suspense.

Later when the family arrives at the Overlook Hotel, the boy is warned by Hallorann, the cook, to avoid Room 217. This is similar to George Orwell's building up suspense about Room 101. There is something sinister about Room 217, Danny is told, and although the reader is not informed *what* is in the room or *why* it is sinister, the warning is enough to make us worry. And because delay is involved—we don't find out what's in the room until much later—the suspense continues for many pages. King makes readers wait a considerable time before revealing the meaning of many of the suspense points in his novels. Often he revives reader worry with a callback, a repeated mention of the danger. For example, the first time Hallorann warns Danny about Room 217 is early in the story. Then Danny thinks about the room a few chapters later when he passes it during the tour. That's a callback. The room is mentioned a few additional times (more callbacks) until the full significance of the horror behind its door is revealed at the payoff. By stringing readers along with callbacks King keeps worry alive and increases suspense.

Suspense and delay are two sides of the same coin, and from a writer's perspective it's very helpful to focus on the delay aspect because once you start thinking about delay you'll realize how important callbacks are. Without callbacks readers might forget your marvelous little hints about the dangers your characters face. Keep those daggers suspended overhead by pointing up at them now and then so that readers stay worried. By studying how King reiterates the issue of Room 217, for instance, you'll learn that repetition is not wrong; indeed, it's *essential* to good narrative and heightened suspense. By noticing how long he waits to reveal the answer to the gaps he inserts into his tales, you'll see that delay can span scores and hundreds of pages, provided you don't let the reader forget ... provided you string him along with callbacks to the material you're leaving out.

The best way to learn what Stephen King does is not to read his book on writing but to read one of his *novels* ... with a pen in hand.

Circle sections that suggests a problem later down the line, such as Hallorann's warning about the Overlook Hotel, or Wendy's worries about her husband's drinking. Then, as you read the book, wait for the callbacks and mark them as you find them. This would include the sections where Danny passes Room 217 again, or where Wendy wonders about her husband's drinking again, and so on. Finally, circle the payoff where the suspense is highest, such as where Danny enters Room 217, or where Jack's madness causes him to attack Wendy with a roque mallet. In this way you'll learn the three essential steps for creating suspense: Hints about worrisome things, callbacks, and payoff. And before you know it people reading *your* books won't be able to sleep nights.

CONCLUSION

Throughout this book we've analyzed classic texts that you can imitate in order to improve your own style. Some of the techniques we've covered include producing first drafts, plot and character development, foreshadowing, point of view, and suspense. Trial and error will certainly allow you to master those tools of the trade that you wish to perfect. Naturally it is to be expected that some of the topics we've covered will be of *more* interest to you than others. The important point is that by now you've acquired the art of analyzing writing *yourself* and you should have the ability to dissect a work, see it with X-ray-like vision, and understand how it functions. When you fix your gaze upon a book it should melt and dissolve and become putty in your hands so that you can mold its techniques into new works of your own design.

As we close our discussion keep in mind that the ancients considered imitation so important that scarcely a book was written by the Romans and Greeks that didn't openly imitate previous works. Quintilian, probably the most prominent Roman rhetorician, heartily encourages imitation. A modern historian summarizes Quintilian's views on imitation concisely and helpfully for the contemporary writer:

> Good imitation was not, however, literal copying, but rather an understanding both of the general spirit of the original and those things that were admirable in previous writers, whether they be choice of language, arrangement, attitude, or even the subject mat-

ter itself. The imitator does not seek a one-to-one correspondence with a single previous model, nor is his imitation to be slavish (this is mere copying) but rather creative: the writer must appropriate the spirit of his model or models and breathe new life into them, to show how something could be better done, or, if not better done, then well done in a different way.[1]

Now I expect that some of the most exciting work lies ahead for you because *you* will be the one selecting which authors to imitate. And in choosing which works to study and be inspired by you will be forming your own style and your own personal artistic vision. If that's not exciting I don't know what is.

Does imitation ever stop? Do good writers ever feel that they have nothing new to learn? Actually, once you master the art of imitation you can rest assured that you'll always be excited by a new book, a new author, a new style, for you will always be able to absorb something of value from them. And in the final analysis you will be able to give back so much more because you've allowed yourself to take risks and flex new writing muscles you never knew you had. By embracing new artists as well as the classics you'll continue to learn from them all. Salinger was doing that with Kafka even *after* he had completed *The Catcher in the Rye*—he was still learning, still in awe of the great writer, in fact *humbled* by his brilliance. Proof positive that good writers *never* stop learning.

I hope that the prospect of venturing forth on your own doesn't make you feel too panicky when contemplating the celebrated writers we've discussed. Remember, we've asked you not only to *imitate* but to *emulate*, that is, to improve upon them.

"But, how can I ever *improve* on someone like Kafka?" you might ask.

Do you know that Salinger asked himself the same thing! But ultimately he got back to work and tried his best to do just that. No great artist flinches for long when confronting the masters. True, a writer might become depressed for a while when he sees how impressive

---

1. Marincola 1997:13-14.

are the works of his predecessors, but such a reaction is perfectly *normal*. In fact, something would be amiss if you *didn't* feel this way; it's a sign of your own skill and competence as a writer to occasionally feel humbled, demonstrating that you're *perceptive* enough to see beauty in the works of others.[2] But if you're a true artist you'll pick yourself up, get over your awe, and use your natural admiration to help yourself see previous works as stepping stones to *your* best work. That is the way of the artist.

Fear not as you strike out on this heroic quest for the summit. The ancient rhetoricians—Quintilian, Cicero, St. Augustine, and a host of others—are all wishing you well. Listen! … Can't you hear them? Can't you hear what they're saying? They *believe* in you, they believe you *can* do it. And for what it's worth, so do I.

---

2. There are countless stories about artists who cried in despair when they saw the greatness of their predecessors. But of course we're all glad that these sensitive souls eventually stopped acting like failures and joined the fray, creating new works of genius of their own.

ACKNOWLEDGEMENTS

It is a pleasure to acknowledge the kindness and assistance received from numerous writers, academics, and scholars, many of whom are well-known experts on a particular author, who have been sufficiently interested in this project to read various chapters and offer encouragement and direction along the way. I would particularly like to thank the following for providing feedback, critiques, and advice during the manuscript's preparation: Richard Currie, Paul C. Doherty, Russell Galen, David Gill, Mark Harmon, Laurie Robertson-Lorant, Ted Morgan, Paul P. Reuben, and John Taliaferro.

The input and thoughts of Konstantin Monastyrsky have been like a lamp in the darkness, illuminating issues of style, plot, and character development that could not have been otherwise made clear to me in any other manner than his frank and often cajoling critiques of my own views. I would also like to express my gratitude to the late Wilson Bryan Key, a friend whose encouragement and advice helped during the bulk of my work on this book and whose writing continues to illuminate a number of important issues related to literary interpretation and the unconscious.

I gratefully thank the librarians at the City University of New York, the College of Staten Island, the CUNY Graduate Center, Boston University, Boston College, and Fordham University. For material unique to their collections I am exceedingly grateful for the courtesies extended to me by the Lilly Library at the University of Indiana for access to the original typescripts of Ian Fleming's novels, and the Ernest Hemingway collection at the John F. Kennedy Presidential Library, Boston, Massachusetts, for access to Hemingway's manuscripts.

I would most especially like to thank Paul C. Doherty, not only for an inspirational course on imitation at Boston College in the early 1980s but also for continued support of my interest in this field of rhetoric. When I was a graduate student at Boston College Law School I received invaluable stylistic advice from the late James L. Houghteling and the late Sanford J. Fox: Their influence helped me fine-tune both the premise and footnotes of the present volume.

The many facilities placed at my disposal by the staff and faculty of the English department at the City University of New York will not soon be forgotten. Mary Reda's constant interest and friendly advice and criticism have made my stay at the College of Staten Island not only intellectually profitable but also very enjoyable, a period to be remembered with great pleasure. I should also like to thank the collegial help and support of Frank Battaglia, Gene Rasmussen, Lenka Rohls, Michael Walters, and Martha Yeager.

I do not know that I could make entirely clear the pleasure I had during the more than two decades that I taught English at Boston College, many of them years during which I conducted research and formed ideas which comprise the foundation of this volume. One man stands out as having made the experience a delight: James A. Woods. A dean with the leadership skills of Ernest Shackleton, he ensured that the process of teaching there was a joy and a learning experience as well.

A good number of students deserve a special word of appreciation for the burdens they have voluntarily undertaken to assist me in collecting materials and reading drafts of this work. In this connection I would particularly like to single out and thank Paulina Glozman for her uncanny editorial insights, and Lee Donegan for his unflagging assistance.

Many in the publishing field have helped me, and I'm deeply grateful to them all. During early stages of my preparation of this book I received invaluable guidance from Michelle Wolfson. Throughout the entire process of preparing the book the advice of Adam Chromy, my literary agent, proved invaluable. I want to especially thank him for being one of the most personable experts I've ever had the pleasure of associating with in the publishing world.

If this book about writing styles and imitation has any grace and style of its own it is largely due to the perceptive understanding and critical input from Scott Francis, editor extraordinaire at Writer's Digest Books—a man whose ability to work with ideas is equaled only by his capacity to deal with their expression in a text, an editor whose insights aided me in innumerable ways and whose considered advice and levelheaded assessment of the manuscript's strengths and weaknesses helped me understand my own argument better and ultimately helped you understand it as well. I'm also grateful for the work of the entire team at Writer's Digest, including Jane Friedman, editorial director, and Kim Catanzarite, whose meticulous copy editing put me to shame on numerous occasions.

I feel that a list of acknowledgments would be incomplete if no mention were made of my appreciation of and my indebtedness to my mother and father for their enthusiastic support and their literary cast of mind, which probably fostered in me, at an early age, an interest in many of the subjects encompassed by this volume. My sister, Susan, provided additional literary feedback, as did my brothers Philip and John. Last but certainly not least I constantly drew invaluable inspiration from the advice of my wife, Marilyn, and the genial presence of my daughter, Kate.

BIBLIOGRAPHY

ALEXANDER, PAUL

1999. *Salinger: A Biography.* Los Angeles: Renaissance Books.

ANDERSON, JOHN DENNIS

2007. *Student Companion to William Faulkner.* Westport, Conn.: Greenwood Press.

ATKINSON, PAUL

1990. *The Ethnographic Imagination: Textual Constructions of Reality.* New York: Routledge.

BAKER, BOB

2004. "Poetry of popular patter." *Los Angeles Times,* May 31:A-1. Available online at articles.latimes.com/2004/may/31/entertainment/et-alliteration31 (accessed August 29, 2008).

BALZAC, HONORÉ DE

1834. *Père Goriot and Eugénie Grandet.* Translated by E.K. Brown, Dorothea Walter and John Watkins. New York: Modern Library, 1946.

1838a. *Traité des Excitants Modernes.* Paris: Éditions du Boucher, 2002.

1838b. "The Pleasures and Pains of Coffee." Translated by Robert Onopa. *Michigan Quarterly Review.* Vol. XXXV, no. 2, Spring 1996, pp. 273-277. Also available online at http://hdl.handle.net/2027/spo.act2080.0035.002:01.

BARRY, KEVIN

2001. *The Dead.* Cork: Cork University Press, Ireland.

BEAHM, GEORGE

1998. *Stephen King: America's Best-Loved Boogeyman.* Kansas City: Andrews McMeel Publishing.

BEEBE, MAURICE, ED.

1960. *Literary Symbolism: An Introduction to the Interpretation of Literature.* San Francisco: Wadsworth Publishing Co.

BEEGEL, SUSAN F., ED.

1992. *Hemingway's Neglected Short Fiction: New Perspectives.* Tuscaloosa: University of Alabama Press.

BELEY, GENE

2006. *Ray Bradbury Uncensored! The Unauthorized Biography.* Lincoln, Nebr.: iUniverse.

BENSTOCK, SHARI

1994. *No Gifts From Chance: A Biography of Edith Wharton.* Austin: University of Texas Press.

BERCOVITCH, SACVAN, AND CYRUS R.K. PATELL, EDS.

1994. *The Cambridge History of American Literature: Prose Writing, 1940–1990.* New York: Cambridge University Press.

BLEIKASTEN, ANDRÉ

1978. "The Heresy of Flannery O'Connor." In *Critical Essays on Flannery O'Connor.* Edited by Melvin J. Friedman and Beverly Lyon Clark. Boston: G.K. Hall & Co., 1985, pp. 138-158.

BLOOM, HAROLD

1997. *The Anxiety of Influence: A Theory of Poetry.* 2nd ed. New York: Oxford University Press.

BLOOM, HAROLD, ED.

2007. *George Orwell's 1984.* New York: Chelsea House.

BLOTNER, JOSEPH

1984. *Faulkner: A Biography.* One-volume edition. Jackson: University Press of Mississippi.

1987. Line and page notes to the corrected edition of *Sanctuary.* New York: Vintage.

BOOKER, CHRISTOPHER

2004. *The Seven Basic Plots: Why We Tell Stories.* New York: Continuum.

BOON, MARCUS

2002. *The Road of Excess: A History of Writers on Drugs.* Cambridge, Mass.: Harvard University Press.

BOWKER, GORDON

2003. *Inside George Orwell.* New York: Palgrave Macmillan.

BOYNTON, ROBERT S., ED.

2005. *The New New Journalism: Conversations With America's Best Nonfiction Writers on Their Craft.* New York: Vintage.

BRADBURY, RAY

1953. *Fahrenheit 451.* New York: Del Rey, 1991.

1957. *Dandelion Wine.* New York: Bantam, 1959.

1962. *Something Wicked This Way Comes.* New York: Bantam, 1963.

1973. *When Elephants Last in the Dooryard Bloomed: Celebrations for Almost Any Day in the Year.* New York: Knopf.

1990. *Zen in the Art of Writing: Releasing the Creative Genius Within You.* New York: Bantam.

2004. *Conversations With Ray Bradbury.* Edited by Steven L. Aggelis. Jackson: University Press of Mississippi.

N.d. Ray Bradbury Interview. Interview by Colin Clark, Web & Publications Editor, National Theatre of Scotland. www.nationaltheatrescotland.com/content/default.asp?page=s452 (accessed December 23, 2008).

BRANCH, WATSON G., ED.

1997. *Herman Melville: The Critical Heritage.* New York: Routledge.

BRANDEN, NATHANIEL

1989. *Judgment Day: My Years With Ayn Rand.* Boston: Houghton Mifflin.

BRAUN, MAXIMILIAN

1976. *Dostojewskij: Das Gesamtwerk als Vielfalt und Einheit.* Göttingen: Vandenhoeck und Ruprecht.

BROOKS, CLEANTH

1963. *William Faulkner: The Yoknapatawpha Country*. Baton Rouge: Louisiana State University Press, 1990.

BROWNE, RENNI, AND DAVE KING

2004. *Self-Editing for Fiction Writers: How to Edit Yourself Into Print*. New York: HarperCollins.

BUDDICOM, JACINTHA

1974. *Eric and Us: A Remembrance of George Orwell*. London: Frewin.

BULMAN, COLIN

2006. *Creative Writing: A Guide and Glossary to Fiction Writing*. Cambridge: Polity.

BURGESS, ANTHONY

1978. *Ernest Hemingway and His World*. New York: Scribner's.

BURROUGHS, EDGAR RICE

1912. *Tarzan of the Apes*. New York: Ballantine, 1963.

1917. *A Princess of Mars*. New York: Ballantine, 1963.

1918. *Out of Time's Abyss*. New York: Ace.

1920. *Thuvia, Maid of Mars*. New York: Ace.

1926. *The Moon Maid*. New York: Ace, 1968.

1928. *The Master Mind of Mars*. New York: Ace.

1931. *A Fighting Man of Mars*. New York: Ace.

1932. *The Land of Hidden Men*. New York: Ace.

1934. *Pirates of Venus*. New York: Ace.

1964. *Beyond the Farthest Star*. New York: Ace.

BUTTRY, DOLORES.

1982. "'Secret Suffering': Knut Hamsun's Allegory of the Creative Artist." *Studies in Short Fiction* 19, no. 1, pp.1-7.

CANE, WILLIAM

2008. *The Birth Order Book of Love*. New York: Da Capo/Perseus Books.

CARPENTER, META.

See Wilde, Meta Carpenter.

CAVITCH, DAVID

1969. *D.H. Lawrence and the New World.* New York: Oxford
University Press.

CHAPMAN, JAMES

2000. *Licence to Thrill: A Cultural History of the James Bond Films.*
New York: Columbia University Press.

CHASLES, PHILARÈTE

1849. "Parisian Critical Sketches: The Actual and Fantastic Voyages of
Herman Melville." In *Herman Melville: The Critical Heritage,* edited by
Watson G. Branch, p. 171. New York: Routledge, 1997.

CITATI, PIETRO

1990. *Kafka.* Translated by Raymond Rosenthal. New York: Knopf.

CLEMEN, WOLFGANG

1972. *Shakespeare's Dramatic Art: Collected Essays.* New York:
Routledge, 2005.

COARD, ROBERT L.

1985. "Edith Wharton's Influence on Sinclair Lewis." *Modern Fiction
Studies,* 31:511-527.

COHN, DORRIT

1978. *Transparent Minds: Narrative Modes for Presenting Consciousness
in Fiction.* Princeton, N.J.: Princeton University Press.

COLES, ROBERT

1967. "Knut Hamsun: The Beginning and the End." *New Republic* 157,
no. 13, pp. 21-24.

COMENTALE, EDWARD P.

2005. "Fleming's Company Man: James Bond and the Management of
Modernism." In *Ian Fleming and James Bond: The Cultural Politics of
007,* edited by Edward P. Comentale, Stephen Watt and Skip Willman,
pp. 3-23. Bloomington: Indiana University Press.

CONTE, GIAN BIAGIO

1986. *The Rhetoric of Imitation: Genre and Poetic Memory in Virgil and
Other Latin Poets.* Translated by Charles Segal. Ithaca, N.Y.: Cornell
University Press.

COOLIDGE, ARCHIBALD C., JR.

1967. *Charles Dickens as Serial Novelist.* Ames: Iowa State University Press.

CORBETT, EDWARD P.J.

1971. *Classical Rhetoric for the Modern Student.* 2nd ed. New York: Oxford University Press.

CORDELL, RICHARD A.

1961. *Somerset Maugham: A Biographical and Critical Study.* Bloomington: Indiana University Press.

COWAN, MICHAEL H., ED.

1968. *Twentieth Century Interpretations of The Sound and the Fury: A Collection of Critical Essays.* Englewood Cliffs, N.J.: Prentice Hall.

CRAWFORD, CATHERINE, ED.

2006. *If You Really Want to Hear About It: Writers on J.D. Salinger and His Work.* New York: Thunder's Mouth Press.

CURTIS, ANTHONY

1974. *The Pattern of Maugham: A Critical Portrait.* New York: Taplinger Publishing Co.

DAVIS, JOE LEE

1953. "Outraged or Embarrassed." In *The Critical Response to Flannery O'Connor,* edited by Douglas Robillard, Jr., pp. 23-24. Westport, Conn.: Praeger, 2004.

DEARBORN, MARY V.

1999. *Mailer: A Biography.* Boston: Houghton Mifflin.

DELBANCO, ANDREW

2005. *Melville: His World and Work.* New York: Knopf.

DICK, PHILIP K.

1965. *The Three Stigmata of Palmer Eldritch.* New York: Vintage Books, 1991.

1968. *Do Androids Dream of Electric Sheep?* (Published as *Blade Runner*) New York, Del Rey, 1982.

1969. *Ubik.* New York: Daw Books, 1983.

1977a. *A Scanner Darkly.* Garden City, N.J.: Double Day.

1977b. Rare Philip K. Dick Interview. Festival du livre de science fiction. September. France. www.youtube.com/watch?v=7Ewcp6Nm-rQ (accessed September 28, 2008).

1981. *VALIS*. New York: Vintage Books.

1995. *The Shifting Realities of Philip K. Dick: Selected Literary and Philosophical Writings*. Edited by Lawrence Sutin. New York: Vintage.

DICKENS, CHARLES

1841. *The Old Curiosity Shop*. Introduction by Peter Preston. Ware, Hertfordshire, England: Wordsworth Editions, 1995.

1848. *Dombey and Son*. New York: Penguin, 1986.

1850. *David Copperfield*. New York: Oxford University Press, 1983.

1853a. *Bleak House*. New York: Bantam, 1983.

1853b. *Bleak House*. Norton Critical Edition, edited by George Ford and Sylvère Monod. New York: Norton, 1977.

DINGES, DAVID F.

2001. "Sleep in Space Flight." *American Journal of Respiratory and Critical Care Medicine*, vol. 164, no. 3, August, pp. 337-338.

DONALDSON, SCOTT

1990. "Preparing for the End: Hemingway's Revisions of 'A Canary for One.'" In *New Critical Approaches to the Short Stories of Ernest Hemingway*, edited by Jackson J. Benson. Durham, N.C.: Duke University Press.

DOSTOEVSKY, FYODOR

1864. *Notes From Underground*. Translated by Mirra Ginsburg. New York: Bantam, 1992.

1866. *Crime and Punishment*. Translated by Sidney Monas. New York: Signet, 1999.

1868. *The Idiot*. Translated by Henry and Olga Carlisle. New York: Signet, 2002.

1880a. *The Karamazov Brothers*. Translated by Ignat Avsey. New York: Oxford University Press, 1994.

1880b. *The Brothers Karamazov: A Novel in Four Parts and an Epilogue*. Translated by David McDuff. New York: Penguin Classics, 2003.

DRISKELL, JAMES E., CAROLYN COPPER, AND AIDAN MORAN

1994. "Does Mental Practice Enhance Performance?" *Journal of Applied Psychology*, vol. 79, no. 4, pp. 481-492.

EDWARDS, BETTY

1999. *The New Drawing on the Right Side of the Brain.* 2nd rev. ed.
New York: Jeremy P. Tarcher/Putnam.

EGRI, LAJOS

1960. *The Art of Dramatic Writing.* New York: Simon & Schuster.

ELLER, JONATHAN R., AND WILLIAM F. TOUPONCE

2004. *Ray Bradbury: The Life of Fiction.* Kent, Ohio:
Kent State University Press.

ELLISON, RALPH

1997. "Elaborating a Personal Myth." In *Readings on Ernest Hemingway,*
edited by Katie de Koster. San Diego: Greenhorn Press.

ERLICH, GLORIA C.

1992. *The Sexual Education of Edith Wharton.* Berkeley:
University of California Press.

EVANS, DAVID H.

2008. *William Faulkner, William James, and the American Pragmatic Tradition.*
Baton Rouge: Louisiana State University Press.

FALK, KATHRYN, ED.

1983. *How to Write a Romance and Get It Published: With Intimate Advice
From the World's Most Popular Romantic Writers.* New York: Crown.

FAULKNER, WILLIAM

1929. *The Sound and the Fury.* New York: Vintage, 1954.

1930. *As I Lay Dying.* New York: Vintage, 1987.

1931. *Sanctuary.* New York: Vintage.

1932. *Light in August.* New York: Modern Library.

1956. "The Art of Fiction No. 12. Interview With Jean Stein vanden
Heuvel." In *The Paris Review,* no. 12, Spring.

FERGUSON, ROBERT

1987. *Enigma: The Life of Knut Hamsun.* New York: Farrar, Straus & Giroux.

FJÅGESUND, PETER

1991. "D.H. Lawrence, Knut Hamsun and Pan." *English Studies* 72, no. 5
(October): pp. 421-425.

FLAUBERT, GUSTAVE

1856. *Madame Bovary.* Translated by Alan Russell. New York: Penguin, 1950.

FLEMING, IAN

1953. *Casino Royale.* New York: Signet.

1954. *Live and Let Die.* New York: Signet.

1957. *From Russia With Love.* New York: Signet.

1958. *Doctor No.* New York: Signet.

1959. *Goldfinger.* New York: Signet.

1963. *On Her Majesty's Secret Service.* New York: Signet.

1964. *You Only Live Twice.* New York: Signet.

FLESCH, RUDOLPH

1949. *The Art of Readable Writing.* New York: Collier Books, 1962.

FLUDERNIK, MONIKA

1996. *Towards a 'Natural' Narratology.* New York: Routledge.

FODOR, SARAH J.

1996. "Marketing Flannery O'Connor: Institutional Politics and Literary Evaluation." In *Flannery O'Connor: New Perspectives,* edited by Sura P. Rath and Mary Neff Shaw, pp. 12-37. Athens: University of Georgia Press.

FORSTER, E.M.

1927. *Aspects of the Novel.* Boston: Houghton Mifflin Harcourt, 1985.

FRYE, NORTHROP

2003. *Northrop Frye on Modern Culture.* Edited by Jan Gorak. Toronto: University of Toronto Press.

GALBRAITH, DAVID

2000. *Architectonics of Imitation in Spenser, Daniel, and Drayton.* Toronto: University of Toronto Press.

GARDNER, JOHN

1983. *On Becoming a Novelist.* New York: Harper & Row.

1985. *The Art of Fiction: Notes on Craft for Young Writers.* New York: Vintage Books.

GENTRY, MARSHALL BRUCE

2006. "He Would Have Been a Good Man: Compassion and Meanness in Truman Capote and Flannery O'Connor." In *Flannery O'Connor's Radical Reality*. Edited by Jan Nordby Gretlund and Karl-Heinz Westarp. Columbia: University of South Carolina Press, pp. 42-55.

GERSON, NOEL B.

1972. *The Prodigal Genius: The Life and Times of Honoré de Balzac*. Garden City, N.Y.: Doubleday.

GIANNONE, RICHARD

1989. *Flannery O'Connor and the Mystery of Love*. Urbana and Chicago: University of Illinois Press.

2000. *Flannery O'Connor: Hermit Novelist*. Urbana: University of Illinois Press.

GLEIM, WILLIAM S.

1938. *The Meaning of Moby Dick*. New York: Russell & Russell, 1962.

GOOD, GRAHAM

1988. *The Observing Self: Rediscovering the Essay*. New York: Routledge.

GOODEN, PHILIP

2008. *Name Dropping: Darwinian Struggles, Oedipal Feelings, and Kafkaesque Ordeals—An A to Z Guide to the Use of Names in Everyday Language*. New York: St. Martin's Press.

GWYNN, FREDERICK L. AND JOSEPH L. BLOTNER, EDS.

1995. *Faulkner in the University*. Charlottesville: University Press of Virginia.

HARRISON, RUSSELL

1994. *Against the American Dream: Essays on Charles Bukowski*. Santa Rosa, Calif.: Black Sparrow Press.

HAMSUN, KNUT

1892. *Mysteries*. Translated by Sverre Lyngstad. New York: Penguin, 2001.

1898. *Victoria*. Translated by Sverre Lyngstad. New York: Penguin, 2005.

HEMINGWAY, ERNEST

1986. *The Garden of Eden*. New York: Collier Books.

1986. *The Garden of Eden*. New York: Collier Books.

2005. *Under Kilimanjaro*. Kent, Ohio: Kent State University Press.

HENDIN, JOSEPHINE

1970. *The World of Flannery O'Connor*. Bloomington: Indiana University Press.

HOWARD, DAVID, AND EDWARD MABLEY

1993. *The Tools of Screenwriting: A Writer's Guide to the Craft and Elements of a Screenplay*. New York: St. Martin's Press.

HOWARD, LEON

1994. "Melville's struggle with the angel." In *The Critical Response to Herman Melville's Moby-Dick* edited by Kevin J. Hayes. Westport, Conn.: Greenwood Press.

HOWARTH, PATRICK

1973. *Play Up and Play the Game: The Heroes of Popular Fiction*. London: Eyre Methuen.

HOTCHNER, A.E.

1966. *Papa Hemingway: A Personal Memoir*. New York: Random House.

1984. *Choice People: The Greats, Near-Greats, and Ingrates I Have Known*. New York: Morrow.

HUGHES, CLAIR

2005. "Consuming Clothes: Edith Wharton's *The House of Mirth*." *Fashion Theory: The Journal of Dress, Body & Culture*, vol. 9, no. 4, pp. 383–406.

HUMMA, JOHN

1983. "The Interpenetrating Metaphor: Nature and Myth in *Lady Chatterley's Lover*." *Publications of the Modern Language Association of America*, vol. 98, no. 1, pp. 77–86.

HURWOOD, BERNHARDT J.

1986. *Writing Becomes Electronic*. New York: Congdon & Weed.

HUXLEY, ALDOUS

1932. *Brave New World & Brave New World Revisited*. New York: Harper & Row, 1965.

HYMAN, STANLEY EDGAR

1966. *Flannery O'Connor*. Minneapolis: University of Minnesota Press.

HIGONNET, PATRICE L.R.

2002. *Paris: Capital of the World.* Translated by Arthur Goldhammer. Cambridge: Harvard University Press.

INGE, M. THOMAS, ED.

1999. *Conversations With William Faulkner.* Jackson: University Press of Mississippi.

JONES, JUDITH PATERSON AND GUINEVERA A. NANCE

1981. *Philip Roth.* New York: Ungar.

JOYCE, JAMES

1916. *A Portrait of the Artist as a Young Man.* New York: B.W. Huebsch.

1922. *Ulysses.* New York: Vintage, 1990.

JUNG, CARL GUSTAV

1964. *Man and His Symbols.* New York: Dell, 1968.

KAFKA, FRANZ

1925a. *The Trial.* Translated by Breon Mitchell. New York: Schocken, 1998.

1925b. *The Trial.* Translated by Willa and Edwin Muir. New York: Vintage, 1964.

1926. *The Castle: A New Translation, Based on the Restored Text.* Translated by Mark Harman. New York: Schocken, 1998.

1927. *Amerika: The Missing Person. A New Translation, Based on the Restored Text.* Translated by Mark Harman. New York: Schocken, 2008.

1979. *The Basic Kafka.* New York: Pocket Books.

KAKUTANI, MICHIKO

1992. "Books of The Times; Lady Chatterley and the Hippie." Book review of *The Trespassers* by Robert Roper. *New York Times,* November 24. Available online at www.nytimes.com/1992/11/24/books/books-of-the-times-lady-chatterley-and-the-hippie.html (accessed January 1, 2009).

KANIN, GARSON

1966. *Remembering Mr. Maugham.* London: Hamish Hamilton.

KAROLIDES, NICHOLAS J., MARGARET BALD, AND DAWN B. SOVA

1999. *100 Banned Books: Censorship Histories of World Literature.* New York: Checkmark Books.

KERT, BERNICE

1983. *The Hemingway Women*. New York: W.W. Norton.

KILLINGER, JOHN

1960. *Hemingway and the Dead Gods: A Study in Existentialism*. Lexington: University of Kentucky Press.

KIM, SHARON

2006. "Edith Wharton and Epiphany." *Journal of Modern Literature*, vol. 29 no. 3 (Spring), pp. 150-175.

KING, STEPHEN

1974. *Carrie*. New York: Pocket Books, 1999.

1977. *The Shining*. New York: Pocket Books, 2001.

1978. *The Stand: The Complete and Uncut Edition*. New York: Doubleday, 1990.

1981. *Cujo*. New York: Signet, 1982.

1987. *Misery*. New York: Signet, 1988.

2000. *On Writing: A Memoir of the Craft*. New York: Simon & Schuster.

KIRSCH, ADAM

2009. "America, 'Amerika.'" *New York Times*, January 2, p. BR23 (New York edition). Also online at www.nytimes.com/2009/01/04/books/review/Kirsch-t.html?pagewanted=1&_r=1 (accessed January 6, 2009).

KROCKEL, CARL

2007. *D.H. Lawrence and Germany: The Politics of Influence*. Amsterdam: Rodopi.

KUBIE, LAWRENCE S.

1958. *Neurotic Distortion of the Creative Process*. Lawrence: University of Kansas Press.

KURZWEIL, RAY, AND TERRY GROSSMAN

2004. *Fantastic Voyage: Live Long Enough to Live Forever*. New York: Rodale.

KUZMANOVICH, ZORAN

2005. "Strong Opinions and Nerve Points: Nabokov's Life and Art." In *The Cambridge Companion to Nabokov*, edited by Julian W. Connolly. New York: Cambridge University Press.

LANIA, LEO

1961. *Hemingway: A Pictorial Biography.* New York: Viking Press.

LANSING, ALFRED

1959. *Endurance: Shackleton's Incredible Voyage.* New York: McGraw-Hill.

LAWRENCE, D.H.

1913. *Sons and Lovers.* New York: Viking, 1968.

1915. *The Rainbow.* New York: Penguin Books, 1981.

1920a. *Mr. Noon.* New York: Penguin Books, 1985.

1920b. *Women in Love.* New York: Penguin Books, 1983.

1923a. *The Fox.* New York: Bantam, 1967.

1923b. *Studies in Classic American Literature.* New York: Penguin Books, 1977.

1928a. *Lady Chatterley's Lover.* New York: Signet, 1962.

1928b. *Lady Chatterley's Lover.* Introduction by Mark Schorer. New York: Grove Press, 1993.

1931. *Apocalypse.* Florence, Italy: G. Orioli.

1998. *The First 'Women in Love.'* Edited by John Worthen and Lindeth Vasey. New York: Cambridge University Press.

LEATHERBARROW, WILLIAM J.

1992. *Fyodor Dostoyevsky: The Brothers Karamazov.* New York: Cambridge University Press.

LEFORT, CLAUDE

2000. *Writing: The Political Test.* Translated by David Ames Curtis. Durham, N.C.: Duke University Press.

LEVINE, CAROLINE

2003. *The Serious Pleasures of Suspense: Victorian Realism and Narrative Doubt.* Charlottesville: University of Virginia Press.

2007. *Provoking Democracy: Why We Need the Arts.* Malden, Mass.: Blackwell Publishing.

LEWIS, R.W.B.

1986. "Note on the Texts." In *Edith Wharton: Novels: The House of Mirth / The Reef / The Custom of the Country / The Age of Innocence.* New York: Library of America.

LIMON, JOHN

1994. *Writing After War: American War Fiction From Realism to Postmodernism*. New York: Oxford University Press.

LOMBARDI, ESTHER

N.d. "The short stories of Edith Wharton provide us with another look at her literary genius." Available online at http://classiclit.about.com/library/weekly/aa030101a.htm (accessed August 23, 2008).

LUNDWALL, SAM J.

1971. *Science Fiction: What It's All About*. New York: Ace.

LUPOFF, RICHARD A.

1968. *Edgar Rice Burroughs: Master of Adventure*. Revised and enlarged edition. New York: Ace.

LYCETT, ANDREW

1995. *Ian Fleming: The Man Behind James Bond*. Atlanta: Turner Publishing.

LYNCH, DAVID

2006. *Catching the Big Fish: Meditation, Consciousness, and Creativity*. New York: Jeremy P. Tarcher/Penguin.

LYNGSTAD, SVERRE

2005. *Knut Hamsun, Novelist: A Critical Assessment*. New York: Peter Lang.

LYNN, KENNETH S.

1987. *Hemingway*. New York: Simon & Schuster.

MADDEN, DAVID

1988. *Revising Fiction: A Handbook for Writers*. New York: New American Library.

MADDOX, BRENDA

1994. *D.H. Lawrence: The Story of a Marriage*. New York: Simon & Schuster.

MALIN, IRVING

1966. "Flannery O'Connor and the Grotesque." In *The Added Dimension: The Art and Mind of Flannery O'Connor*, edited by Melvin J. Friedman and Lewis A. Lawson. New York: Fordham University Press.

MARINCOLA, JOHN

1997. *Authority and Tradition in Ancient Historiography*. New York: Cambridge University Press.

MARTINSEN, DEBORAH A.

2003. *Surprised by Shame: Dostoevsky's Liars and Narrative Exposure.* Columbus, Ohio: Ohio State University Press.

MAUGHAM, W. SOMERSET

1915. *Of Human Bondage.* New York: Signet, 1991.

1919. *The Moon and Sixpence.* New York: Vintage, 2000.

1938. *The Summing Up.* Garden City, N.Y.: Doubleday, Doran & Co.

1944. *The Razor's Edge.* New York: Penguin, 1992.

1949. *A Writer's Notebook.* New York: Arno Press, 1977.

MAUROIS, ANDRÉ

1965. *Prometheus: The Life of Balzac.* Translated by Norman Denny. New York: Carroll & Graf Publishers.

MAYNARD, JOYCE

1998. *At Home in the World: A Memoir.* New York: Picador.

McKEE, ROBERT

1997. *Story: Substance, Structure, Style and the Principles of Screenwriting.* New York: ReganBooks.

McLUHAN, MARSHALL

1964. *Understanding Media: The Extensions of Man.* 2nd ed. New York: Routledge, 2001.

MEANS, KATHRYN

2000. "Margaret Mitchell and Tom Wolfe: Scarlett and The Right Stuff in Atlanta." In *Literary Trips: Following in the Footsteps of Fame,* edited by Victoria Brooks. Vancouver, B.C., Canada: Greatest Escapes Publishng.

MELETINSKY, ELEAZAR M.

1998. *The Poetics of Myth.* Translated by Guy Lanoue and Alexandre Sadetsky. New York: Routledge.

MELTZER, MILTON

2006. *Herman Melville: A Biography.* Minneapolis: Twenty-First Century Books.

MELVILLE, HERMAN

1851. *Moby-Dick; or, The Whale.* New York: Signet Classic, 1998.

MEREDITH, ROBERT C., AND JOHN D. FITZGERALD

1972. *Structuring Your Novel: From Basic Idea to Finished Manuscript*. New York: Barnes & Noble Books.

MEYERS, JEFFREY

1990. *D.H. Lawrence: A Biography*. New York: Knopf.

2004. *Somerset Maugham: A Life*. New York: Knopf.

MILLER, MARLOWE A.

2006. *Masterpieces of British Modernism*. Westport, CT: Greenwood Publishing Group.

MILLS, PAUL

1996. *Writing in Action*. New York: Routledge.

MITCHELL, MARGARET

1936. *Gone With the Wind*. New York: Avon, 1973.

MODLESKI, TANIA

1982. *Loving With a Vengeance: Mass-Produced Fantasies for Women*. Hamden: Conn.: Archon Books.

MOGEN, DAVID

1986. *Ray Bradbury*. Boston: Twayne.

MORGAN, TED

1980. *Maugham*. New York: Simon & Schuster.

MOYNAHAN, JULIAN

1959. "Lady Chatterley's Lover: The Deed of Life." *ELH*, vol. 26, no. 1 (March), pp. 66–90.

MURPHY, JAMES J., RICHARD A. KATULA, FORBES I. HILL, AND DONOVAN J. OCHS

2003. *A Synoptic History of Classical Rhetoric*. Philadelphia: Lawrence Erlbaum Associates Inc.

MURRAY, HENRY A.

1951. "In nomine diaboli." In *Moby-Dick Centennial Essays*. Dallas: Southern Methodist University Press, 1953.

NABOKOV, VLADIMIR

1980. *Lectures on Literature*. Edited by Fredson Bowers. New York: Harcourt.

NOBLE, JUNE, AND WILLIAM NOBLE

1985. *Steal This Plot: A Writer's Guide to Story Structure and Plagiarism.* Middlebury, Vt.: Paul S. Eriksson.

OATES, JOYCE CAROL

1966. "Where Are You Going, Where Have You Been?" In *Classic Short Fiction*, edited by Charles H. Bohner, pp. 821–832. Englewood Cliffs, N.J.: Prentice Hall, 1986.

1973. "The Visionary Art of Flannery O'Connor." In *Flannery O'Connor: Modern Critical Views*, edited by Harold Bloom. New York: Chelsea House, 1986.

1988. "The Hemingway Mystique" in *Brett Ashley: Major Literary Characters*, edited by Howard Bloom. New York: Chelsea House, 1991.

O'CONNOR, FLANNERY

1960. *The Violent Bear It Away.* In *3 by Flannery O'Connor: Wise Blood, The Violent Bear It Away, Everything That Rises Must Converge.* New York: New American Library, 1983.

1961. "Everything That Rises Must Converge" In *3 by Flannery O'Connor: Wise Blood, The Violent Bear It Away, Everything That Rises Must Converge.* New York: New American Library, 1983.

ORWELL, GEORGE

1945. *Animal Farm.* New York: Signet.

1949. *Nineteen Eighty-Four.* New York: Signet, 1961.

2005. *Why I Write.* New York: Penguin Books.

PAGE, ANN E.K., ED.

2004. *Keeping Patients Safe: Transforming the Work Environment of Nurses.* Washington, D.C.: National Academies Press.

PALMER, CHRISTOPHER

2003. *Philip K. Dick: Exhilaration and Terror of the Postmodern.* Liverpool: Liverpool University Press.

PARINI, JAY

2004. *One Matchless Time: A Life of William Faulkner.* New York: HarperCollins.

PARKER, HERSHEL

1996. *Herman Melville: A Biography. Volume I, 1819–1851.* Baltimore: Johns Hopkins University Press.

PATERSON, JUDITH HILLMAN

See Jones, Judith P.

PINSKY, MICHAEL

2003. *Future Present: Ethics And/As Science Fiction.* Madison, N.J.: Fairleigh Dickinson University Press.

POPLAWSKI, PAUL, ED.

2001. *Writing the Body in D.H. Lawrence: Essays on Language, Representation, and Sexuality.* New York: Greenwood Press.

PRESTON, PETER, AND PETER HOARE, ED.

1989. *D.H. Lawrence in the Modern World.* New York: Cambridge University Press.

PRITCHETT, V.S.

1973. *Balzac.* New York: Knopf.

PROFFER, CARL R.

1968. *Keys to Lolita.* Bloomington: Indiana University Press.

PYRON, DARDEN ASBURY

1991. *Southern Daughter: The Life of Margaret Mitchell.* New York: Oxford University Press.

RAND, AYN

2000. *The Art of Fiction: A Guide for Writers and Readers.* New York: Plume.

RATH, SURA P., AND MARY NEFF SHAW, EDS.

1996. *Flannery O'Connor: New Perspectives.* Athens: University of Georgia Press.

REES, ELLEN

2008. "Knut Hamsun, Novelist: A Critical Assessment [book review]." *Scandinavian Studies,* vol. 80, no. 1 (Spring), pp. 109–112.

REIFF, RAYCHEL HAUGRUD

2008. *J.D. Salinger: The Catcher in the Rye and Other Works.* Tarrytown, N.Y.: Marshall Cavendish Benchmark.

REISS, HANS

1978. *The Writer's Task From Nietzsche to Brecht.* London: Macmillan.

REISSENWEBER, BRANDI

2003. "Character: Casting Shadows." In *Writing Fiction: The Practical Guide From New York's Acclaimed Creative Writing School,* edited by Alexander Steele, pp. 25-51. New York: Bloomsbury.

REYNOLDS, BARBARA

2006. *Dante: The Poet, the Political Thinker, the Man.* London: I.B. Tauris.

REYNOLDS, MICHAEL S.

1988. *The Sun Also Rises: A Novel of the Twenties.* Boston: Twayne.

RIMMON-KENAN, SHLOMITH

1983. *Narrative Fiction: Contemporary Poetics.* London and New York: Methuen.

RIO-JELLIFFE, R.

2001. *Obscurity's Myriad Components: The Theory and Practice of William Faulkner.* Lewisburg, Pa.: Bucknell University Press.

ROBERTSON-LORANT, LAURIE

1996. *Melville: A Biography.* New York: Clarkson Potter.

ROBSON, ERNEST M.

1959. *The Orchestra of the Language.* New York: Thomas Yoseloff.

ROLLESTON, JAMES

1986. "Kafka's Time Machines." In *Franz Kafka (1883–1983): His Craft and Thought,* edited by Roman Struc and J.C. Yardley. Waterloo, Ont., Canada: Wilfrid Laurier University Press, pp. 25-48.

ROTH, PHILIP

1992. *Conversations With Philip Roth.* Edited by George J. Searles. Jackson: University Press of Mississippi.

RUSSELL, SHARON A.

2002. *Revisiting Stephen King: A Critical Companion.* 2nd ed. Westport, Conn.: Greenwood Press.

SAFIRE, WILLIAM

2008. "Inartful." *New York Times,* July 20, p. MM14 (New York edition). Also available at www.nytimes.com/2008/07/20/magazine/20wwln-safire-t.html (accessed January 10, 2009).

SAHELIAN, RAY

1997. *Pregnenolone: Nature's Feel Good Hormone.* Garden City Park, N.Y.:
Avery Publishing Group.

SALINGER, J.D.

1951. *The Catcher in the Rye.* New York: Bantam, 1966.

1953. *Nine Stories.* Boston: Little, Brown.

1961. *Franny and Zooey.* Boston: Little, Brown.

SALINGER, MARGARET A.

2000. *Dream Catcher: A Memoir.* New York: Washington Square Press.

SCOTT, R. NEIL

2002. *Flannery O'Connor: An Annotated Reference Guide to Criticism.*
Milledgeville, Ga.: Timberlane Books.

SCRIBNER, CHARLES, III

1996. Preface to *The Only Thing that Counts: The Ernest Hemingway /
Maxwell Perkins Correspondence 1925–1947.* New York: Scribner.

SCURA, DOROTHY M., ED.

1990. *Conversations With Tom Wolfe.* Jackson: University Press of Mississippi.

SHERRILL, ROWLAND A.

1986. "The Career of Ishmael's Self-Transcendence." In *Herman Melville's
Moby-Dick,* edited by Harold Bloom. New York: Chelsea House.

SHNEIDMAN, EDWIN S.

1986. "Melville's Cognitive Style: The Logic of *Moby-Dick.*" In
A Companion to Melville Studies, edited by John Bryant. New York:
Greenwood Press, 1986.

SILVERMAN, FRANKLIN H.

1999. *Publishing for Tenure and Beyond.* Westport, Conn.: Praeger.

SIMMONS, ERNEST J.

1940. *Dostoevsky: The Making of a Novelist.* London and New York:
Oxford University Press.

SIMPSON, MELISSA

2005. *Flannery O'Connor: A Biography.* Westport, Conn.:
Greenwood Press.

SMITH, SAM F.

2006. "Joseph Conrad Anecdote." http://forreststokes.com/ wordpress/?p=131 (accessed March 15, 2008).

SPILKA, MARK

1963. *Dickens and Kafka: A Mutual Interpretation.* Bloomington: Indiana University Press.

SULLOWAY, FRANK J.

1996. *Born to Rebel: Birth Order, Family Dynamics, and Creative Lives.* New York: Pantheon.

SUTIN, LAWRENCE

1989. *Divine Invasions: A Life of Philip K. Dick.* New York: Harmony Books.

SVOBODA, FREDERIC JOSEPH

1983. *Hemingway & The Sun Also Rises: The Crafting of a Style.* Lawrence: University Press of Kansas.

1991. "The Most Difficult Job of Revision." In *Brett Ashley: Major Literary Characters,* edited by Howard Bloom. New York: Chelsea House.

SWIGGART, PETER

1962. *The Art of Faulkner's Novels.* Austin: University of Texas Press.

TALIAFERRO, JOHN

1999. *Tarzan Forever: The Life of Edgar Rice Burroughs, Creator of Tarzan.* New York: Scribner.

TAYLOR, D.J.

2003. *Orwell: The Life.* New York: Henry Holt.

TAYLOR, HELEN

1989. *Scarlett's Women: Gone With the Wind and Its Female Fans.* New Brunswick, N.J.: Rutgers University Press.

TERRAS, VICTOR

1981. *A Karamazov Companion: Commentary on the Genesis, Language, and Style of Dostoevksy's Novel.* Madison: University of Wisconsin Press.

THORNTON, WELDON

1993. *D.H. Lawrence: A Study of the Short Fiction.* New York: Twayne.

VINCENT, HOWARD PATON

1949. *The Trying-Out of Moby-Dick.* Carbondale: Southern Illinois University Press, 1965.

WEGENER, FREDERICK

1995. "Edith Wharton and the Difficult Writing of *The Writing of Fiction.*" in *Modern Language Studies,* 25:2 (Spring), pp. 60–72.

WEINGARTEN, MARC

2006. *The Gang That Wouldn't Write Straight: Wolfe, Thompson, Didion, and the New Journalism Revolution.* New York: Crown.

WELLER, SAM

2005. *The Bradbury Chronicles: The Life of Ray Bradbury.* New York: William Morrow.

WEST, DAVID, AND TONY WOODMAN, EDS.

1979. *Creative Imitation and Latin Literature.* New York: Cambridge University Press.

WHARTON, EDITH

1911. *Ethan Frome.* New York: Collier Books, 1987.

1920. *The Age of Innocence.* New York: Barnes & Noble Classics, 2004.

1928. *The Children.* New York: Scribner, 1997.

1934. *A Backward Glance.* New York: D. Appleton-Century Company.

WHITE, EDMUND

1996. "Knut Hamsun." *Review of Contemporary Fiction* 16, no. 3, pp. 21–26.

WHITT, MARGARET EARLEY

1995. *Understanding Flannery O'Connor.* Columbia: University of South Carolina Press.

WILDE, META CARPENTER, AND ORIN BORSTEN

1976. *A Loving Gentleman: The Love Story of William Faulkner and Meta Carpenter.* New York: Simon & Schuster.

WILLIAMS, JEFFREY

1998. *Theory and the Novel: Narrative Reflexivity in the British Tradition.* New York: Cambridge University Press.

WILLIAMS, TENNESSEE.

1975. *Memoirs.* Garden City, N.Y.: Doubleday.

WOLFE, TOM

1979. *The Right Stuff.* New York: Bantam.

1987. *The Bonfire of the Vanities.* New York: Bantam.

1998. *A Man in Full.* New York: Bantam.

2000. *Hooking Up.* New York: Picador.

WOLFE, TOM, AND E.W. JOHNSON, EDS.

1973. *The New Journalism.* New York: Harper & Row.

WOODCOCK, GEORGE

1966. *The Crystal Spirit: A Study of George Orwell.* Montreal:
Black Rose Books, 2005.

WORDSWORTH, WILLIAM

1802. Preface to *Lyrical Ballads.* London: Biggs and Cottle.

YAGODA, BEN

2000. *About Town: The New Yorker and the World It Made.* New York: Scribner.

YOUNG, JANE JAFFE

1999. *D.H. Lawrence on Screen: Re-Visioning Prose Style in the Films of the
Rocking-Horse Winner, Sons and Lovers, and Women in Love.* New York:
Peter Lang.

YOUNG, PHILIP

1966. *Ernest Hemingway: A Reconsideration.* University Park: Pennsylvania
State University Press.

ZAGAR, MONIKA

1998. "Knut Hamsun's Taming of the Shrew: A Reading of Drowning Tamara." *Scandinavian Studies* 70, no. 3 (Fall): 337-359. Academic
Search Premier, EBSCOhost (accessed December 9, 2008).

ZUCKERMAN, ALBERT

1994. *Writing the Blockbuster Novel.* Cincinnati: Writer's Digest Books.

ZWEIG, STEFAN

1946. *Balzac.* Translated by William and Dorothy Rose. New York:
Viking Press.

INDEX

ABOUT THE AUTHOR

William Cane has had a distinguished career as a professor of English at CUNY and Boston College, where he helped a generation of students improve their prose by imitating great writers. Cane is the author of six books, including the international bestseller *The Art of Kissing*. A highly sought-after speaker on the college lecture circuit, he has appeared on almost every major television talk show, including *Today*, *The View*, and *CBS This Morning*. He lives in Jersey City with his wife and daughter.